Acknowledgments

In the Name of God was written largely due to the assistance of
two fine institutions and five tolerant men. Thomas Hughes, Larry
Fabian and Mike O'Hare at the Carnegie Endowment for International Peace in Washington provided me with two marvelously
tranquil years between 1986 and 1988 to reflect on the broader
political trends of the Middle East as well as on the role of religion
in politics in the late twentieth century and the genesis of modern
terrorism. They also generously provided the time and resources to
visit Iran in 1987. After leaving Carnegie, I decided there should be
a more permanent record of my research and adventures in a land
so off-limits to most Americans. Robert Gottlieb, editor of *The New
Yorker*, and John Bennett, a *New Yorker* editor as funny as he is
thoughtful, twice endorsed my ventures to Tehran in 1988 to complete the cycle of a study that, by propitious accident, had begun in
1973. This book would have been impossible without the encouragement of all five.

For endless advice and editing suggestions, I am deeply indebted
to four very special colleagues: Pauline Baker and Geoffrey Kemp
at Carnegie, and David Ottaway and Caryle Murphy of *The Washington Post*. I also owe special thanks to several mentors who educated and encouraged me along the way: Lt. Col. Augustus Richard
Norton of the U.S. Military Academy at West Point; Professor R.
K. Ramazani at the University of Virginia; Professor Roy Mottahedeh, director of the Center for Middle Eastern Studies at Harvard

University; Professor Shaul Bakhash of George Mason University; Jerrold Green, director of the Center for Middle East Studies at the University of Arizona; and Professor Nikkie Keddie of the University of California at Los Angeles. I drew heavily on their scholarship and expertise, and I am grateful for their contributions in reading parts or all of the manuscript. Eric Hooglund, an Iran specialist formerly with the National Security Archive, was of enormous assistance in providing historic perspective and reading over the manuscript for inaccuracies, big and small. Anthony Cordesman, whose books constitute the bible on the Gulf war, was particularly helpful in correcting my course whenever I veered in the wrong direction on the Middle East's longest modern conflict. And Brian Jenkins of the Rand Corporation has offered endless advice about the trends and tactics of Middle East terrorism. And, as always, special thanks to William Royce of the Voice of America's Farsi Service for his linguistic expertise and helpful reflections.

Several participants in various crises during the first decade of Iran's revolution also read the manuscript or were prepared to discuss the historic moments in which they were involved. Gary Sick, who served as the Iran specialist on the National Security Council during the early stages of the revolution and the hostage crisis, generously provided insight on the revolution's first decade. I also appreciate the help of former hostages Bruce Laingen, Mike Metrinko and Colonel Leland Holland for assistance with information on the 1979–81 hostage crisis. On the Reagan administration's Iran initiative in 1985–86 and its aftermath, I owe special thanks to former National Security Advisor Robert McFarlane and to two former senior staff directors for the Middle East on the National Security Council, Ambassador Robert Oakley and Howard Teicher. Gerald F. Seib of *The Wall Street Journal* helped with the period covering his 1987 detention in Iran.

Several U.S. military, intelligence and State Department officials, who all asked to remain anonymous, were also generous with their time and their knowledge. The same applies to many of their counterparts in the Middle East and Europe. They deserve so much more than this simple line.

Needless to say, this book could not have been written without access to or assistance from hundreds of Iranians whom I have met over the past fifteen years. They came from all walks of life, and many defied official policy toward the United States to help me better understand Iran, not only its revolution. Because of the controversial nature of this book, I have unilaterally decided against

ALSO BY ROBIN WRIGHT:

SACRED RAGE:
THE WRATH OF MILITANT ISLAM

Robin Wright

In the Name of God

The Khomeini Decade

SIMON AND SCHUSTER

New York   London   Toronto   Sydney   Tokyo

SIMON AND SCHUSTER
Simon & Schuster Building
Rockefeller Center
1230 Avenue of the Americas
New York, New York 10020

Designed by Levavi & Levavi, Inc.
Manufactured in the United States of America
10 9 8 7 6 5 4 3 2 1

Library of Congress Cataloging in Publication Data
Wright, Robin B.
   In the name of God: the Khomeini decade/Robin Wright.
      p.   cm.
   Includes bibliographical references.
   1. Iran—Politics and government—1979–   I. Title.
DS318.825.W75   1989
955.05′4—dc20   89-21632
                                                        CIP

ISBN 0-671-67235-5

naming any of them; I would not want any to suffer because of my interpretations of events or my conclusions—with which some would certainly disagree. Again, my silent thanks will, unfortunately, have to suffice.

Several researchers also provided invaluable help. In their spare time, librarians Jane Lowenthal and John McHarris at Carnegie, Aleta Embrey at *The Los Angeles Times* and Betsy Folkins of the Middle East Institute managed to come up with the data that I needed to complete this book. Three interns at Carnegie—Mona Yacoubian, Mona Ghali and Keith Bickel—were also diligent and tolerant of my need for minutiae on a place about which there is limited accurate information.

Two wonderful editors are ultimately responsible for helping me give shape and substance to this book. Alice Mayhew's support and encouragement were a constant source of inspiration, and George Hodgman deserves sainthood for tolerating the temperament of a writer working under tight deadlines.

Last but never least has been the inexhaustible love and encouragement of my mother.

To the memory of a thoughtful law professor who advised his students as well as his children to approach all problems "by standing on top of the world and looking down" and who was so much more than my father.

Contents

Cast of Characters*

∽∝∾

Ali, Imam: Son-in-law and cousin of the Prophet Mohammad, after whom Shi'ism was named; the Shi'a—or, as originally known, Shi'at Ali—means followers of Ali. The dispute over leadership of the new Islamic world after the Prophet's death in the seventh century led to the biggest schism ever within Islam.

Bahonar, Mohammad Javad: Third prime minister of the Islamic Republic; killed in a 1981 bombing.

Bahramani, Ali Hashemi: Nephew of Rafsanjani and the "second channel" in the arms-for-hostages negotiations.

Bakhtiar, Shapour: Appointed prime minister of a caretaker government before the exile of Mohammad Reza Shah Pahlavi; forced out eleven days after Ayatollah Khomeini's return in 1979; fled to exile in Paris.

Bani-Sadr, Abolhassan: First president of the Islamic Republic; ousted in 1981; fled to exile in Paris.

Bazargan, Mehdi: First prime minister of the Islamic Republic; resigned after nine months because of the seizure of the United States embassy.

Beheshti, Mohammad: Supreme Court Chief Justice and Islamic Republican Party ideologue; killed in a 1981 bombing.

---

* Iranian names are spelled according to phonetic transliterations of Farsi, or Persian. Readers may be confused by different spellings of similar names. Hussein, for example, is the same name as Hosain; Hussein is the Arabic transliteration; Hosain is Farsi. Although the two languages use the same alphabet, the pronunciation is different. The Prophet's name in Arabic is most often spelled Muhammed or Mohammed; in Farsi, it is Mohammad.

Berri, Nabih: Leader of the Shi'ite Lebanese Amal movement.

Borujerdi, Mohammad Hosain: Grand Ayatollah who preceded Khomeini; died in 1961.

Ghorbanifar, Manuchehr: Iranian exiled businessman and intermediary in the arms-for-hostages swap.

Hashemi, Mehdi: Head of the World Islamic Movement; arrested in 1986 on charges of treason and murder; his allies allegedly leaked news of the visit to Iran by former National Security advisor Robert McFarlane; executed in 1987.

Hashemi, Mohammad: Brother of *Majlis* Speaker Ali Akbar Hashemi Rafsanjani and head of the Voice and Vision of Iran.

Hosain, Imam: Grandson of the Prophet Mohammad and son of Imam Ali, the followers of whom founded Shi'ism; martyred in a seventh-century clash with the Umayyad dynasty at Karbala.

Hussein, Saddam: President of Iraq since 1979.

Khamenei, Ali: Third president of the Islamic Republic, 1981–89; selected as Ayatollah Khomeini's successor in June 1989.

Khomeini, Ahmad: Son and chief of staff of Ayatollah Khomeini.

Khomeini, Batoul: Wife of Ayatollah Khomeini.

Khomeini, Mustafa: Son of Ayatollah Khomeini and his father's chief of staff until his death in Iraq in 1977.

Khomeini, Ruhollah: Iran's Supreme Jurisprudent, popularly known as the imam.

Mahallati, Mohammad: The Islamic Republic's United Nations ambassador, 1988–9.

Mohtashami, Ali Akbar: Iran's ambassador to Syria in the mid-1980s and later Minister of Interior.

Montazeri, Hosain Ali: Heir apparent to Ayatollah Khomeini, selected in 1985, forced to resign in 1989.

Mughniyah, Imad: A leader of Islamic Jihad, or Islamic Holy War, a pro-Iranian Lebanese Shi'ite cell believed to have abducted many of the American hostages in Lebanon.

Musavi, Mir Hosain: Fourth prime minister of the Islamic Republic, since 1981.

Musawi, Hussein: Leader of Lebanon's Islamic Amal.

Pahlavi, Mohammad Reza: Second and last shah of the Pahlavi dynasty; forced into exile in 1979, died in 1980.

Pahlavi, Reza: First shah of the Pahlavi dynasty; forced into exile in 1941; died in South Africa in 1944.

Qotbzadeh, Sadeq: Foreign minister under Bani-Sadr; arrested and executed in 1982 for plotting to overthrow the regime.

Rafiqdoost, Mohsen: Revolutionary Guards commander elevated to cabinet minister in 1982; ousted in a no-confidence vote in 1988.

Rafsanjani, Ali Akbar Hashemi: Speaker of Iran's parliament since 1980 and appointed commander-in-chief in 1988.

Raja'i, Mohammad Ali: Second prime minister and second president of the Islamic Republic; killed in a 1981 bombing.

Rajavi, Masoud: Head of the Mojahedin-e Khalq, or People's Holy Warriors, an Islamic Marxist group.

Sadr, Musa: Lebanese Shi'ite imam and founder of the Amal movement.

Shariatmadari, Kazem: Grand ayatollah stripped of title in 1982 because of opposition to Khomeini.

Velayati, Ali Akbar: Iran's foreign minister since 1981.

Yazdi, Ibrahim: Foreign minister under Bazargan in 1979; quit after the U.S. embassy takeover.

Prologue

"Never was any such event so inevitable, yet so completely unforeseen."

—Alexis de Tocqueville,
on the French revolution

On one of the last days of my last trip to Iran in 1988, I went up to the Roof of Tehran, the point atop the snow-capped Elburz Mountains reached by antiquated cable car. From the vantage point of ten thousand feet, where the air was cool and hard even on a steamy July day, it offered a place to reflect on a country that I had been wandering in and out of for almost fifteen years.

I had first visited Tehran in 1973, during the height of Iran's alliance with the West. Iran, then, seemed to make sense. In the complex and turbulent Middle East, where so many were so often hateful or suspicious of the United States and other Western nations, Iran was a comfortable place for most foreigners. During the Pahlavi dynasty, the two shahs had transformed Tehran. Trappings of Western lifestyles and technology had been mixed with the political intrigue and the exotica of the Orient.

In 1973, two gigantic carpets hanging from the rafters of Tehran's Great Bazaar symbolized Iran's interdependence and interaction with the outside world, particularly with the West. One had been

intricately woven in the shape of the shah's face, the other was of
John F. Kennedy. Since Mohammad Reza Shah Pahlavi's corona-
tion in 1941, the Iranian capital had assumed the role of crossroads
between East and West formerly reserved for other Iranian cities or
Middle East capitals. In 1943, Tehran had been a logical site for the
precursor to superpower summitry, the first conference of allied
leaders Franklin Roosevelt, Winston Churchill and Joseph Stalin.
Both Roosevelt and Churchill had major downtown thoroughfares
named after them. After the war, Queen Elizabeth was similarly
honored during a state visit; world leaders began to stop frequently
in Tehran.

By 1973, jumbo jets were landing daily in Tehran from New York
and Paris, Tokyo and Beijing. Westerners could stay at a Hilton or
an Intercontinental, eat the finest French cuisine or Kentucky Fried
Chicken, and play the night away at assorted nightclubs and casi-
nos. As East and West vied for stronger political and economic ties
with this Middle East oil power, Tehran became an enticing center
of international trade and politics. "All the themes of those spy
novels set in Istanbul were actually taking place in Tehran," a noted
Iranian commentator once joked.[1] The capital was the symbol of
Iran's entry into the twentieth century.

All that changed in 1979, when a revolution led by Ayatollah
Ruhollah Khomeini stripped Mohammad Reza Shah Pahlavi of his
power and Iran of its vibrant reputation. Overnight, the newly austere Islamic Republic became off-limits, and the changes began.
Over the next decade, a new set of images, strong and persistent,
became synonymous with Iran: Hostage seizures. Suicide bombings. Teenagers serving as human minesweepers on the battlefront.
Women hidden behind black chadors. Mullahs toting rifles and leading mobs in chants of "Death to America."

For me, the changes were most striking on January 21, 1981.
Along with a small crowd of journalists, I stood on the Algiers
airport tarmac near the steps of the plane that brought the fifty-two
American hostages from Tehran on their stopover to freedom following the final suspense-filled days of the negotiations in Algeria.
I remember scrutinizing their faces as they disembarked one-by-
one in the wee hours of a cold, rainy night for their formal transfer
from Algerian custody; I wanted an explanation of what had happened to Iran's long and proud traditions to explain this nightmare.
Even the hostages' subsequent accounts offered few answers about
the dimensions and import of this revolution. Later that year I
moved to the Middle East, using Beirut as my base. The next four

years coincided with the emergence and spread of Islamic fundamentalism throughout the region. Much of it, as much indirectly as
directly, seemed tied to Iran.

And so I decided to go back, beginning an odyssey that led to this
book. It included visits to the war front in my own chador, required
of even foreign women but rather cumbersome when traipsing
through swampland or trying to dash from Iraqi bombers' line of
fire. It included an almost surreal discussion with the Revolutionary
Guards cabinet minister about Iran's role in the 1983 Marine bombing in Beirut, in which I had lost friends. And it included attending
more than one revolutionary celebration in which I watched the
stars and stripes burned and heard my country berated and threatened.

The only restraints I had on any visit were time and a tediously
slow bureaucracy. But, over the years, I managed to taste a wide
range of Iranian life, including parliament, university classes, Muslim Friday prayer sermons and an Armenian Christian wedding,
research institutions, amusement parks, military installations,
banks, Iranian television, the shah's former palace, several government ministries and dozens of private homes. I visited bazaars,
cemeteries, florists, schools, factories, picnic grounds, mosques, hospitals, groceries, restaurants, and even former tourist attractions
that I had toured in 1973. Along the way, I met Iranian carpet
merchants, policemen, musicians, biochemists, salesgirls, mullahs,
political scientists, diplomats, newspaper editors, civil servants,
housewives, doctors, maids and many more ordinary Iranians, each
of whom had a different perspective on the revolution. I also had
encounters with the revolutionary komitehs, the committees that
police moral and political conduct, and talked about Khomeini's life
with members of his family.

Determining how Iranians really felt about their revolution was
not easy. An Asian diplomat offered me some advice which he, in
turn, had been given shortly after his posting to Tehran by another
envoy: "Don't make the mistake of thinking that the longer you've
been here, the more you understand Iran. Most of our intelligence
reporting has been wrong all along and not just since the revolution.
Yours will be too. None of us understands the Iranians."

I remembered that advice one searingly hot evening in 1988
when I sat with a friend who is a civil servant in a tatty and barren
Tehran café. Over coffee cake and melon juice, he told me of his
disillusionment with the government. He had marched and protested to bring down the shah, and he had been among the millions

who greeted Khomeini upon his return. But now, he said, he was fed up. He had not voted in the spring parliamentary elections; he had not even followed who was running. He wanted to end the eight-year war with Iraq; he said he would sneak his son out of Iran rather than see him join the military when he came of age if the war was still raging. He wanted better relations with the outside world, including the Great Satan. Although he did not like the shah, he repeatedly made the point that life had been better during Pahlavi rule. Then he was briefly called away by a passing friend. When he came back, he was ashen-faced. The BBC and Radio Israel had reported (erroneously, as it turned out) that Khomeini was dead. He sat down slowly and did not say anything for several minutes. "This," he then pronounced, "is terrible for my country."

Understanding Iran, either as a revolution or as a monarchy, has not been easy for the West. We thought that we understood it once, but we were chastened and then humiliated. "You thought you understood Iran because the shah spoke English and because his cabinet had read Shakespeare," an Iranian journalist told me in 1988. "You thought he was good because you could see a reflection of yourself in him. But he understood Iran as little as you did, and that's why you both failed."

•

In their eagerness to change societies and to break with the past, revolutions have traditionally held off the outside world during the first traumatic years. Xenophobic Iran has not deviated from the pattern. Indeed, the revolution was so full of hatred that its actions elicited abhorrence and fear rather than grudging respect from the West. Despite the outside world's tendency to revile the theocracy and the man who created it, however, Iran's revolution cannot be ignored or dismissed. For the Middle East, it is arguably one of the three most important turning points of the century. The collapse of the five-century-old Ottoman Empire and the creation of the state of Israel are the other two. The revolution's impact, however, has not been limited to the region. Virtually no part of the world has been untouched by the revolution's repercussions because of its effect on oil prices, on the patterns of terrorism and modern warfare, on Third World politics and on the emergence of religious fundamentalism, not only within Islam.

Iran is, also, simply too valuable to be ignored. First, its geo-strategic position is of even greater significance, particularly to the West, than its vast oil wealth. Its frontiers, which bridge the Arab world with the Indian subcontinent, have for millennia been central to political, military and commercial developments. Its position and the traditions of its Aryan people, the Indo-European race whence Iran gets its name, have long made Iran the crossroads of culture and geography.

Ancient Persia was pivotal to Alexander the Great's drive into India in the fourth century B.C. Its conquest by Arab armies in the seventh century gave the then new Islamic Empire access to central and eastern Asia. Persia was invaded by the Turks in the eleventh, sixteenth and eighteenth centuries, conquered by Genghis Khan's Mongol army in the thirteenth century and by Tamerlane in the fourteenth century, challenged by the Afghanis in the eighteenth century and, in the twentieth century, occupied by Britain and the Soviet Union. More recently, the Persian Corridor was the most viable supply route for U.S. Lend Lease aid to the Soviet Union during World War II; forty thousand American soldiers were deployed in Iran to keep the train link open.

Since World War II, Iran's value has further increased, for two reasons. First, petroleum became essential to the movement of modern armies and to the development of modern industry. Free access to oil was essential to both political and economic power. Second, as the U.S.-Soviet superpower rivalry evolved, Iran's location became even more vital. To the north, Iran shares a twelve-hundred-mile border with the Soviet Union that includes the volatile, predominantly Muslim Soviet central republics, the oil-rich Caucasus and the Caspian, the world's largest inland sea. In the postwar era, keeping Iran free of Soviet influence evolved into a Western priority. In 1946, the first crisis of the then new United Nations Security Council produced a resolution calling for a Soviet withdrawal from the northern Iranian provinces occupied during World War II; President Harry S Truman also issued an ultimatum to Joseph Stalin to leave Iran. The subsequent Cold War arguably had its origins in this confrontation.[2]

The need for oil and the superpowers' scramble for influence worldwide further increased the value of the Middle East, especially of Iran. Its five other frontiers became important for more than trade and transit. To the west, Iran's 730-mile border with Iraq is an entry point into the Arab world's Fertile Crescent, while strategic Turkey is a vital member of NATO. To the east are unstable Afghanistan, which witnessed Asia's second-bloodiest war in the 1980s, and Pakistan, one of the United States' closest Asian allies. Iran's southern frontier along the Persian Gulf, through which more than 40 percent of the Free World's oil passes daily, is the longest of the six countries that rim the strategic waterway. Iran also, in effect, controls the Strait of Hormuz, the so-called chokepoint for Gulf oil exports.

Roughly one-fifth the size of the United States, Iran ranks fifteenth among the world's nations in geographic mass. With a growth rate estimated at 4 percent, its population is among the world's top twenty-five. Of the eight main Gulf nations, Iran's population of fifty-two million is the largest, roughly twice the total of all the other Gulf nations, and the most diverse.

In terms of natural wealth, Iran holds 10 percent of the world's known oil reserves, an estimated sixty-five billion barrels. At the time of the revolution, Iran was the world's fourth-largest producer of petroleum. It accounted for about 11 percent of global output and 27 percent of Middle East production. Unlike the basically single-product economies of the Arabian Peninsula, however, its resources also include the world's second-largest reserve of natural gas and other minerals as well as commercial agriculture and a small industrial base. In other words, no nation can afford to ignore Iran, regardless of who is in power.

•

At least in part because of Iran's many assets, Khomeini's Islamic Republic made it through the first decade in three uneven stages. The first stage, from 1979 to 1982, was the period of survival. The revolution defied the pundits' predictions of an early demise due either to the mullahs' political inexperience or to a plethora of domestic and foreign challenges. Most ominous for Iran was the fact that the theologians came to power knowing virtually nothing about running a state or administering an enormous bureaucracy. Indeed, the idea was virtually anathema. Iranian Shi'a had traditionally avoided direct participation in government as demeaning to spiritual authority. Khomeini's upheaval thus represented not only a revolution in Iran but also a revolution within Shi'ism.

During this stage, survival was often a literal issue, politically and physically. As it became clear that the United States was losing its foremost ally in the region, the Carter administration briefly toyed with the idea of trying to reverse the tide. After the shah's exit, it considered re-creating the conditions of 1953, when the shah had also been forced to leave Iran. The Central Intelligence Agency had helped to topple the regime challenging the Pahlavi dynasty and then to bring the shah back after only a few days.

In January 1979, however, the United States opted to dispatch General Robert Huyser, who had close contacts with Iranian military leaders, to Tehran. He was instructed to ensure that the military supported Bakhtiar's caretaker government; if it fell, he was to ensure "that the military took action."[3] In the end, however, the military was too divided and too demoralized to act. Five days after the military's disintegration allowed Khomeini's backers formally to assume office, Washington announced its intention to maintain diplomatic relations with the new Islamic regime. The tense diplomatic ties, however, quickly disintegrated after the takeover of the American embassy in November and the aborted military rescue of fifty-two hostages the following spring.

The revolutionaries had barely written a new constitution and elected their first government when it faced another military threat: Iraq's 1980 invasion. Tehran could hardly afford a war. The regular Iranian military had been decimated by defections, mass purges and executions; the new Revolutionary Guards had limited training and inferior arms. Within the first few weeks, Iraq seized thousands of square miles of Iranian territory, including large chunks in Iran's oil-rich southern Khuzistan Province.

The threats were not only external. Khomeini's domestic opponents, including many who had been his allies in ousting the shah, also tried to overthrow the new government. Two massive bombs in June and August 1981 eliminated a president, a prime minister, ten cabinet officials and twenty-seven members of parliament. Because of internal wrangling and assassinations, Iran held three presidential elections in a twenty-one-month period in 1980 and 1981, the last two within ten weeks. Iran's third president, Ali Khamenei, has walked with a cane and his right hand has dangled uselessly at his side since a small bomb planted in a tape recorder went off as he was giving a Friday prayer sermon in 1981.* In a single four-month period in 1981, the Iranian press reported that more than a thousand government officials, including mullahs, judges, political officials, Islamic Republic Party leaders and Khomeini aides, had been killed.[4]

•

The second stage, from 1983 to the end of 1986, marked the revolution's period of expansion, when the imam and his adjutants transformed Iran and profoundly shook up the region. Politically, Khomeini radically altered the status quo in the Middle East by transforming a staunchly pro-Western monarchy into a feistily in-

---

* At a breakfast Khamenei held with reporters at the Waldorf-Astoria Hotel in September 1987, on the day after his United Nations address, a bodyguard had to lean over the president and cut up his food like a parent for a child.

dependent theocracy. Domestically, rule by Islam was institution-
alized on the basis of a republican constitution with a democratic
veneer. The fabric of society was, meanwhile, overhauled so that
school curricula, banking laws, penal codes and even standards of
dress and public behavior conformed to Islam.

Militarily, the Islamic Republic's armed forces managed to turn
the tide of the war in their favor. Nibbling away at Iraqi territory,
the many branches of the Iranian military turned the Persian Gulf
conflict into the bloodiest of modern Middle East wars. By 1986,
many Western military analysts had begun to predict that Iraq had
few hopes of defeating Iran—and that the Islamic Republic might
actually be capable of winning the war.

Economically, Iran managed to endure four staggering obstacles:
First, oil prices plummeted from thirty-five dollars per barrel in
1980–81 to as low as nine dollars per barrel in 1986. Second,
billions of dollars in capital evaporated during the exodus of more
than a million Iranians, including many of the best educated and
most experienced, who were scared away by the revolution. Third,
war costs estimated to average about $10 billion a year sapped the
economy, especially after Iraq's heavy bombardment of Iran's oil
facilities and industrial sectors. Finally, foreign assistance and in-
vestment in development schemes were drastically cut. Yet, although its foreign reserves dropped to minimal levels, Iran managed
to pay off the shah's foreign debt, which at its peak in 1978, the
year before the revolution, had reached $7.4 billion.[5] The Islamic
Republic had eliminated its debt, the mullahs liked to boast, at a
time when the United States, Iran's former mentor, had become the
world's largest foreign debtor nation.

During this period, Iran ended its role as protector of the Persian
Gulf; almost overnight, it became the greatest threat to the status
quo in the Middle East. Tehran made no secret of its support for
Islamic extremist groups in Saudi Arabia, Kuwait, Bahrain and elsewhere that were seeking to challenge or to overthrow the conservative sheikhdoms. Directly and indirectly, the Islamic Republic
was linked with coup plots, assassination attempts and a series of
successful bombings carried out in several Arab states. In the Gulf
and Lebanon as well as in other parts of the Muslim world, militant
Islam rather quickly came to be viewed as a more serious threat
than either Soviet expansionism or Israeli Zionism.

In the process, Iran redefined the nature of warfare by weaker
Third World nations against the superpowers and their allies. Under
Iranian tutelage, political violence and terrorism crossed a threshold

in the 1980s. New tactics of mass hostage seizures and suicide bombings were introduced by Islamic zealots and later adopted by secular, occasionally even rival, groups. Terrorists also no longer limited their demands to regional governments or foes, as had been the pattern among most Latin American, European and other Middle East groups during the 1960s and 1970s.[6] They increasingly sought to intimidate or to reshape Western nations' foreign policies.[7]

The Islamic Republic also challenged both Moscow and Washington. "We must settle our accounts with great and superpowers and show them that we can take on the whole world ideologically, despite all the painful problems that face us," Khomeini pledged upon his return to Iran.[8] The greatest humiliations for two U.S. presidents involved Iran: Jimmy Carter was not reelected in large part because of the 1979–81 takeover of the American embassy in Tehran during which fifty-two Americans were held hostage for 444 days. The biggest embarrassment of Ronald Reagan's two-term presidency was the 1985–86 arms-for-hostages swap with Iran.

Meanwhile, Moscow was often infuriated by Iranian aid to the Mojahedin, or "holy warriors," during the Soviet Union's eight-year invasion and occupation of Afghanistan. After Pakistan, Iran provided the second-highest level of assistance to the Afghani opposition of any regional nation; Iran also absorbed more than two million refugees. The Islamic Republic did not discriminate between superpowers in cutting old ties. Just as Tehran had ended its membership in the pro-Western CENTO alliance, it also abrogated a key section of the 1921 treaty providing Moscow with the right to intervene militarily against any anti-Soviet threat emanating from Iran. And the mullahs never showed signs of being intimidated by Soviet pressure. Indeed, Tehran boldly expelled eighteen Soviet diplomats in 1983 and simultaneously banished the communist Tudeh Party, which had held out longer than all other opposition groups. For the first time, Iran had the upper hand in dealing with both superpowers. Both nations' attempts at reconciliation were repeatedly rejected as insufficiently obliging.

•

For all it had achieved, however, the revolution began to falter during its third stage, a period of retreat, from late 1986 to mid-1988. The cost of the arrogance and the isolation that had been so essential to the imam's dream had been enormous. At several junctures, the Islamic Republic's future seemed as tenuous as it had in the days and moments just after Khomeini's return.

The Islamic Republic began to lose the war with Iraq. By the summer of 1988, it had given up most of the ground it had gained in the previous six years, often at a staggering toll in human life. On land, the battlefront was almost exactly back to where it had begun in 1980. And in the Persian Gulf, the 1987 deployment of more than two dozen American warships—along with additional contingents from Britain, France, Holland, Belgium and Italy—had curbed Iran's ability to strike ships doing business with Iraq's allies and benefactors.

The setbacks also affected equipment and personnel. Operation Staunch, the U.S. arms embargo that was reimposed after the disastrous arms-for-hostages swap, had made many crucial weapons either beyond reach or too expensive. By 1988, Iraq had a five-to-one advantage in tanks, a nine-to-one edge in heavy artillery, and a six-to-one advantage in warplanes.[9] Iraq's increasing use of chemical warfare and its escalating missile attacks on civilian residential areas—the so-called war of the cities—further sapped the Iranian will to fight. By 1988, the Revolutionary Guard Corps, the mullahs' military prop, was made up mostly of conscripts, not volunteers.[10] Iran had limited if any means of recovering militarily.

The 1987 American embargo on Iranian oil and other vital exports, including the nation's celebrated carpets and caviar, added to the growing financial squeeze. Washington pressured other industrialized democracies to follow its lead. Even with stiff discounts, Iran had increasing problems selling its oil. Development schemes had to be put indefinitely on the back burner. Meanwhile, many of the economic reforms that had been at the heart of the revolution were, years later, still on hold. The economy was so unstable in mid-1988, during the final throes of the war, that the black-market rate for the American dollar had soared to more than twenty times the legal rate of exchange.[11]

Even more seriously, the revolution was losing steam. The four-story-high portraits of the imam, his dark brow usually furrowed and his hand often raised in exhortation, and the artful street posters, which depicted the Islamic masses marching all the way to Jerusalem, had become faded or frayed, a fair reflection of diminishing public fervor. To ensure turnouts at elections, students and workers were often bused, without advance notice or subsequent choice, to polling places.[12] To keep crowd attendance high at public rallies and Friday prayers, the war wounded and martyrs' families were rounded up. The revolutionary komitehs, the neighborhood groups that policed political and moral conduct, had to become ever more vigilant about everything from women's slack observance of Islamic dress codes to political protests. In 1987 and 1988, small demonstrations, usually over high prices and the war, were reported in several major cities. Khomeini's revolution appeared to be on a precipice.

•

At the end of its first decade, the twentieth century's only theocracy attempted a form of rapprochement, with its own population as well as with the outside world. It initially appeared to be the beginning of a fourth phase, motivated in part by the necessity of military and economic hardships and in part by the mullahs' growing political maturity. The formal turning point was Iran's abrupt decision in mid-1988 to accept an unconditional cease-fire in the war with Iraq.

In small ways and large, the Islamic Republic began to come to terms with its regional rivals and with the outside world. A new dialogue with its neighbors along the Arabian Peninsula indicated that Iran was coming to terms with its place in the region. Relations were also reestablished or upgraded with France, Canada and Britain. European hostages held by pro-Iranian groups in Lebanon were gradually released, always after Iranian intervention. And trade talks were held with a host of nations, a seeming reversal of Iran's foreign policy motto of "Neither East nor West."

The revolution also became less severe at home. Voltaire, Samuel Johnson and John Keats were quoted alongside great Muslim philosophers in the *Tehran Times'* "Thoughts of the Day" column. Quiet purges were conducted of many komitehs.[13] The bazaaris, or merchant class, were given guarantees that the government would not nationalize all foreign trade. The shift even extended to women's dress. Violations of modest Islamic dress codes, which would earlier have led to public reprimands or temporary detentions, became less harsh. Pale shades of nail polish became permissible.

The changes made it seem that, after a decade-long political spasm, Iran was gradually returning to normality. Then, as the Islamic Republic celebrated its tenth anniversary, Khomeini just as abruptly reversed course again. In a move that enraged the West, he condemned Salman Rushdie, author of *The Satanic Verses*, to death on the grounds that his novel amounted to blasphemy against Islam. The subsequent international reaction led Tehran to break relations with Britain and to renew its calls for defiance of the outside world. In a step that undermined his own succession as well as the Islamic Republic's future, the imam then fired his heir apparent and warned the Tehran government not to waver from the revolution's original goals. With those two actions, the momentum created since the war's end seven months earlier was, at least temporarily, lost.

The Rushdie edict was not without historic parallels. Mao Zedong's draconian measures during China's Cultural Revolution shortly before his death also happened in the context of debates over an opening to the West. Both Mao and Khomeini did not want to see their revolutionary ideals compromised by the exigencies of the state, which history has proven, mostly recently in the Soviet Union and Eastern Europe, must happen for a modern revolution to survive. In China's case, Mao's actions were a political spasm; the next generation of leaders moved quickly to better diplomatic and economic ties with the outside world. In Iran, it may be another decade before the outside world can judge Khomeini's draconian actions.

What had appeared to be a new phase in Iran's revolution quickly ended, however, with the ayatollah's death on June 3, 1989. The next generation of leaders inherited a legacy of mixed signals from which to shape the post-Khomeini era.

•

Iran will always be an aberration in relation to both the Middle East and southern Asia, the two regions it bridges. It is a culture and a society literally unto itself. Two great mountain ranges, the Elburz and the Zagros, and three great bodies of water, the Caspian Sea, the Persian Gulf and the Indian Ocean, have helped maintain a sense of geographic separateness. Iranians accepted an "outside" religion to replace the native Zoroastrian faith and they have, over the centuries, adapted others' ways to their own. But the proud sense of history, the Persian language, and the unique Indo-European racial identity of the majority of its people have prevented assimilation by all the outside powers that have conquered the land.

Even a decade of revolution had not changed life as much as the outside world might have expected. From the Roof of Tehran at dusk, the Iranian capital twinkled with light. Concentrations of red, green and yellow neons shone from the main business district, still bustling in the early evening. The northern suburbs were illuminated by apartment complexes and luxury villas proliferating up the sides of the Elburz range, while lights flickered from the maze of mud-brick homes and shanties encroaching on the arid, dusty desert on the distant skyline. A small cluster of high rises glistened from the city center; another in the foothills indicated the former tourist district. Just below, hikers using flashlights were making their way down the steep brown slopes before dark, and the bar-becue fires of picnickers at mountainside retreats glowed warmly.

As I looked down from the Roof of Tehran, it was clear that the capital, like the rest of Iran, had, so far, survived the traumas of a revolution. But then, Iranians have always been survivors. Rarely has the French saying "The more things change, the more they are the same" applied to any one place for so long.

Whatever the status of diplomatic relations between Iran and the outside world, understanding its people and its history is no less important now than it was during its era of openness under the shah. This book is written in the hope that a better understanding of Iran's volatile revolutionary decade, in the context of its past, will sooner rather than later lead to an equilibrium in relations—between peoples if not between governments. This time, hopefully, it will not be because we are looking for reflections of ourselves.

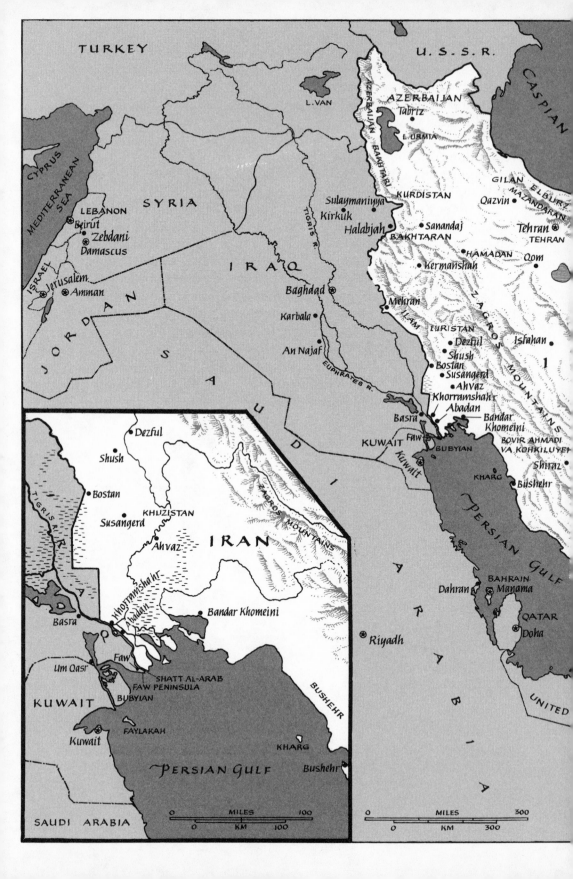

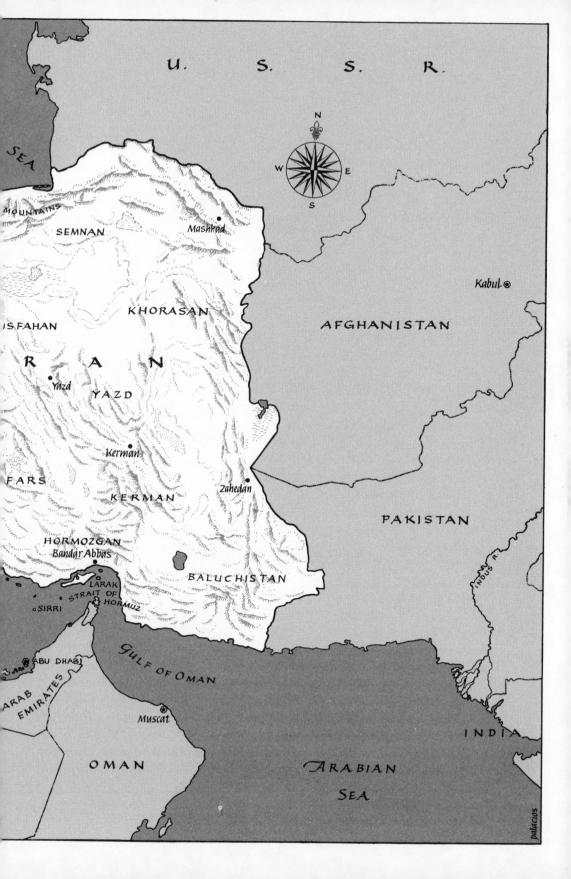

CHAPTER ONE

The Khomeini Revolution

ↄ·ↄ

"Do not step on a Persian carpet or a mullah, for
its value increases."

—Persian proverb[1]

"This time either Islam triumphs or we disappear."

—Ayatollah Khomeini[2]

On February 1, 1979, a brisk winter day in Tehran, the most powerful nation in the Persian Gulf was in limbo. Sixteen days earlier, Mohammad Reza Shah Pahlavi, with a small jar of Iranian soil in his hand and Empress Farah Diba at his side, had reluctantly abandoned the Peacock Throne on an "open-ended vacation." The momentum of a crusade aimed at ending twenty-five hundred years of monarchial rule had finally forced him out. The shah had left behind a hastily formed caretaker government, but its ability to hold on to power was in doubt. Iran was still paralyzed by nationwide strikes, and the unity and loyalty of the military were uncertain. February 1 was finally to test whether the vestiges of the monarchy could survive. After more than fourteen years in forced exile as punishment for his caustic campaign against the Pahlavi dynasty, Ayatollah Ruhollah Mustafavi al-Musavi Khomeini was scheduled to come home.

The imam's return had initially appeared doubtful; it had already been delayed twice. The fledgling three-week-old government, fearful of the impact Khomeini's presence would have, had pleaded for more time on a day-to-day basis. It first proposed a three-month delay, which the ayatollah rejected. It then stalled, listing excuses ranging from an air controllers' strike to bad weather. But with the unwavering certainty demonstrated throughout his banishment, Khomeini gave notice that he would not tolerate any further delays.

Air France then had doubts about being able to land in Tehran. The airline agreed to charter a jumbo aircraft to the Khomeini entourage only on condition that the number of passengers was limited to half capacity so that the fuel load could be doubled—in case the plane had to turn back. Iranian women and children, including Khomeini's wife, Batoul, were barred from the plane to avoid endangering their lives.[3] As the red, blue, and white 747 approached the Iranian capital, the precautions seemed to be justified. "We have just received a warning over the aircraft radio that the Iranian air force has orders to shoot us down directly [when] we enter Iranian airspace," one of Khomeini's aides announced to the local and foreign press on board.[4] The plane was forced to circle for a half hour before it was finally allowed to land; the pilot also flew low over the capital to ensure that tanks had been cleared from the runway.[5]

Since opposition to the shah had exploded more than a year earlier, however, a revolution had seemed increasingly inevitable. Students and leftists had launched nationwide demonstrations, which had often ended in bloody riots, confrontations with Iranian troops, and deaths. Bazaaris and bankers had shut down key businesses, stagnating the economy. Strikes had paralyzed the oil industry and government services such as the post office and the customs department. The accumulated effect was to immobilize the state; even the central heating in the shah's favorite palace had been cut off. By January 1979 the momentum was unstoppable.[6]

Prime Minister Shapour Bakhtiar, head of the caretaker government, tried. "The government will not spare any effort, nor is any sacrifice too great, to guarantee the unity of Iran," he warned on the day Khomeini returned. "I will not allow the country to be governed by any force other than legitimate authority."[7] The shah's backers also made a final, fledgling effort. Television coverage of Khomeini's arrival at the airport, watched by millions outside Tehran, was disrupted, reportedly by royalists. For a half hour the shah's picture, accompanied by a silence in stark contrast to the uproar among Khomeini's backers on the streets, appeared on Iranian television screens.

Elite units of Iran's military, by 1979 the sixth largest in the world with the most extensive arsenal in the region, attempted a show of strength in the final hours. Columns up to two miles long of army tanks and trucks loaded with troops, bayonets affixed to their rifles, rumbled along Tehran's tree-lined boulevards to demonstrate that the government was not prepared to capitulate. But, like earlier attempts to check the vigor of the antishah movement, it was all too late. The military had already begun to crumble. Members of the shah's personal Imperial Guard appeared ready for a fight, but there were even more indications of defections. Thousands of ordinary army soldiers had stuck carnations, a symbol of nonbelligerency, into their gun muzzles, while vans carrying Royal Air Force troops were brazenly decorated with Khomeini posters.

Despite the bitter cold, public outpourings of support were rapturous from the moment the Air France jumbo was first sighted by people who had been waiting in the streets for up to twelve hours. Tehran echoed with the cacophony of cheering and car honking in long and repetitive bursts. Crowds chanted *Agha Amad,* or "The respectful one has come," and *Allahu Akbar* or "God is great," a phrase that was to become the revolution's credo, shouted in both elation and anger.

As Khomeini's motorcade inched along a twenty-mile route through the capital, many men and women sobbed openly, the joy mixed with disbelief. Above the din, street vendors loudly hawked Khomeini pennants, portraits and pins. Despite the deployment of fifty thousand volunteer marshalls, identifiable by green armbands and often by newly fashionable beards, Iranians mobbed the convoy. Hundreds ran alongside until they dropped from exhaustion. Even conservative estimates numbered the crowd at no less than three million. Iranians wanted change, and the ayatollah's return marked the moment for catharsis.

The *New York Times* compared the public display to the parades for aviator Charles Lindbergh after his first transatlantic flight and to the welcome accorded General Charles de Gaulle upon his return to Paris after World War II.[8] "He is the light of our lives," a high school mathematics teacher told the *Times,* which reported that this sentiment reflected "the feelings of millions."[9] A *Washington Post* correspondent was sufficiently moved to write, "Not since Lenin was sent across Germany in a sealed train in 1917 to Petrograd's Finland Station to lead the Bolsheviks against the czar has a revo-

lutionary leader's return to his homeland seemed so full of portent
as Khomeini's arrival in Iran." [10]

A decade later those words seemed uncannily prescient. Only
once before in this century had a revolution, the Russian upheaval,
so stunned and frightened the outside world. None of the more than
twenty revolutions in the Third World since World War II,[11] including those in Cuba, Vietnam and Nicaragua, had reverberated with
such energy or innovative potential. And only twice in modern
history had political conventions been so shaken by a new ideology.
In rejecting the Bourbons of France, the Jacobins of the eighteenth
century introduced equality and civil liberty as the basis of modern
democracy. The Bolsheviks of the early twentieth century over-
threw the Russian Romanovs in favor of classless egalitarianism.

Yet few interested parties, either inside or outside Iran, fully
understood exactly what Khomeini's return did portend. From the
beginning, the Iranian revolution was an uncomfortable aberration
in the pattern of modern revolutions; it did not invoke identifiable
symbols or seek goals synonymous with revolutions of the previous
two centuries. Like the Jacobins and Bolsheviks, Iran's theocrats
sought to oust a decadent and decaying monarchy. Yet the alternative they advocated deviated from the Greco-Roman legacy and
from the Judeo-Christian values that, together, formed the basis for
all other revolutions since the Age of Enlightenment.[12] The introduction of Islam as a contemporary idiom of political opposition
and the creation in the twentieth century of an *Islamic republic*—
unprecedented in either religious or political history—as a viable
means of governance was even more disturbing for both East and
West.

To the outside world the disquieting issue was not just that the
political spectrum, defined in the postwar era by a familiar and
occasionally complacent tension between variations of democracy
and socialism, was suddenly being challenged by an ideology that
did not fit labels of either left or right. Nor was it that, in an age
when the world's political spectrum was divided between a consti-
tutionally secular nation and an ideologically atheist state, Khomeini's zealous religious ideology seemed obsolete. More disturbing
was the fact that this revolution's agenda did not fit contemporary
political theory. The widely accepted intention of revolution was
progress, or moving forward the human condition. But neither
bourgeois nor proletarian,[13] Iran's upheaval, which appeared to be
designed mainly to restore the glories and values of the seventh-

century Islamic empire, did not seem to be in keeping with the spirit of the modern age.

For all the fervor in Iran on February 1, 1979, few outsiders believed this revolution had the qualities to endure for very long. Its vulnerability was symbolized when, exhausted by the night flight and the excitement and weakened by heart troubles that had plagued him for a decade, Khomeini fainted at the airport.[14]

Politically and physically, the imam simply did not fit the mold of modern revolutionary leaders that included Lenin, Mao, Castro and Nicaragua's young Ortega brothers, who also came to power in 1979. Khomeini was also an aberration from other successful Middle East revolutionaries, such as Algeria's Ahmed Ben Bella, Egypt's Gamal Abdel Nasser and Libya's Moammar Qaddafi, who had all chosen varying forms of socialism to rule their states.*

Unlike the younger and more energetic figures who had led other twentieth-century revolutions, Khomeini had not even entered the political arena until he was sixty. The imam, as his followers had anointed him to the consternation of many other ayatollahs, was a leading activist for less than four years before his expulsion by the shah in 1964. He then spent fourteen years in exile. He was nearly eighty when he returned to overthrow the remnants of the monarchy. Khomeini may have had the fire of his younger counterparts, but he hardly had the stamina of those who led long, grueling marches across China or guerrilla campaigns from Cuba's tropical mountains. Indeed, he had not even been present during Iran's struggle.

In his own country Khomeini's singular focus on re-creating a pure Islamic society free of attachments to the world's major powers also made him seem an unlikely national leader. Descendants of the Aryans, who settled in Iran some two millennia ago, have always prided themselves on their contacts with and knowledge of the outside world. Even the poor and the rural peasants have a surprisingly informed sense of the world and their place in it. Iranians of all classes also like to tell foreigners that they have never

* The only other Muslim leader to transform a Middle East nation through religion in this century had been Abdel Aziz ibn Saud. In the 1920s and 1930s, ibn Saud had forged the new nation of Saudi Arabia from a collection of warring tribal fiefdoms under the fundamentalist Wahhabi Islamic banner. The Islamic legal code, known as the Sharia, which literally translates from Arabic as "the path to the watering place," was installed as the law of the land. But ibn Saud chose to establish a monarchy to rule the new nation; Sunni clerics were advisers rather than leaders. Ibn Saud's massive family eventually became the rulers of the most powerful kingdom in the Arabian Peninsula.

really felt at home in the Middle East—after no less than three millennia. Some talk openly about their superiority over the Arabs to their west and the Asians to their east. A few complain bitterly of the imposition of Arabic script on their Indo-European language, Farsi.

A few have even protested that they were forced in the seventh century to accept Islam, in place of the native Zoroastrian religion, by the expanding Islamic Empire. The protests, however, usually relate to the power of outsiders over Iranians rather than to any disregard for Islam. Historically, Iran has rarely acquiesced willingly to outsiders; most invaders instead ended up being absorbed by Iran. In the twentieth century, many Iranians also appeared comfortable mixing with Europeans and Americans, wearing their fashions, selling their wares, and adapting their technology to Iranian commerce and development. By the 1970s, Iranians increasingly appeared to be looking outward, not inward.

Khomeini, however, was not a relic of the past; he was very much a product and a symbol of the twentieth century. In the issues that sparked it and in the technology used to spread it, his was also the most modern of revolutions. The imam's emergence was a response to domestic issues that had simmered throughout the century as well as to international trends in the postwar period.

Throughout the early years of his life, and again at the end, the ayatollah represented only a minority in Iran. But at one juncture, Khomeini personified the political, social and moral upheaval that energetically addressed fundamental questions of existence for both the Iranian individual and the Iranian state in the twentieth century. And for the crucial first decade of Iran's revolution, his vision shaped a nation. The emergence of the imam, whose life spanned almost nine decades of the twentieth century, was neither a fluke nor an anomaly. His life was very much a part of Iran's story.

•

When the imam was born in 1902, he was known, simply, as Ruhollah, the sixth child of Hajar and Mustafa.[15] Ruhollah means "soul of God"; surnames were largely unused in a country then still called Persia. His mother, Hajar, gave birth in the family's mud-brick home, the most common rural dwelling at the turn of the century, in the small backwater town of Khomein. The family was never wealthy, but it did have religious status, a traditional route to power. Both his grandfather and his father, who was murdered less than five months after Ruhollah's birth, were mullahs "of the Musavis"—or, as written locally, al-Musavi—a family line that descended from the Prophet Mohammad. Such noble heritage entitled them to wear a black turban, rather than the white headwear of an ordinary cleric.

The imam's life ultimately overlapped with a dozen national crises. The first happened when he was still a child, and Persia was shaken by its first twentieth-century revolution. Although the Constitutional Revolution of 1905–11 was, in fact, no more than a reform movement, the issues and the opposition's methods eerily foreshadowed the flashpoints and tactics that ultimately brought Khomeini to power seven decades later. Indeed, the 1979 revolution was in some ways an extension of the earlier upheaval.

The Constitutional Revolution was largely a reaction to Persia's domination by foreign powers, particularly the British and the Russians. In exchange for financial aid to pay for European-inspired reforms and the monarchy's needs, the weak Qajar shahs had doled out political and economic concessions. By 1905, Britain held oil rights in the south while, in the north, Russia commanded the Persian Cossack Brigade, the most and arguably only competent branch of the military. Other foreigners were also brought in to help run the country. To curtail the powers that allowed the king to give away the country and to rid Persia of a foreign presence that challenged religious and social traditions, a powerful alliance of the clergy, the intelligentsia and bazaar merchants launched a protest.[16]

The mounting tension finally erupted in 1905 after a coalition of mullahs and merchants criticized the government and demanded greater rights. The denouement followed the arrest of an opposition mullah—just one of many indications of the clergy's power. In an ensuing protest, police killed a religious student. During the funeral procession for the young shahid, or martyr, through the streets of Tehran, Cossack troops opened fire, enraging the crowds. For the next three weeks, the protest gained momentum among the population, while the shah's government came under mounting pressure from paralyzing general strikes. In August 1906, the Qajar monarch was forced to accept the opposition's demand for Persia's first constitution and its first parliament—both of which limited the king's powers.[17]

But the constitutionalists and their parliament were no more effective than the Qajar king at controlling the unwieldy nation. The fragmented opposition alliance also disintegrated as the mullahs grew disillusioned with reforms that appeared to create a secular, Western-style democracy. The constitution, based on a Belgian model, was increasingly seen as a threat to Islam.

Because Islam makes no distinction between the powers of Caesar and God, religion had long been a strong political force as well
as a form of nationalism in Iran. Shi'ism had been a source of
national identity—even among those less than devout—since it was
first introduced in 1501 by the then new Safavid dynasty as the
state religion. At the time, it was used mainly to create a sense of
united identity separate from the then threatening Ottoman Empire, which was ruled by Sunni Muslims. Iran had been the only
country in the Gulf region not absorbed by the Ottomans.

The new constitution acknowledged Islam in three clauses: First,
all legislation would be vetted by five learned clergy. Second, press
laws and education curricula had to be formulated so that they
included nothing offensive to Islam. And third, the king, all ministers and all judges had to be members of the Twelver branch of
Shi'ite Islam.[18] But leading mullahs recognized that the constitution's otherwise secular goals also limited their powers. By 1911,
the opposition movement had dissipated because of the defection
of key clergy, domestic strife and the occupation by British and
Russian troops of southern and northern Persia. The revolution was
over—for the time being.[19]

As the Constitutional Revolution unraveled in Tehran, Khomeini
was already studying the Koran. Like all male children of his time
who wanted an education, he attended a religious school. "Every
child at the traditional school would read a part of the Koran every
day," his older brother, who also became an ayatollah, later recalled. "The imam completed the Koran at the age of seven. . . . He
had extraordinary ingenuity and talent."[20] Once, in a meeting six
decades later with an Iranian soccer team, Khomeini alluded to his
own brief and fledgling attempt at sports.[21] But as a teenager he
spent most of his time studying theology, logic and literature and
writing poetry about nature, friendship and religion. His early life
was simple and rather austere. The ascetic habits that he learned as
a youth—a few rugs on which to work and sleep and a meager diet
of yogurt, goat cheese, lentils and fruit—would continue throughout his life.[22]

The imam's teenage years coincided with another period of national turmoil. Persia declared its neutrality during World War I,
but the nation was nonetheless a battleground for conflicting interests: the British and Russians were pitted against Ottoman and pro-
German forces. Meanwhile, the Qajar dynasty was on its last legs,
impotent to intervene or to restore its sovereignty. The nation was
also deeply divided. Persia still had a few strong and legendary

cities. Among them were Shiraz, famous for its roses and the lyrical verse of the fourteenth-century poet Hafez, and Isfahan, the oasis full of poplars and willows and exotic, blue-tiled monuments to Iran's many dynasties. But most of the country was made up of feudal fiefdoms, tribes and ethnic groups whose rivalries ran deep. Any sense of nationhood was based on a dominant religion rather than on a sense of common purpose or unity associated with a king.

Khomeini came of age in the 1920s as the decaying 131-year-old Qajar dynasty finally crumbled. The period also marked the emergence of two men whose disparate versions for Iran were to clash a half century later. In 1921, as Khomeini moved to Qom, the drab theological center near Tehran, to complete his religious studies, a self-educated army colonel named Reza Khan gained national prominence as one of four men who rose to assume power from the crumbling government. Five years later, the young Khomeini qualified as a mullah just as Reza Khan formally replaced the Qajar dynasty and crowned himself Reza Shah, the first king of the new Pahlavi dynasty.[23]

The name Pahlavi comes from the Persian language used before the seventh-century Arab invasion; it means "heroic." A tall, athletic soldier born near the Caspian Sea, Reza Shah had a commanding sense of authority and a forceful will. He also had great ambitions. Politically, he sought to modernize ancient Persia by breaking the hold of tradition, both social and religious, that he believed prevented progress. He sought to create a strong central state loyal to no quarter but the monarch.[24] Economically, he wanted Iran's oil resources, discovered by British geologists in 1908, as well as new industries to supplement, and eventually to replace, the centuries-old dependence on regional trade, agriculture and handicrafts. Socially, the scope of the innovations that Reza Shah envisioned were reflected in his bold order that foreigners refer to Persia as Iran.

The transformation, however, was often disconcerting. Reza Shah demonstrated marked contempt for tradition, especially Islam. Streets were plowed through mosques and religious institutions, bazaars and other old quarters. Religious judges and taxes and Islamic laws were secularized, often according to European standards under the control of the central state; the clergy was thus deprived of major sources of power, income and input into the system. Elementary and religious schools run by the mullahs were put under a government ministry and their curricula standardized, again based on European models. Tribal leaders also lost power to the new class of civil servants installed to run the provinces and towns. Pastoral tribes were told to end nomadic migrations; many were forcibly disarmed; and some were imprisoned. To enforce his policies, the first Pahlavi king built a new army, based on conscription and paid for with a new national taxation.[25]

No issue appeared too small for his attention. Reza Shah restored the old Persian solar calendar in place of the Arabic lunar standard used by Muslims elsewhere. He purged Arabic words from Farsi. Inspired by the overhaul of society in Kamal Ataturk's Turkey after the collapse of the Ottoman Empire, he banned the veil and commanded that both sexes adopt Western dress. In general, Westernization became synonymous with civilization—in a country with a civilization that dated back thousands of years.[26] Reza Shah also ordered the entire population to take family names for the first time, preferably Iranian rather than Arabic or Islamic. In 1926, in identification booklet 2744, the future imam was registered as Ruhollah Mustafavi, the surname taken from his father Mustafa.[27] *

Reza Shah succeeded on several fronts: foreign troops withdrew and Britain ceded control of Iran's Gulf coast. He reorganized the army, standardized and upgraded education, developed new industries and built a national transportation system.[28] He molded a backward nation and brought it into the twentieth century. But while Reza Shah managed to wrest control of the army, the parliament and other instruments of power, he was unable to subvert one community—the clergy.

Khomeini came from just the kind of environment that Reza Shah's reforms most disrupted, and the young cleric was as intent a young man as the new king. By the 1930s, as Reza Shah was in the full throes of modernization, Khomeini had quietly but methodically begun campaigning to preserve beliefs long central to the Iranian way of life.[29] His forum was limited to the mosque and the Qom seminary where he taught, and his campaign was only an academic exercise at this stage. But in response to the king's innovations, the young mullah countered that a new society could not be created in a vacuum, or without understanding and incorporating the past. After thirteen centuries, Islam could not simply be set aside. As Reza Shah grew more aloof in the company of a new elite,

---

* The introduction of surnames was not standardized. Khomeini's older brother, Morteza, for example, took the name Pasandideh, which in Farsi means, roughly, "pleasing."

Khomeini was expanding his contacts and building a grassroots network among growing numbers of students and the faithful.

The young mullah already showed the signs of rigid discipline and absolute dedication to Islam that were to make him famous—and feared. As his daughter, Zahra Mustafavi, recalled decades later, "From when I was a child of four until now that I am almost fifty, I cannot remember a muezzin's call not being followed by the imam saying his prayers. I can remember him saying prayers during the hot nights and fasting even when no one else was fasting." Religion even played a role in his marriage. He was almost thirty when he married Batoul, the thirteen-year-old daughter of a noted Tehran ayatollah who came from a family that also descended from the Prophet Mohammad. Like most Iranian marriages, it was arranged, in this case through clerical contacts.

Khomeini's personal life was just as regimented. "He goes walking three times a day and each time for twenty minutes. When he gets back he looks at his watch to see if it is twenty minutes, otherwise he goes back for a few more steps to get it complete," his daughter said. "He's so punctual that if he doesn't turn up for lunch at exactly ten past everyone will get worried, because his work is regulated in such a way that he turned up for lunch at exactly that time every day. He goes to bed exactly on time. He eats exactly on time. And he wakes up exactly on time. He changes his frock every time he comes back from the mosque."[30]

Despite his hostility toward Reza Shah, Khomeini never directly confronted the first Pahlavi king, who abdicated in 1941 after sixteen years on the Peacock Throne. Reza Shah's downfall, perhaps ironically, was not due to his ruthless implementation of domestic reforms but was instead the result of his foreign policy. In an attempt to counter the long-standing influence of the neighboring Soviet Union and Britain, the Iranian monarch turned to the Germans. He was attracted to their industry and expertise as a model for his own nation. He was also swayed by German ideas, specifically the notion that Aryans, which he believed were his own people's roots, were superior to other races.[31] In part because of their alarm over the Iranian monarch's pro-Nazi sentiments after the outbreak of World War II, and in part because of their territorial ambitions, the Soviet Union and Britain invaded Iran in 1941 and forced Reza Shah to abdicate in favor of his twenty-two-year-old son, Mohammad Reza. He was then forced to abandon Iran for exile in South Africa, where he died three years later.

Shortly after Reza Shah's abdication, Khomeini published *Secrets Exposed,* his most important work thus far. It was also his first public political statement, in which he had no kind words for the Pahlavi era. He wrote,

> Wherever you go and whomever you encounter, from the street-sweeper to the highest official, you will see nothing but disordered thought, confused ideas, contradictory opinions, self-interest, lechery, immodesty, criminality, treachery, and thousands of associated vices. . . . Given such circumstances, it should not be expected that the government would be regarded as just and legitimate in religious circles. . . . In short, these idiotic and treacherous rulers, these officials—high and low—these reprobates and smugglers must change in order for the country to change.

But Khomeini, now almost forty, was still in the minority. As he rather woefully admitted in his book, "There is much to be said, much that is weighing on my mind. But where are the ears to listen to me? Where is the perception to understand me?"[32] His time had not yet come.

•

The second and more subtle conflict in the imam's life grew out of his experience in middle age. It centered not on the new Pahlavi king but on differences with his own colleagues. The ayatollah—who was now well known by the name Khomeini, after the town from which he came, as was common practice among mullahs—favored a vigorous, even aggressive application of Islam. "Faith consists of this form of belief that compels man to action," he once explained.[33] In his classes in Qom, he exhorted students to tackle contemporary political and social problems as a religious duty.[34]

Khomeini's obsession, throughout his life, had been the survival of Islam, not just as a faith but as a way of life. Islam has always been a particularly vibrant religion. Unique among the world's major monotheistic faiths, its tenets include laws to govern politics and society as well as a set of spiritual beliefs. It covers business deals and banking, hygiene, marriage and divorce, defense and taxes, penal codes, even family relationships. As a result, Reza Shah's programs to secularize and modernize society threatened not just the turnout at prayer services on Friday, the Muslim sabbath; they also undermined the structure of Islamic society and its code of conduct. Khomeini believed that man's acts of evil were the result of estrangement from the values encouraged by Islam.

Khomeini also understood the two qualities unique to Shi'ite Islam that provided a means to counterattack. First, Shi'ism has always had a revolutionary potential because of the mobilizing power of its mullahs. Unlike the Sunni clergy, who serve mainly as advisors to the faithful, Shi'ite theologians are empowered to interpret religious law and duty for their followers. Their word, in theory, is law. Second, Shi'ism has historically often been an idiom of social protest,[35] beginning with its original commitment to fight injustice and to challenge secular authority when it errs. For thirteen centuries, this duty has been central to the faith because of the parable of Hosain, one of the three most revered figures in Shi'ite history.

Hosain was the grandson of the Prophet and the son of Ali, who married Mohammad's daughter. The Shi'a—or, as it was originally written, Shi'at Ali—means "followers of Ali." The Shi'a broke away from the single Islamic movement because of a political dispute over who should lead the new faith after the Prophet's death.

The Shi'a argued that the caliph, or God's representative on earth, should descend through the Prophet's family. Since Mohammad had no sons, this meant Ali, who was the Prophet's cousin as well as his son-in-law. The argument was based mainly on the presumed righteousness of the Prophet's family. The mainstream Sunni, however, advocated leadership selected by the Prophet's associates or by a council of religious scholars. Ali was eventually selected to be the fourth caliph, but he was assassinated less than five years later. The single Islamic strain then irrevocably split, and the caliphate again moved outside the Prophet's family to the new Umayyad dynasty.[36]

The small Shi'ite community, however, did not give up its quest to lead the Islamic world. In A.D. 680, nineteen years after Ali's murder, Hosain decided to challenge the perceived injustice of the Umayyad's Sunni rule. But his small group of seventy-two, which included women and children, were no match for the thousands of well-armed Umayyad troops loyal to the caliph Yazid. At Karbala, now a city in southern Iraq, Hosain and his followers were massacred.

Hosain's defiant act contributed an important legacy to the Shi'ite community. As the ultimate martyr, having fought despite the foreknowledge that he would face a swift and bloody defeat, Hosain established the precedent of dying for belief rather than living with injustice. Revolt against tyranny, even if it meant sacrificing one's life in the process, became a duty to God.[37] The Shi'a, who now account for between 12 and 15 percent of the world's estimated nine hundred million Muslims, inherited the belief that they were victims of authority and persecution. The importance of Hosain's martyrdom is still evident today. Just as Christians commemorate Jesus bearing the cross before his crucifixion, devout Shi'ite communities throughout the world reenact the martyrdom of Hosain at Karbala every year in an Islamic passion play during the festival of Ashura.

Khomeini modeled his beliefs and his later campaign on the Hosain paradigm. "Every day is Ashura and every place is Karbala" was one of his rallying cries. He specifically argued that the clergy should be more assertive in fighting the injustice represented by the Pahlavi dynasty—whatever the cost. Years later, he argued that the mullahs should have a role in matters of state, in keeping with the tradition of Mohammad, who was both prophet and sovereign. He believed that religion should not only direct the life of the individual but that faith should also guide the life of the community of men—or the state. And, by 1979, he clearly hoped that his revolution would restore the rightful leadership of the Islamic world to the Shi'a.

Other Iranian mullahs, however, did not agree with his vision. Throughout the 1940s and 1950s, Khomeini was still in the minority. Although he became an ayatollah in the 1950s,* he was effectively forced to remain on the sidelines due to convention. The accepted Shi'ite code of conduct for clerics required deference to the leading ayatollah, and Grand Ayatollah Mohammad Hosain Borujerdi, who had been Iran's highest-ranking mullah since 1947, was a distinctly apolitical figure. He had once summoned some two thousand mullahs to a conference in Qom, where they passed his resolution, although not unanimously, prohibiting clerical involvement in Iranian politics.[38]

Khomeini continued to speak out during this period, but few beyond his circle of students listened since he lacked supreme authority. It was not until Borujerdi's death in 1961, four decades after Khomeini became a mullah, that the way opened for a new generation of clerical leadership—and a new degree of activism. Within a year, Khomeini was vying for a greater share of power.

•

* Ayatollah, which means "sign of God" or "mirror of God," is the ranking title granted Shi'ite clerics. It is gained by general acknowledgment of a mullah's scholarship and piety rather than by appointment or election.

In an ironic parallel with the simultaneous emergence of Khomeini as a mullah and Reza Shah as Iran's new king in the 1920s, the ayatollah made his move in the early 1960s just as the second Pahlavi king began to tighten his hold on power.

Mohammad Reza Shah Pahlavi had initially been a weak figure, beholden to the foreign powers who put him on the throne in 1941 and dependent on his ministers and parliament to run the state. During his first dozen years on the Peacock Throne, many of the powers centralized by his father were reassumed by the tribes, clans and clergy. Parties and ideas repressed under Reza Shah proliferated. During this vigorous period of political activity, the political spectrum ranged from the communist Tudeh Party to the widely popular National Front, a four-party coalition that advocated constitutional democracy and rejected all forms of foreign intervention or control, notably of oil, which had been under concession to the British since it was discovered.[39]

The National Front represented several of the ideas—such as limiting the monarch's power and ending foreign domination—advocated during the 1906 Constitutional Revolution. The party's popularity had brought Prime Minister Mohammad Mosaddeq to power in 1951. Within two years, however, the European-educated son of an aristocratic family had begun to lose the support of traditionalists. The clergy and the bazaaris particularly were suspicious of his program and angered by his cavalier disregard of custom, including Islam.[40] In an attempt to hold off the opposition, the premier increasingly resorted to the same dictatorial tactics used by Reza Shah.

Mosaddeq soon came into open conflict with the second Pahlavi monarch, who tried to have the prime minister dismissed. The ploy backfired, at least briefly, and the shah was instead forced to flee to Rome. But Mosaddeq had also frightened Iran's main foreign mentors. Alarmed by his nationalization of Iranian oil, London and Washington moved to oust him. The CIA orchestrated riots that forced Mosaddeq's resignation in 1953 and allowed the young shah to return less than a week after his abrupt departure. The role of the United States in the coup d'état marked the first stage of Washington's intervention in Iran, which many Iranians, including Khomeini, would never forget.

With growing United States support in the 1960s, Mohammad Reza Shah became more aggressive in pushing the Western-oriented modernization programs initiated by his father—whom he held in awe.[41] Under American prodding and with much fanfare, he introduced his White Revolution in 1963. The six-point package centered around land reform, largely in favor of rural peasants. It also, however, included granting women the vote and the right to run for office, the privatization of state-owned factories, profit-sharing for industrial workers, a literacy campaign, and national-ization of forests and water resources.[42] The reforms did provide significant changes, particularly in the construction of new factories, schools, roads, bridges and dams. But many, such as land redistri-bution, were superficial.

The White Revolution also led to greater foreign, namely Amer-ican, involvement and to greater power for the shah. The tradition-ally independent clergy once again became anxious that Islam would be suppressed or even disappear from the mainstream of Iranian life. Opposition also grew among the general public because the reforms did not address basic demands for political participation and social justice.

At a time when most religious and secular opponents appeared either unwilling or unable to take on the shah, Khomeini used the White Revolution finally to propel himself and his ideas to the forefront. On the defensive during Reza Shah's reign and con-strained in his use of Islam during Borujerdi's lifetime, the ayatollah was for the first time free to go on the offensive, using Islam as his idiom. Portraying himself as the conscience of a nation being mis-led, Khomeini framed the shah's actions in the context of deviations from God's will and violations of the historic faith.

Khomeini was bold, even audacious. During celebrations to mark the Iranian New Year in March 1963, he issued a *fatwa*, or religious edict, that addressed the shah's White Revolution. Calling many of the reforms "a serious threat to Islam," he urged all believers to boycott the New Year celebrations. "In order to warn the Muslim community of the imminent dangers facing the Koran and this coun-try of the Koran, I declare the New Year to be a period not of festivities but of mourning. Oh Allah, I have performed my first duty and if you allow me to live longer and permit me, I shall shoulder other tasks in the future."[43] It was no small boast; his initiative began to redefine the format of opposition in Iran.

The shah struck back. In an attempt to silence the clergy, he had more than sixty mullahs detained. Hundreds of theology stu-dents, normally exempt from national service, were ordered to report to the army. Government funds to select clergy were cut off. Security was tightened around Qom, where Khomeini and other mullahs taught.[44] The shah publicly called the mullahs "black reactionaries."

Khomeini then threw down the gauntlet. In June 1963, during the Ashura commemoration of Hosain's martyrdom, always the most emotional Shi'ite holiday, he responded to the shah in a passionate oratory. "We have come to the conclusion that this regime also has a more basic aim: they are fundamentally opposed to Islam itself and the existence of a religious class," he said. Addressing the shah directly, he added,

> You miserable wretch, forty-five years of your life have passed. Isn't it time for you to think and reflect a little, to ponder about where all of this is leading you, to learn a lesson from the experience of your father? I hope to God that you did not have in mind the religious scholars when you said, "The reactionaries are like an impure animal," because if you did, it will be difficult for us to tolerate you much longer, and you will find yourself in a predicament. . . . The nation will not allow you to continue this way.[45]

It was the boldest public attack on the shah during his twenty-three years in power. Two days later Khomeini was arrested, sparking demonstrations throughout the country and creating a new aura around the rebel ayatollah, who spent the next ten months in jail.[46] Khomeini's followers now date the revolution not to 1979 but to the 1963 incidents that led to the imam's imprisonment.

In many ways, the shah helped make Khomeini, who, throughout most of his life, had been eclipsed by other leaders, both secular and religious. Now the ayatollah jumped several rungs up the ladder of public esteem. First, his initial arrest created public appeal and drew attention to his agenda. Public outrage helped him to circumvent his peers and other suspicious clergy, including many of greater scholarship or with greater followings. Second, the shah simultaneously alienated even those clergy who disagreed with Khomeini by ignoring the traditional internal balance of power. The clergy has been one of the three power blocs that Iranian rulers over the previous three centuries have traditionally needed to survive. The ayatollah eventually replaced the shah because of his strength of character and his vision, but also because the monarch forgot this basic historic fact.

The politics of petrodollars further disrupted this finely tuned balance of power between the monarchy and the clergy. The dramatic 1973 price hike, which quadrupled in response to Western support for Israel during the latest Arab-Israeli war, allowed the monarchy new independence from its former sources of revenue and support. The shah felt free once again to strip the clergy and the bazaaris of many of their remaining powers.

Rising oil revenues also led the shah to introduce ambitious new schemes for development, largely with outside help. Foreign multinationals began to challenge the bazaar's dominance of trade and imports, while foreigners increasingly replaced the mullahs as advisors to the shah. The loss of the clergy's influence and the challenges to Iranian tradition further provoked the mullahs' opposition.

The shah's relationship with the United States also inadvertently contributed to Khomeini's rise. The final break between the shah and the ayatollah centered on legislation passed by Iran's parliament in October 1964. A controversial bill granted all U.S. military personnel and their dependents immunity from prosecution for crimes committed in Iran. The imam passionately denounced the statute as a violation of domestic and international law. Since the bill's passage appeared to be linked with a $200 million loan the shah wanted in order to further arm and modernize Iran, Khomeini also charged the government with, literally, selling out.

"Our dignity has been trampled underfoot; the dignity of Iran has been destroyed," he said in a speech to followers in front of his residence in Qom. The measure, he charged,

> reduced the Iranian people to a level lower than that of an American dog. If someone runs over a dog belonging to an American, he will be prosecuted. Even if the shah himself were to run over a dog belonging to an American, he would be prosecuted. But if an American cook runs over the shah, the head of state, no one will have the right to interfere with him. . . . Are we to be trampled underfoot by the boots of America simply because we are a weak nation and have no dollars? [47]

Again he played the conscience of Iran, questioning whether it had abandoned its values and sold its soul.

In the kind of anti–United States diatribe that would later become familiar to Americans, but which was virtually ignored at the time, he also said,

> Let the American president know that in the eyes of the Iranian people, he is the most repulsive member of the human race today

because of the injustice he has imposed on our Muslim nation. Today the Qoran has become his enemy. The Iranian nation has become his enemy. Let the American government know that its name has been ruined and disgraced in Iran.[48]

On November 4, 1964, the ayatollah was detained and then deported to Turkey. Khomeini never forgot that his humiliating banishment, in effect the selling out of the local clergy, was a price that the shah was more than willing to pay for closer relations with the United States. The date would come back to haunt Americans; exactly fifteen years later, Iranian students commemorating Khomeini's expulsion attacked the U.S. embassy in Tehran and took the staff hostage in a drama that would drag on for almost fifteen months.

•

The ayatollah's exile was ignominious. He spent the first seven months in Turkey, the next twelve years in the Iraqi holy city of Najaf and, after his expulsion from Iraq at the behest of the shah, the final four months in a Paris suburb. Always an outsider and often shunned by the local populations, Khomeini lived simply, teaching a small corps of students and living with his wife, eldest son, Mustafa, and a few followers in simple accommodations.

At home, the bloom of oil wealth, which began producing billions rather than just millions of hard dollars in revenues, also focused attention elsewhere. At the height of the shah's glory in the early 1970s, per capita income in Iran increased to two thousand dollars, a Third World high. The student population reached an estimated ten million, including a hundred thousand university students. The number of industries quadrupled. And tens of thousands of acres of farmland were redistributed to some three million peasant families.[49]

But there was also a downside. Massive migrations to the cities led to housing shortages and slums. Unemployment, corruption and inflation soared. The gap between the rich, epitomized by an elite corps of families surrounding the Pahlavis, and the poor, notably those still in rural sectors, grew wider. More fundamentally, the second Pahlavi king was increasingly perceived as having accelerated the pace of petrodollar-funded development to a stage that compromised Iran's proud and independent identity. The shah had pledged that Iran would be competitive, economically and militarily, with France by 1993.[50] By the 1970s, it was already heading rapidly in that direction.

Few Iranians rejected the focus on modernization, but opposition grew to the heavy emphasis on Westernization with which advancement had become synonymous. The same sense of nationalist pride and cultural uniqueness that led to resentment of Arabs, Mongols, Turks, Afghanis, Russians and British during past incursions into Iran sparked animosity in the 1970s toward what was locally perceived as a different kind of subjugation by powers further afield. Alienation became widespread, leading to growing public sentiment that something was intrinsically wrong.

From exile, Khomeini played to the new mood. Borrowing from a young intellectual, Khomeini popularized the term "Westoxication." In a typical speech, he addressed "the dazzling effect that the material progress of the imperialist countries has had on some members of our society." He told those assembled at his Najaf lectures,

> When the moon landings took place, they concluded that Muslims would jettison their laws! But what is the connection between going to the moon and the laws of Islam. . . . Let them go all the way to Mars or beyond the Milky Way; they will still be deprived of true happiness, moral virtue, and spiritual advancement and be unable to solve their own social problems. For the solution of social problems and the relief of human misery require foundations in faith and morals; merely acquiring material power and wealth, conquering nature and space, have no effect in this regard. . . . So as soon as someone goes somewhere or invents something, we should not hurry to abandon our religion and its laws, which regulate the life of man and provide for his well-being in this world and the hereafter.[51]

His most famous message was provoked by the shah's ostentatious 1971 celebrations of Persia's twenty-five hundred years of continuous monarchy, dating back to Cyrus the Great. At a cost of at least $200 million, the celebration was billed as the "greatest gathering of heads of state in history."[52] The Persepolis fete also, however, came at a time of serious famine in the provinces of Baluchistan and Sistan as well as Fars, where the commemoration was held. Presidents and princes from sixty-nine nations feasted on caviar and roast peacock catered by Maxim's in Paris and drank *première classe* French wine out of Baccarat crystal.[53] Meanwhile, Iranians were largely outsiders.

Khomeini was scathing. "Islam is fundamentally opposed to the whole notion of monarchy," he said.

> Anyone who studies the manner in which the Prophet established the government of Islam will realize that Islam came in order to

destroy these palaces of tyranny. Monarchy is one of the most shameful and disgraceful reactionary manifestations. Are millions of the people's wealth to be spent on these absurd celebrations? Are the people of Iran to have a festival for those whose behavior has been a scandal throughout history and who are a cause of crime and oppression, of abomination and corruption in the present age? . . . The crimes of the kings of Iran have blackened the pages of history.[54]

His 1971 attack represented the broadening of Khomeini's focus from a single individual to an entire system of government. He charged that the shah's authority was illegitimate and even anti-Islamic, an allegation that later had a profound impact on the broader Islamic fundamentalist movement in the Middle East as well as on the Islamic Republic's foreign policy.

The ayatollah shrewdly used Islamic tradition both to chastise the shah and to keep his own image alive. Of particular importance was the parallel he drew between his exile and the Prophet Mohammad's hegira in the seventh century.[55] Under pressure from local tribesmen who ridiculed his claims of having received revelations from God via the archangel Gabriel, Mohammad had been forced to retreat from Mecca to Medina, now cities in Saudi Arabia, to meditate and to mobilize . The Prophet, however, had pledged that he and his small band of followers would return to Mecca, which he did a decade later in triumph to begin the building of the first Islamic government.[56] Khomeini also promised to return and, this time, to restore the glories of Islam's first empire. For many of the faithful, the ayatollah's name evoked anticipation of renewed greatness. The comparison served to elevate Khomeini to a higher spiritual plane, while the shah's mistakes made the monarch appear increasingly human and vulnerable.

Religion also provided the structure for Khomeini's campaign. As the shah cracked down on secular opposition groups, the mosque became one of the last refuges for dissent—a pattern that later became familiar in other parts of the Middle East. During Khomeini's three decades as a teacher, he had also built up a powerful lobbying force in the form of *talabehs*. *Talabehs* are students who are paid by the mullahs supervising their studies; theological students are, in effect, all on scholarship. The more *talabehs* a mullah has, the more prestigious is his position, the more powerful are his edicts, and the greater the income he is likely to draw from followers. Khomeini had more than a thousand former students, many of whom formed a tightly knit network after his expulsion to continue the campaign he had started. For their opposition many served multiple jail terms.

To the age-old practices of his faith, however, the ayatollah added modern touches. Through mimeographed and photocopied texts and, later, on tape cassettes and videos, he provided his former *talabehs* with regular pronouncements on events in Iran for clandestine distribution. He also used technology to keep current, as his daughter recalled. "Just because I am his daughter, we do not have a conversation each time I see him. We go into the room and say hello and just sit there because he is either listening to the radio or watching TV. He's not free for even a minute. Even in the bathroom he has the radio with him."[57] During his final four months in Paris, Khomeini also made extensive use of a sophisticated telephone system, which had been installed by an American company, to maintain links with the simmering revolution.

•

The final stage of the conflict between Khomeini and the Pahlavi family began, for the ayatollah, with the death of Mustafa, his first son and chief of staff, in October 1977. Although Mustafa was buried in Iraq and Khomeini was still banned from Iran, memorial services were organized in Tehran and other Iranian cities forty days after Mustafa's death, in accordance with Shi'ite custom. The services underscored how deeply the tenets and traditions of the Shi'ite faith were still ingrained in Iran, despite the shah's efforts to secularize society.

At the Tehran service for Mustafa Khomeini, the presiding cleric also called on the faithful to pray for the imminent return of "our one and only leader, the defender of the faith and the great combatant of Islam, Grand Ayatollah Khomeini."[58] At a time when the fragmented opposition needed unity and a single symbol around which to mobilize, Mustafa's death helped to turn the limelight toward Khomeini. Until this event, the disparate movement— which ranged from Marxist to fundamentalist—had lacked a specific direction or format. They had not yet found an effective idiom around which to unite. After Mustafa's death, however, the pattern of the uprising began to take on a distinctly Shi'ite flavor.

Two important Shi'ite traditions based on the parable of Hosain —the belief in martyrdom and the cycle of Shi'ite mourning—particularly contributed to the timing and momentum of the revolution's climax. During the fourteen months preceding the shah's ouster, those who died in clashes with security forces were said to be carrying on the noble tradition of Hosain, while the shah was increasingly equated with the Umayyad caliph Yazid, the personification of injustice. The Shi'ite practice of mourning, which is marked on the third, seventh and fortieth days after a death, then created a cycle that was difficult for the shah to break.

Once again, the shah's actions provided the flashpoint. On New Year's Eve 1977, six weeks after the memorial services for Mustafa Khomeini, President Jimmy Carter visited Tehran and toasted the shah for creating "an island of stability in one of the more troubled areas of the world. This is a great tribute to you, Your Majesty, and to your leadership, and to the respect, admiration and love which your people give to you." [59] With this hearty endorsement, the Iranian monarch decided to try again to discredit Khomeini and the Iranian clergy. Although the shah adhered to Shi'ite traditions, at least in public, his hostility toward the clergy had turned into hatred. In a conversation with the American ambassador, he referred to them as "ragheads." [60]

In early January 1978, a letter appeared in a Tehran newspaper. It specifically portrayed Khomeini as a poet of licentious love sonnets with homosexual tendencies, a foreigner with Indian roots* and an agent of the British. The letter also attacked the clergy in general as a group of "black reactionaries" and "a race of parasites, engaged in sodomy, usury and drunk most of the time." [61] Historical accounts vary about whether the shah masterminded the article through his Ministry of Information, but the imam's supporters had few doubts: the shah had declared open war on the symbols of Islam. The next day, clerics and religious students in Qom launched what was to become the first of several demonstrations that would last through the spring. By official count, two were killed in that day's confrontations with police; the opposition alleged that seventy died.

After the Qom riots, the mechanism for the next confrontation was the final round of Shi'ite mourning forty days later, when final rites were held for the Qom martyrs. In the Azerbaijani capital of Tabriz, services turned into protests and, after a student was killed, into new riots. The army finally had to be dispatched to end a two-day rampage against government offices and banks, liquor stores and movie theaters. Another round of martyrs, up to a hundred according to some eyewitnesses, were commemorated with new disturbances and new deaths another forty days later in March. The violence spread to cities throughout Iran as the pattern continued

* Khomeini's grandfather had lived for a period in Kashmir.

sporadically through the summer and fall. The sequence contributed to the establishment of Islam as the idiom of political opposition in Iran. As practiced by Iranian Shi'a, mourning is not simply a
time to react with sadness; particularly in times of conflict, it is also
a time of renewal.

By September 7, 1978, the shah felt he had no alternative but to
proclaim martial law. Word of the ban on all demonstrations, however, had not been widely publicized by the time protestors assembled early the next morning at Tehran's Jaleh Square, not far from
the parliament. When they refused to disperse, Iranian security
forces opened fire. The government said less than a hundred died;
the mullahs put the total at over ten thousand;[62] more reliable
figures estimated the number of deaths in the hundreds.[63] But the
Jaleh Square incident in the capital was still the bloodiest single
confrontation thus far between Khomeini's backers and the shah's
forces. Iranian history books now refer to it as Black Friday.

The outrage over the Black Friday martyrs led to the loss of the
last remnants of support for the monarchy and the virtual collapse
of the government. The fall of 1978 was marked by widening
strikes in the oil industry, the bazaar and other vital economic
centers. Some Iranian royalists appeared to understand what was
happening. According to one account, more than a hundred thousand Iranians abandoned Iran in the final four months, from October to the day of Khomeini's return on February 1, 1979.[64]

The shah tried several desperate tacks. He switched governments.
He ordered the arrest of more than 130 former government leaders,
including a premier and an intelligence chief. He won Iraqi assistance in getting Khomeini even farther away from Iran; Baghdad
expelled him. The ayatollah ended up in Paris. In November, the
shah, in a nationwide television address, also conceded that corruption had plagued his regime and he asked for forgiveness. In a final
dramatic moment, he told the nation, "As the shah of Iran as well
as an Iranian citizen, I cannot but approve your revolution." He
promised further change.[65] But it was too late. Despite some last-
ditch and often-conflicting ploys on the advice of the shah's family,
friends and foreign governments, all that remained was to find a
caretaker so that he could leave.

•

Although it had appeared through most of his four-decade-long
campaign that the ayatollah would not succeed, several factors gave
him an edge. First, Khomeini represented the strong and charismatic
leadership that Iranians have looked to since the days of Cyrus the

Great and Darius in the sixth century B.C.; weak rulers have fared poorly in Iran. Throughout his reign, the shah dithered indecisively between superficial reforms and repressive crackdowns. As American ambassador William Sullivan, who met regularly with the shah during the final days, concluded, "He was truly not cast to be a leader of men or the nation in times of crisis." [66] In contrast, throughout his life, the ayatollah had consistently provided a vigorous alternative.

Second, although no contemporary world leader would appear to have had less charm, Khomeini also genuinely had charisma. His mass appeal stemmed from his impassioned eloquence and absolute sense of righteousness. Ironically like Ronald Reagan, the imam was also "the great communicator." In public addresses and taped messages, he could speak as one of the people, not above them, and he used the familiar and comforting idiom of a religion that offers answers to questions of theology as well as of daily life. Even for many of those who rejected his Islamic message, Khomeini initially won respect for his unwavering commitment to Iranian political independence and cultural dignity. At the time, most Iranians believed that he genuinely had their interests at heart.

The outside world never reconciled with his appeal. "We never tried to understand the man or what he was about," commented a leading European ambassador in Tehran in 1988 about the outside world's reaction to the ayatollah. "We felt we didn't have to. His persona told us everything we wanted to know, and it was all negative. In the context of Iran, however, he has been brilliant, as hard as that may be to swallow. [67]

Third, Khomeini employed the framework of an ideology that dated back thirteen centuries. Unlike Marxism, variations of which have been the dominant force behind revolutions elsewhere in the twentieth century, the use of Islam involved no conversions or reeducation. Khomeini used Shi'ite myths and beliefs to set the pace and to provide the flashpoints around which the revolution unfolded, just as he would use them again to provide the themes and justification for many of his theocracy's actions.

In the final stage, the potent combination of a charismatic alternative leadership and an indigenous idiom of opposition gave the revolution particular legitimacy and forcefulness. It also made Iran's upheaval virtually unavoidable. The shah departed Iran on January 16, 1979, ending five decades of Pahlavi rule and two and a half millennia of monarchy. At least for the time being, Khomeini had ensured that Islam would, indeed, not disappear.

CHAPTER TWO

Hostages and Purges

ᘒᘒᘒ

"We must purify society in order to renew it."
—Ayatollah Mahdavi-Kani
of the Revolutionary Council[1]

"I have no authority to impose anything on my people, for Islam does not permit me to act as a dictator."
—Ayatollah Khomeini[2]

Colonel Leland Holland, the stocky, muscular army attaché at the American embassy in Tehran, recalled being uneasy in the first days of February 1979 following Khomeini's return. "Armed bands of komitehs and Revolutionary Guards were roaming the streets. There was no law, no order, and no respect for authority. It just kept getting rougher and rougher. I was shot at near the embassy gate. Every day it was getting more and more like Vietnam."[3] As in other revolutions, the initial period was indeed wild and almost breathless in its intensity. Recovering from several months of martial law and years of periodic crackdowns, Iranians reveled in their new rights of free speech and a free press, of right of association and assembly, and of political expression—often to bloody extremes.

Holland recalled looking out the embassy window one day as a group of tattily clad youths stopped a vintage Buick on Roosevelt Avenue. "They pulled the guy out of the car and shot him," he said. They just left him there. There was no attempt to clean it up or do anything with the body. It was left sprawled on the street. Then they set fire to the car."[4] Holland never found out the victim's identity; his best guess was that he, or perhaps the car's owner, was somehow associated with the monarchy.

Students, leftists and Islamic zealots elsewhere were capricious and uncontrolled in their reaction to the shah's ouster. Mobs attacked and ransacked the fortress headquarters and the safe houses of SAVAK, the shah's notorious secret police. Military bases and police stations throughout Iran, even in the rural provinces, were overrun. Armories were raided, often with assistance from the soaring number of deserters, and arms were widely distributed to a population previously barred from owning guns. In a reenactment of the assault on Paris's Bastille, Tehran's notorious Evin Prison was stormed and hundreds of inmates freed. In the Elburz foothills, the shah's favorite Niavaran Palace, along with other opulent Pahlavi properties, were seized. Both rabble and intelligentsia were bent on avenging the victims, excesses and tyranny of the shah.

The revolutionaries, however, were also intent on ridding Iran of the shah's proxy, Prime Minister Shapour Bakhtiar, a former National Front politician who had reluctantly taken the job in order to allow his old rival to leave. But Bakhtiar's gamble, which cost him many allies and friends as well as his reputation, soon failed; upon his return, the ayatollah appointed his own Provisional Revolutionary Government. The remnants of the caretaker regime battled, sometimes literally, to prevent a takeover by the Khomeini entourage. The tension between the two governments—one official, the other de facto—played out during the first eleven days of February in Iran's once formidable military. Skirmishes on streets and at bases flared for days between shah loyalists in the military and defectors as orders and counterorders flowed from the two centers of power.

Bakhtiar's fate was finally determined during a particularly vicious clash between air force cadets and technicians, who had gone to Khomeini's headquarters to pledge their loyalty, and the shah's famed Imperial Guards, nicknamed the Immortals. The tension within the military climaxed on February 9, 1979, when the airmen tried to take over Doshan Tappeh Air Force Base. The Immortals, handpicked for their loyalty to the monarchy as well as for their physical strength, had been the most determined holdouts after the shah left. They were the logical choice to put down the rebellion.

Instead, however, the Immortals were overwhelmed by the airmen and recently armed civilians and revolutionaries who joined the fracas during two days of fierce battles. The outcome signaled the turning point for the military. After hours of anguishing debate at the highest levels, the Supreme Military Council announced on February 11 that, to prevent further bloodshed, it would order all troops to return to their barracks; the army would no longer attempt to intervene in the political crisis. Bakhtiar, who had earlier told the American ambassador that he intended to "steal" the revolution away from Khomeini,[5] had lost his last prop. He was forced into hiding and, after several days underground, he fled to Paris; Bakhtiar had held on to power for only six weeks. Eleven days after his return, Khomeini was officially in control.

After ousting the ancien régime, the revolutionaries, still full of angry energy, had one other immediate goal: to strike at the shah's main political prop—the United States. The conditions and timing initially appeared ripe. With the army neutralized, the twenty-seven-acre American embassy compound in the heart of downtown Tehran became one of dozens of diplomatic facilities left without much protection. The limited guard detail included only thirteen American Marines and a handful of Iranian police stationed nearby. The complex they were to protect included a two-story red brick chancery, a consulate, the ambassador's residence as well as his deputy's home and four other staff houses, two warehouses, a commissary, an office building, staff quarters for the Marine guards, a motor pool and assorted other smaller buildings. The American mission was so big it had its own athletic field, two pools, woods and two tennis courts.

After the Bakhtiar government's collapse, American Ambassador William Sullivan told his staff that he anticipated an attack on the compound; he also warned Washington of the possibility.[6] "The embassy was a fat target," Holland recounted. "We had a feeling that we were going to be tested." But two days passed, and nothing happened. On February 14, after hearing street rumors, Holland wrote a memo expressing his renewed concern. It was not universally welcomed—or believed. On February 14, a political officer at the embassy scolded Holland. "The ayatollah broadcast an appeal this morning for everyone to turn in their guns," the diplomat told him. "The ayatollah says that the revolution is over." [7] But events later that day proved Holland to be all too prescient.

At 10:30 A.M., a barrage of automatic gunfire suddenly echoed throughout the compound. Glass shattered; bullets ripped through furniture and ricocheted off walls. A coordinated attack had been mounted from all sides from positions atop high-rise buildings surrounding the American mission. Stunned diplomats and staff hit the floor. "Good God, we have a war here," was Holland's first thought. [8] "People were coming over the walls shooting," said Colonel Thomas Schaefer, another defense attaché. "I can honestly say that attack sounded worse than any firefight I ever heard in Vietnam." [9]

Sullivan ordered the Marine guards not to shoot back unless their own lives were endangered. Vastly outnumbered and outgunned, the Americans had virtually no chance of holding off the attackers or winning a gunfight. As the envoys madly scrambled to shred crucial diplomatic documents, the Marines fired round after round of tear gas at the encircling mob. The Iranians, however, still managed to breach the compound's inner security by battering down the metal doors. Sullivan finally ordered his staff to surrender.

But the battle was not over. Although accounts of the next few minutes differ, the embassy press officer later recalled that, shortly after the Americans were hauled into the ambassador's office and lined against the wall, a bullet whizzed through a window and struck the picture of then U.S. Secretary of State Cyrus Vance. The frame clattered to the floor. A counterattack had begun. Ibrahim Yazdi, a naturalized American pharmacist who had returned from Houston, Texas, to be at Khomeini's side and who would soon be named foreign minister, led the assault. After learning about the attack, he had mobilized a group of Tehran University students to liberate the embassy. Once again, the compound was under fire—this time as rival groups of Iranians fought it out.

The original captors soon surrendered to Yazdi's group; they negotiated safe conduct out of the embassy in exchange for agreeing not to hurt the Americans. The ordeal was over in a few hours, and the second group of Iranians apologized for the incident, which they blamed, in classic understatement, on "undisciplined elements" of the revolution. "In times of revolution, mistakes occur," Yazdi told the Americans. "Right now it is impossible for the government to control every group in Iran. But the Provisional Government of

Iran did not want this to happen. We will try to ensure your safety."[10]

Later, Khomeini even dispatched a delegation of mullahs to the embassy to convey his apologies for actions "contrary to his wishes" and his relief that no Americans had been killed. The Iranian delegation suggested that two of the mullahs stay behind to help prevent future incidents, and Yazdi offered to transfer the entire embassy staff to a safer site. Sullivan turned down both offers, although he did accept a bodyguard and two units of forty men each from among Yazdi's revolutionaries to protect the embassy fence.[11]

Nevertheless, the banner headline in one of Tehran's evening papers that night declared, AMERICAN EMBASSY FALLS. Assaults against United States targets had also not been limited to Tehran. The Tabriz consulate was also attacked, and Americans at a sensitive United States monitoring station near the Soviet border were briefly taken hostage.[12] The incidents were a chilling harbinger of things to come.

•

The early chaos was not restricted to Iran's streets. Since the antishah movement hardly constituted a monolithic force, the turmoil also extended inside the revolution. The upheaval had originally brought together an amalgam of Iranian society: communists as well as bazaar merchants, Islamic modernists as well as rabid fundamentalists, leftist students as well as the professional middle class and, most important to Khomeini, the *mostazafin*, or the "disinherited" slum dwellers and peasants, who had gained little from Iran's oil wealth or the shah's modernizing reforms. But the multifaceted movement, which had naturally grown together in opposition, also naturally began to disintegrate after its original goal was achieved. The revolution's inherent contradictions surfaced as the disparate sectors' expectations came into conflict; each had a different vision of utopia.

Like other revolutions, Iran's upheaval was initially awkward and bloody as the nation spent the first nine months sorting out just who should rule and how. In theory, Mehdi Bazargan, a French-educated engineer, was in charge of this process. At seventy-two, Bazargan was a seasoned politician. A diminutive but intense man with a balding pate, he had headed the Iran Party, one of four factions in the National Front that had thrived in the early 1950s. He later founded the Freedom Movement. A former professor at Tehran University and the managing director of the National Iranian Oil

Company during the Mosaddeq era, Bazargan's revolutionary and Islamic credentials were irreproachable. He had gone to jail years before Khomeini and was again imprisoned for opposing the shah's White Revolution in the 1960s.[13] An early supporter and organizer of various Islamic societies, he devoted spare time to the subject of the compatibility between Islam and modern science.[14]

Bazargan's Provisional Revolutionary Government moved quickly on issues of obvious consensus after the fall of the shah's caretaker government. Iran pulled out of the pro-Western Central Treaty Organization (CENTO). Relations were severed with South Africa and Israel; Jerusalem's mission was turned over to the Palestine Liberation Organization. Oil exports, disrupted by months of strikes, were resumed.

Within two months of Khomeini's return, Iran also held a two-day referendum on the form of the new state. Backed by several secular parties as well as by moderate mullahs, Bazargan argued that the electorate should be given a choice between at least two forms of government. In the end, however, Khomeini insisted on only one option: the electorate voted either "yes" or "no" on whether Iran should become an Islamic Republic. Reports circulated widely that the red ballot, signifying rejection of an Islamic Republic, was unavailable at several polling stations and that the affirmative green ballot was the only one issued by Revolutionary Guards.[15] With revolutionary euphoria still high, however, millions of other Iranians also did not seem to mind the ballot's limitations. According to government tallies, 98 percent of the more than twenty million voters said "yes."* Khomeini pronounced April 1, 1979, the day the results were announced, as the first day of "the government of God."

The first major step in the transition should have been a signal to Bazargan of things to come, particularly of how his decisions might be defied, or worse, ignored. Although the prime minister understood that he was basically a temporary leader, he was ill equipped to handle the diversity and rivalry within the revolution's constituency during the transition. His mandate was to pull the diverse sectors together after the political and economic havoc created by fourteen months of demonstrations and crippling strikes. Specifically, he was to oversee the writing of a new constitution and na-

---

* The official tally was believable in part because those groups that opposed an Islamic Republic announced a boycott of the poll, and individuals who resisted the idea had either left the country or stayed home. Nevertheless, almost 90 percent of the electorate turned out.

tional elections for a new chief of state and parliament.[16] He truly wanted to heal the nation and to include all quarters in the process.

In a revolutionary context, Bazargan, a capable and thoughtful politician, was too ineffectual and too naive. His own following was also too small to provide him with any leverage. Finally, he was too moderate. Forces of moderation, which usually gain temporary control, have rarely survived modern revolutions. In France, Lafayette and the Girodins were pushed aside by Robespierre and the Jacobins; in the Soviet Union, the Kadets and Kerensky were overwhelmed by Lenin and the Bolsheviks.[17] Iran was no exception. From the beginning, radical organizations and undercurrents challenged Bazargan's pragmatic course. The prime minister knew he was under pressure from a plethora of groups, ranging from leftists and ethnic communities to Islamic socialists.* What he did not count on was subterfuge and sabotage from the quarters he originally thought were his biggest backers: the mullahs.

The first major tension played out along the same lines as the clash between different Iranian groups at the American embassy: more pragmatic elements who favored gradual change and hardline, committed zealots who wanted to extend the revolution to its logical conclusion. At the highest level, the opposing ambitions were represented by Bazargan's Provisional Revolutionary Government on the one side and the Revolutionary Council on the other.

Composed of between sixteen and nineteen members, the Revolutionary Council had originally been organized by Khomeini during his final weeks of exile in Paris. The supersecret body was made up of the leading clerics and supporters whom the imam most trusted. Bazargan, ironically, was one of its original members. But after his appointment by the Revolutionary Council as premier, Bazargan and the other secular council members who formed part of the first Provisional Government cabinet were replaced. The two bodies were supposed to work in tandem, and they originally did. The Revolutionary Council provided guidelines and rulings for changes, which the Provisional Government enacted in the daily running of the state. But the cooperation soon became co-optation.

The breakdown evolved over disputes ranging from punishment of the shah's associates to ambassadorial appointments.[18] The issues might have seemed trivial in the context of the broader mission, but

---

* Islamic socialists, the most prominent of whom were the Mojahedin-e Khalq, or People's Holy Warriors, blended Islam and Marxism.

they were, in fact, at the very heart of the revolutionary transition: Was the goal merely to oust the Pahlavi dynasty and then quickly get back to business? Or was it, after the shah's exit, to remake society?

The Provisional Government wanted an orderly transition in which justice was dispensed according to the human rights code that the shah had abused. Many members of the Revolutionary Council, however, advocated rapid retribution against those who carried out the shah's unjust orders. Bazargan wanted envoys skilled in diplomacy or, at minimum, seasoned in politics and international affairs. The Revolutionary Council, however, preferred ideologues who were prepared, if necessary, to defy international convention.

The differences were reflected in the February 14 attack on the American embassy. Although they envisioned a change in the Tehran-Washington relationship, most members of the Provisional Government were prepared to maintain relations with the United States, to continue selling it Iranian oil and, in turn, to carry on Iranian purchases of American military equipment. Ibrahim Yazdi had been willing to order an attack on his own revolutionary colleagues to preserve the connection. The more ardent revolutionaries, however, threw caution to the wind. Whatever the cost to Iran economically, militarily, or diplomatically, they sought to assert national independence by ridding the country of the Great Satan. It was a natural extension of the revolution since, they believed, the shah had been put back on the throne in 1953 and then survived another twenty-six years courtesy of the United States.

Although it represented only a small fraction of those involved in the shah's ouster, the Revolutionary Council always had the edge over the broader-based Provisional Government. Bazargan had to rely on the tired machinery of the ancien régime.[19] The Revolutionary Council, however, was strengthened by the activities of three vigorous new revolutionary organizations, whose misadventures helped precipitate the break.

At the top of the list were the komitehs, or committees, that had sprung up around neighborhood mosques and among students and workers to organize the antishah strikes and demonstrations. After Khomeini's return, the komitehs evolved into a rival authority to the police and gendarmerie, both too weakened to countermand them. Many were basically vigilantes determined to prevent a counterrevolution. The revolution's early excesses were often tied to these ad hoc groups, which set out to enforce obedience or submission to the new orthodoxy.[20] The komitehs often arbitrarily arrested men and women, and occasionally children, for anything from suspected prostitution to antirevolutionary activities, which were rarely specified. Homes were searched for incriminating evidence, including liquor and chessboards, the latter banned because the pieces were associated with the monarchy. Passengers were harassed at impromptu komiteh roadblocks, which scrutinized identity papers in the hunt for potential saboteurs. Anyone suspected of less than absolute loyalty was in danger of being terrorized.

At first, the komitehs were, literally, out of control. Loyal to a local mullah or, occasionally in the early stages, to a leftist group, they were largely unsupervised. They also proliferated as it became clear that membership was a route to the new brand of power. In Tehran alone, estimates of the number of komitehs ranged wildly from a thousand to forty-five hundred.[21] Nationwide, Bazargan once said, "The committees are everywhere, and no one knows how many exist, not even the imam himself."[22] The premier constantly criticized them and pleaded for restraint.

The Provisional Government's attempts to rein them in, however, backfired. A series of purges and edicts limiting their activities instead streamlined and purified the komitehs.[23] Leftists and Islamic socialists were largely eliminated, leaving mainly fundamentalists in control. As the komitehs gradually came under the de facto control of the Revolutionary Council, they took on paragovernment functions, such as intervening in neighborhood or local labor disputes and distribution of basic goods. They became, in some ways, a rough equivalent of the Russian soviets, or councils, and France's Jacobin societies, through which the more militant Russian and French revolutionaries built up an alternative government and eventually consolidated their hold on power over the moderates.

Next on the list were the tribunals, which were responsible for some of the most heinous acts. Sadeq Khalkhali, the most notorious revolutionary tribunal judge, once explained the courts' outlook: "Human rights mean that unsuitable individuals should be liquidated so that others can live free."[24] On February 15, the day after the attack on the American embassy, the court carried out its first executions. Revolutionary justice was swift and bloody. At the former girls' school compound where the Khomeini entourage had set up its temporary headquarters, four ranking military commanders, accused of multiple counts of "corruption on earth" and "crimes against God," were tried secretly—reportedly without the right of defense attorneys. Early the next morning, they were taken up on the roof and shot. Military and SAVAK officers, cabinet ministers, former members of parliament, and other officials in the shah's regime later faced a similar fate.

Bazargan pleaded for an end to the tribunals' bloodletting, which was another threat to his own powers. He publicly called the executions "irreligious, inhuman and disgraceful."[25] Khomeini intervened twice to quiet the domestic and international uproar, which included public condemnation from more moderate mullahs and a resolution by the U.S. Senate. The courts were reorganized under the Revolutionary Council, and their jurisdiction limited to antirevolutionary crimes.

Khomeini later declared that capital punishment should be limited to those responsible for killings during the shah's rule.[26] But the executions continued unabated. During the revolution's first nine months, almost six hundred Iranians faced the firing squad. "The Revolutionary Courts were born out of the anger of the Iranian people, and these people will not accept any principles outside Islamic principles," commented Khalkhali. "There is no room in the Revolutionary Courts for defense lawyers because they keep quoting laws to play for time, and this tries the patience of the people."[27]

Last on the list of organizations driving the revolution was the Revolutionary Guards Corps, or Sepah Pasdaran, the military arm of the Revolutionary Council. While the komitehs and the tribunals grew out of a need to preempt potential dangers and the desire for retribution, the Pasdaran was formally created in May 1979 in response to a genuine threat. The Revolutionary Council chairman, one of Khomeini's former *talabeh* students, had been assassinated a few days earlier, and another prominent council member, Ali Akbar Hashemi Rafsanjani, was shot at and injured the same month. The revolutionary mullahs needed a loyal support unit to protect them. Despite massive purges and desertions, the regular military was still viewed with suspicion by the Revolutionary Council—for good reason, as it later turned out.

In contrast to the smart, American-style khakis and uniforms of the Iranian army, navy and air force, the Pasdaran wore plain green fatigues without insignia, medals, rank or even epaulets. A simple yellow-and-blue badge, often encased in plastic, was attached to the breast pocket. Although both their training and their arms were minimal at first, the Pasdaran quickly gained greater stature as a powerful internal security force. Besides providing bodyguards for the mullahs and security for their facilities, the Pasdaran also played a crucial role in quelling some of the ethnic uprisings and in running the burgeoning prisons.[28] Originally strictly volunteers and closely vetted, the Pasdars were in some ways the Iranian counterparts to the political commissars Lenin used as an ideological force in the Russian army.[29]

During the first nine months, the four revolutionary organizations strengthened their positions through edicts from the top and through harassment and terror from the bottom. In the process, they eventually evolved into a rival state apparatus. The dispute between the Revolutionary Council and the Provisional Government rapidly grew into a full-scale power struggle, the first of several that were to become a trademark of the revolution throughout its first decade, albeit among different quarters. The militant revolutionaries not only gained more power, they also developed the institutions to back them up.

Well-intentioned but weak, Bazargan lacked both the charisma and the authority to control the revolution's course. He could not even get the hundreds of thousands of Iranians who had refused to pay their taxes, utility bills or bus fares during the final months before the shah left to resume payments. His repeated appeals were countered by Khomeini's speeches suggesting that the *mostazafin* should not have to sacrifice further to pay taxes.[30] Bazargan never stood a chance. His frustrated cabinet ministers slowly began to drift away. The other institutions Bazargan had inherited—the army and police, the civil service and courts, and the executive-branch ministries—had been sufficiently decimated or intimidated that his Provisional Government was increasingly vulnerable.

Bazargan attempted pragmatic compromise. He brought members of the Revolutionary Council into his cabinet. He offered his resignation at least three times, only to be told by Khomeini on each occasion to go back and try again. He appealed to the imam, in person and in a string of sometimes whining letters, to provide guidance to settle the disputes. He even went public. By August 1979, he complained that his government was "a knife without a blade. Power must rest with one responsible body, not with many komitehs or the imam."[31] The imam's calculated reluctance to intervene on Bazargan's behalf further endangered the prime minister's already tenuous hold on power, which slipped further as he spent more and more of his time on the defensive. It seemed only a matter of time before Bazargan would have to give up—just as his moderate predecessors in other revolutionary environments had also had to surrender to the inevitable course of revolutions.

•

During the summer of 1979, Colonel Holland detected the first hint of public disenchantment about the revolution as expectations went unfulfilled. "The luster had begun to wear off a bit," he recalled.[32] "The economy had ground to a halt, and some of the kick had gone out of the revolution." The shape of the changes ahead was beginning to crystallize—and alienate. The government nationalized private banks, private insurance companies and some private industrial sectors. Relations deteriorated with both superpowers. New press restrictions imposed terms of imprisonment for criticizing Islam; they also prohibited anyone associated with the shah from publishing. More than two dozen publications were closed down by the end of the summer. Political groups that had marched against the shah but were outside the tight Khomeini inner circle were increasingly looked upon as the opposition. Several offices were raided. In return, the mullahs became the target of the first attacks and assassination attempts.

The most volatile issue during this period was the form of a new constitution.* Everyone wanted in on the debate, from women's groups to artists and book dealers. Two drafts had been put forward in April and June 1979. Both sparked fierce reaction from a variety of sources on a variety of issues: more moderate mullahs opposed provisions for clerical dominance in government. They were content to have government run by experienced technocrats, with the clergy offering guidance from afar. Islamic socialists proposed strict centralization and regulation of the economy on behalf of the masses. Ethnic minorities demanded provisions for greater autonomy in their regions. Fearful that a strong president, as the drafts called for, would merely replicate the monarchy, legal experts argued instead for a strong parliament. They also advocated an elected rather than an appointed judiciary. According to one account, sixty-two draft constitutions and more than four thousand constitutional proposals were put forward.[33]

At this stage, it was not at all clear that Khomeini intended for the Islamic Republic to become a theocracy, or a state ruled by the clergy. Indeed, after his return, Khomeini went back to the Qom seminary and the simple mud-brick home where he had taught and

---

* Some quarters had argued that the constitution should have been drafted before Iranians were asked to vote on whether Iran should become an Islamic Republic, a proposal that the hard-line clergy effectively vetoed. It was a shrewd tactic, which preempted opposition arguments, for an Islamic Republic, of course, had to have an Islamic constitution.

lived before his exile. He communicated with the Bazargan government as well as with other parties vying for power through his second son and new chief of staff, Ahmad, or when interested parties made the pilgrimage from Tehran to Qom. Khomeini seemed content to leave the workings of government in the hands of the Tehran technocrats, while his role was at first limited to guide or counselor during disputes.

The ayatollah's only writing on Islamic government, published long before the revolution had even seemed possible, never mentioned a theocracy. "We do not say that government must be in the hands of the Islamic Jurisprudent. Rather we say that government must be run in accordance with God's law," he said. Supervision by religious leaders, he noted, "in no way conflicts with public order, the stability of government, or the interests of the country."[34]

Khomeini's interviews during his final months in exile also did not indicate that he planned to establish a theocracy. "Our intention is not that religious leaders should themselves administer the state, but that they should guide the people in determining what the demands of Islam are," he told *Le Monde*. He told another interviewer that the clergy "should not participate in government."[35] Both of the first two constitutional drafts called for a strong president to lead the nation; neither contained a provision for the leading Muslim jurist, or *Veliyat-e Faqih*,* to be the ultimate arbiter of power over all three branches of government.

One of the mysteries of the revolution's first nine months centers on Khomeini's real intentions. Did he plan to accept the original constitution and only later introduce the concept of a theocracy with a *faqih*—meaning himself—at its helm? Or was he indeed content with the drafts' original provisions, which would have relegated him to the sidelines? The evidence indicates that the imam's goals were still limited. He had accepted the second draft and was prepared, after all, to submit it to a national referendum.

But, again following the pattern of earlier revolutions, the opposition forced further debate. After dissenters argued against accepting the second draft, the Revolutionary Council was forced into a compromise: Let the population go to the polls to choose a panel of

---

* The concept of a *faqih* is alien to Western societies. As British scholar Sir John Malcolm wrote in the nineteenth century about the status of the ayatollahs, "It is not easy to describe persons who fill no office, receive no appointment, who have no specific duties, but who are called—from their superior learning, piety and virtue—by the silent but unanimous suffrage of the inhabitants . . . to be their guides in religion and their protectors against the violence and oppression of their rulers, and who receive from those by whose feeling they are elevated a respect and duty." The *faqih* emerged from this group.

seventy-three experts, a so-called Assembly of Experts,* who would sort through the different positions and write a final draft to put to the nation. From the dissenters' vantage point, it was a classic mistake. Rafsanjani, a Revolutionary Council member, correctly warned them, "You will regret your own decision." [36]

Rather than being trampled by the opposition forces, the hard-liners' resolve only hardened. First, they manipulated the list of candidates so that it was heavily weighted in their favor. Although more than a thousand candidates were eventually cleared to run, several parties boycotted the poll, charging harassment and preferential selection of candidates. As a result, the new Islamic Republic Party (IRP), which represented the views of Khomeini and the Revolutionary Council, won control of about two-thirds of the seats. The revolutionary zealots then used the Assembly of Experts as an opportunity not to mediate differences but to push for their own changes and to increase their own powers. The result was a third constitutional draft more militant and more theocratic than either of the first two.

The final version called for a top-heavy bureaucracy laden with checks and balances; it was also, in every detail, thoroughly Islamic. Chapter one stipulates that government is based on faith in one God and that "man should submit to His will." To the customary three branches of government—an executive, a legislature and a judiciary—was added a fourth, the twelve-member Council of Guardians. Six theologians were appointed by Khomeini and six by the parliament. Mandated to verify that all legislation complied with Islamic tenets, it had total veto power over parliament. The president of the Supreme Court also had to be a "just theologian." The Bill of Rights was, on the surface, generous on individual freedoms, except that all actions deemed anti-Islamic were automatically banned.

But the most important—and controversial—issue was ultimate authority. The original drafts had called for a strong presidency; in the final version, the presidency was weakened and real leadership transferred to a *faqih,* a Supreme Jurisprudent, or a council of between three and five ayatollahs. The *faqih* is, in effect, all-powerful. His appointment powers are extensive over the judiciary, the military and the Council of Guardians; he also has de facto veto power over candidates running for virtually any office and the right to

---

* The Assembly was not all Muslim. In what became a model for the parliament, the Christian, Jewish and Zoroastrian communities also had specially allocated seats.

dismiss the president. He holds the title of commander-in-chief. Unlike other branches of government, his term is unlimited.*

The concept of a *faqih* was revolutionary within Shi'a Islam. Shi'ism had always distanced itself from the conventional state. In the absence of the twelfth imam, the faith did call for a qualified alternative to lead the community—although always independently from the government. Khomeini defied tradition, however, by translating this role to leadership of the state. Heavily influenced by Plato's *Republic*, which he had studied as a young theologian, Khomeini adapted the concept of a philosopher-king for a system led by those best qualified and most conversant on Islamic law.[37] Specifically, Iran's philosopher-kings were the clerics. The final draft constitution gave the *faqih* jurisdiction not only over the religious institutions and interpretation of religious doctrine, it also gave him the final word on government actions taken by the executive, legislative and judicial branches.

The reaction to this provision, drawn up in the early fall of 1979, was widespread and fierce. The more moderate or modernist clergy were among the most vocal opponents, although dissent also spread among leftists, religious minorities, ethnic groups and other quarters. In October, Bazargan publicly warned of "a dictatorship of the clergy." He even tried to convince Khomeini to dismiss the Assembly of Experts on the pretext of procedural problems, but the ayatollah refused.[38]

Khomeini also rejected out-of-hand growing criticism that Iran was going to once again fall under the rule of a dictator. The opposition was too fragmented to effectively block the proposal, but by October the momentum behind it was the most serious threat to date to institutionalizing clerical rule. The mullahs were aware that the national referendum on the constitution, set for December and already threatened with boycotts by several of Khomeini's former allies, could be embarrassing at a time when the fragile revolution needed to show widespread support in order to survive.

•

As rival forces in Iran clashed over the framework for the Islamic Republic's future, another drama was playing out on the other side of the world. The beleaguered shah, riddled with lymphatic cancer and shunned by most of his old allies, was having problems finding a home to end his wandering exile. After brief residences in Egypt,

---

* In contrast, the president was limited to a maximum of two four-year terms, members of the unicameral parliament to an unlimited number of four-year terms, the Supreme Judicial Council to five years and the Council of Guardians to six years.

Morocco and the Bahamas, he tried Mexico. But renewed pressures from the shah's old American allies—Henry Kissinger, David Rockefeller and others—were mounting on the Carter administration to provide at least humanitarian aid to a long-standing U.S. ally. The American embassy in Tehran had repeatedly and vehemently warned of the consequences of admitting him to the United States. But Washington eventually succumbed and, on October 22, 1979, allowed the shah and his family to fly to New York for treatment.

After the aborted Valentine's Day occupation of the embassy, the United States had maintained fragile relations with the Islamic Republic. Chants of *Marg bar Amrika,* or "Death to America," were common in public gatherings, and in August a couple of rounds of rocket-propelled grenades had landed in the embassy compound grounds. But the Carter administration maintained quiet channels of communication with Bazargan and his aides. At the same time, however, the United States avoided or ignored many of the key mullahs and revolutionary organizations. There is no known record of any meeting between American political or intelligence emissaries and Khomeini, either when he was in exile or after his return to Iran. The United States consistently failed to deal directly with him or what he represented.

The shah's move came at a particularly sensitive time domestically. Controversy raged over the constitution. The diverse factions that together had staged the revolution were increasingly taking potshots, both verbal and literal, at each other. Bazargan became totally frustrated and despondent about the rival government that had made his job virtually impossible. Simmering public disenchantment with the way the revolution was unfolding became visible in demonstrations. Several issues needed a focus or a catalyst for resolution.

News of the shah's travel to New York stimulated xenophobic fears in Iran about the United States' intentions.* Many Iranians, not only those associated with the new regime, still feared that Washington was waiting in anticipation of the appropriate moment to intervene. Even among Iranians opposed to or disillusioned by

---

* Although Iranians always feared and fiercely resisted foreign invasions and domination, their apprehension about the West dates back to the late nineteenth century and Britain's commercial thrust into Iran. In 1872, Baron Paul Julius von Reuter, founder of the British news agency, won a monopoly to exploit Iranian mines and forests and to run the Iranian railway, banks and customs. In 1891, a British company was granted a monopoly of Iranian tobacco. In both cases, the clergy led successful opposition campaigns against the concessions.

the revolution, the ability to stand up to the United States had strong nationalistic appeal. Many admired America and wanted to visit or to get educations there, but they did not want to be its surrogates. Cries went out throughout Iran for the United States to hand over the deposed shah. To further complicate the crisis, Bazargan led an Iranian delegation to Algeria, where, among other things, he met with President Carter's National Security advisor, Zbigniew Brzezinski, on November 1. News of the meeting was broadcast that night on Iranian television. The trip wires were set.

November 4, 1979, marked a double anniversary in Iran. Fifteen years earlier Khomeini had been sent into exile for protesting Iran's policy of diplomatic immunity for American military personnel. And one year earlier a particularly bloody clash erupted between the shah's security forces and young demonstrators at Tehran University, which was about two miles from the American embassy compound. Several protestors had been killed by American-trained Iranian troops. So emotions were already running high; the United States' offer of refuge to the shah further fueled those passions. Once again, the U.S. diplomatic mission became the obvious target.

After the Valentine's Day attack almost nine months earlier, the American embassy had been heavily fortified. Bullet-proof glass was installed and many windows sealed; new armor-plated doors were put in to prevent penetration. Before leaving Tehran for retirement, Ambassador Sullivan had warned Washington months earlier that initial appeals to allow the shah into the United States would almost certainly result in the seizure of American diplomats.[39]

Yet neither the Americans in Tehran nor the Carter administration had fully read the warning signs. Indeed, diplomats' wives, who had been evacuated during the uprising against the shah, had just been told that they could soon return to Iran. The United States was even sufficiently emboldened to request diplomatic immunity for the embassy's military personnel again; that very morning, two top envoys had also gone to the Iranian Foreign Ministry to make, among several representations, a formal request over the same controversial issue that had ultimately led to Khomeini's deportation exactly fifteen years earlier.

November 4 was a hazy, dank, lethargic day. Shortly after 10:00 A.M., a large crowd burst through the embassy's front gate. Compared with the February assault, there was initially little alarm at the compound. Unlike the earlier incident, there was no wild gunfire and no frenzied crawling over the compound's eight-foot fence.

Colonel Holland and others recalled that the first demonstrators were all women. Walking several abreast, their all-enveloping black chadors billowing, they paraded in neat order around the grounds to the shouts of "Death to America."[40] Political Officer Mike Metrinko assumed it would be a brief encounter. He decided that he would still be able to keep a luncheon engagement.[41] Others also initially thought it was just a matter of sitting it out.

But unlike the February attack, which was basically an emotional outburst, the November 4 takeover was much better planned. Nine days earlier, some eighty students, largely from Polytechnique University,[42] had assembled in a northern Tehran suburb to discuss a course of action to protest the shah's admission to the United States as well as disturbing recent "tendencies" within the revolution. Bazargan was seen as having led the nation astray again, in part because of his dealings with the United States. A catalyst was needed to set the revolution back on course and to ensure that the fundamentalists' position was not derailed by dissent on the constitution.

After heated debate, the students agreed to stage a sit-in at the American embassy. They would try, they also agreed, to hold out for three to five days. The planning was meticulous. Students were recruited from a cross-section of Tehran colleges. Maps of the United States mission were printed, and special armbands and identity cards distributed. A prominent mullah was consulted and brought into the planning.[43] The planners even thought of making large stenciled prints of Khomeini to attach to the chests of the demonstrators. They realized that, if violence broke out, a photo of a youth killed from a bullet fired through a picture of the imam's face would play right into the hands of the demonstrators—and have awesome repercussions for the United States.

The Americans never really had a chance. Apparently with the help of inside information, the demonstrators knew exactly which basement window in the main chancery could be penetrated; it was an emergency fire exit. They also knew which buildings in the compound were without security and that the Marine guards were housed in an apartment building across the street; they took those vulnerable positions—and Americans—first. The first hostages were all blindfolded and their wrists tied; some, pistols pointed at their heads, were paraded around the chancery to force out the others. Diplomats and Iranian staff in the two main buildings tried to hold out, at least until they could shred classified documents. This time, however, the attackers had also learned how to counter tear gas by lighting smoky fires to dissipate the fumes. There seemed no way to keep them back. Finally, once again, the Americans were forced to let the Iranians into the secured areas.

The first moments were uncertain; the hostages and their captors were both unsure of what to do next. Some of the Americans were roughed up, others were reassured that nothing was going to happen. "Don't be scared. We won't hurt you," an American communications officer was told. "We just want to teach you. We will bring you Khomeini's thoughts. We will teach you about God. We will teach the CIA not to do these terrible things to our country."[44] The most striking aspect of the discourse on that first day, however, was the enormous gap between the Iranians and the Americans after more than three decades of close relations between their governments.

After listening to an anti-American tirade from one of his female captors, the embassy press officer told her to calm down and, reaching for a gallon of scotch, offered her a drink; liquor is anathema to a devout Muslim. In another exchange, one of the male captors inquired about the meaning of the witches, skeletons and goblins hung on the walls of a room in the ambassador's residence. They were left over from a Halloween party a few days earlier. Despite the explanation that it was a fete when candy was distributed to children, he was apparently not convinced. Pointing at a skeleton, the captor asked again, "You do this for children?" In a more brutal moment, another captor ripped out a television cord and slapped one of the American military personnel across the bottom of his shoeless foot. "This is the way the shah's army tortured innocent Iranians," he told the hostage.[45] Both the Iranian military and intelligence services had been trained by the United States, and many revolutionaries blamed the Americans for their actions.

One of the few Americans who spoke Farsi had some unusual exchanges in discussions with his captors about Islam and then Christianity. "Most of them were curious," he recalled. "They were very interested in the Biblical idea of turning the other cheek. . . . They wanted me to explain that." He described them as typical of other Iranian youths he had met from small towns who had been brought up in strict traditional homes. "Most of them had probably never seen an American before. I think a lot of them were surprised to find out that we didn't have horns. They didn't know what an American was like, and some probably didn't even know where America is. They expected us to be some kind of monsters."[46]

The Iranians' attitude was summed up in their conversation with a consular official over an American scheme to build poor roads in Iran so that, they charged, Iranians would be killed. The consular official countered that Iranians were simply lousy drivers. "Over and over again they came back to the idea that the shah had ruined their country, and America was responsible for the shah," he later recalled. "Every evil that had ever befallen Iran was America's fault." [47]

Throughout the day, many of the Americans waited anxiously to be liberated. Three United States envoys were still at the Foreign Ministry; they had decided to stay put and to try to persuade the authorities to take action. But Ibrahim Yazdi, who had led the earlier counterattack and was now foreign minister, was unable to rescue the Americans this time around. "I think his unwillingness to do so was probably the best testimony of just how low the Provisional Revolutionary Government had fallen," said one of the diplomats. "They just had no credibility with anyone at all. Yazdi recognized that; hence his refusal to get involved." [48] Added Metrinko, the embassy political officer, "By this stage, he was simply being excluded from the decision-making process by the inner circle, which was the real government and which used the facade of the Provisional Government as part of its sound-and-light show." [49]

The Students Following the Imam's Line, as the captors announced themselves, were clearly euphoric about their conquest of the "den of spies," as they dubbed the embassy. In some ways, this was symbolically as important an achievement as ridding Iran of the shah. It was the fulfillment of the revolution, for the omnipotent Great Satan had been humiliated and beaten. In brazen pronouncements to the tens of thousands who turned out the next morning to show their support, the youths demanded that the United States hand over the former monarch. He would, they announced, be tried by a revolutionary tribunal. As well planned as the embassy seizure had been, however, the youths clearly had no plans about what to do once it was taken—which some of them talked about openly in front of the hostages.

In its early attempts to resolve the crisis, the Carter administration recognized only the foreign-policy side of the crisis, not the captors' domestic agenda. The young zealots, who were of similar thinking if not all originally from the same Islamic society or komiteh, were testing the waters or, as one hostage put it, forcing "a showdown between the government and its opponents." [50] Specifically, the seizure forced Khomeini's hand. He had not ordered the takeover, but the outcome of the crisis was now up to him.

The embassy occupation provided the most visible indication thus far of the imam's style of leadership and of his role in the early stages of the revolution. "His style of leadership has always been to lead from the rear," the embassy's political officer later recounted. "Khomeini is inclined to look and see which way the winds are blowing, and then endorse the strongest current, or what appears to be the strongest current."[51] The ayatollah was rarely decisive unless he thought a move had clear-cut support from either the majority or the most important quarters.

For two days, the suspense mounted. Bazargan once again pleaded for intervention, knowing that the Provisional Government was at stake. Meanwhile, the students orchestrated their own campaign to prove that the seizure was truly popular and in the long-term interests of the revolution. The scene outside the embassy became a festival of hatred. Graffiti was scrawled in English and Farsi across the high brick wall as chanting crowds roared their approval. A long line of speakers was brought in to condemn the Great Satan and, implicitly, to back the captors. Various mullahs, including Khomeini's son Ahmad, were escorted through the compound to view the still-bound hostages as well as the documents and "spy devices" the captors had seized. "We were waiting to see if [the government] would expel us or make problems," a student leader conceded at a press conference.[52]

In the end, the takeover proved to be the stimulus needed to break the political stalemate in Iran. On November 6, Tehran Radio announced that Khomeini had given his blessing to the seizure of the den of spies. Several hostages later recalled the wild cheering that erupted among their captors. "What we are doing is a great thing! We are blessed by Allah!" one of the students told a hostage.[53] He appeared to be rather stunned by the pronouncement. But another news bulletin brought even more chilling news for the hostages. Bazargan and Yazdi had resigned; the Revolutionary Council, whose membership was finally revealed, was now in official control.

A month later, the proposed Islamic constitution was put to the nation for a vote. The timing was deliberate; the mullahs called for the referendum on the day after Ashura, the emotional commemoration of Hosain's martyrdom when Shi'ite fervor is always at a peak. The climate in Iran, however, had changed dramatically since the seizure of the embassy; the ayatollah's opponents had been at last temporarily silenced. Events in the Islamic Republic once again dominated the world press. Third World nations were taking more notice, while prominent world figures sought time with the leadership over the hostage crisis. The fervor that had dissipated since Khomeini's return was again evident in demonstrations by tens of thousands in front of the American compound. Despite their domestic economic problems and political differences, the revolutionaries knew they had the upper hand internationally. The new momentum helped counter opposition to the constitution. Although the turnout was lower than the referendum on an Islamic republic, the document won 99.5 percent approval from almost sixteen million voters. The revolutionary spirit had been revived, and the hostages' fate sealed for 444 days—until they were no longer of use to the mullahs in realizing the rest of their domestic agenda.

CHAPTER THREE

God Against the Infidels

ๆฆ

"Victory is not achieved by swords; it can be achieved only by blood. Victory is not achieved by large populations; it is achieved by strength of faith."

—Ayatollah Khomeini[1]

"We are all your soldiers, Khomeini. Our ears are open to your commands."

—Parliamentary deputies
at premier session[2]

Throughout the spring and summer of 1980, Tehran and Baghdad had taken to taunting each other, in words and occasionally through artillery barrages. With bombast and bravado, Tehran Radio described new Iraqi President Saddam Hussein as "a puppet of satan" and "mentally ill"; his government colleagues were alternately referred to as "fascist butchers" and "the gangsters and tyrants of Baghdad."[3] Ayatollah Khomeini brazenly called on Iraq's Shi'ite majority to launch a jihad against the socialist infidels of Iraq's ruling Baath Party.*

* *Baath* means "renaissance" in Arabic. The Baath Party, founded in the 1950s, seized power in Iraq in 1968. Its pan-Arab ideology is socialist and secular. A rival version of Baathism is also the ruling ideology in Syria.

Baghdad had responded in kind, unleashing a propaganda war against Iran and allowing Iranian dissidents access to radio stations to incite Iran's armed forces and other groups to rebel. Iraqi radio referred to Iran's ruling mullahs as "racist Persians" and warned of their danger to the entire twenty-two-nation Arab bloc. Iraq tried to stir up opposition among Iran's ethnic minorities and among Iran's Arab population in oil-rich Khuzistan Province. Tens of thousands of guns to aid potential insurgents were smuggled across the border as part of Iraq's support and encouragement of its Arab brothers.[4]

The childish rhetoric on both sides seemed almost silly, but the tension was potentially threatening. Together, the two Persian Gulf powers exported between three and five million barrels of oil each day, most of it to the West. An escalation might also disrupt freedom of navigation through the strategic Strait of Hormuz, the narrow channel through which more than 40 percent of the industrialized democracies' oil imports passed. Finally, the volatile region had already been tormented by more than thirty years of Arab-Israeli wars, and the Soviet Union's 1979 invasion of Afghanistan had created near panic in the neighboring Persian Gulf and in the Asian subcontinent. The Middle East did not need a new hot spot.

The international consensus was that the dispute would probably remain symbolic and localized along the frontier. Historically, the demarcation line between the Arab world and the Persians had been the scene of dozens of border disputes and wars over ethnic, religious, territorial and ideological differences. This round of tension seemed merely an extension of the long-standing rivalry. On September 21, 1980, U.S. Defense Secretary Harold Brown acknowledged that the fighting had "gone beyond skirmishing," but he contended that the conflict was "not a major war."[5] So the Iranian leadership was not the only party stunned when, at dawn the very next day, an estimated fifty thousand Iraqi troops pushed hard and fast across four strategic junctures along the desert and swampland border with Iran. The infantry assault was backed up by waves of Iraqi strikes on Iran's major military installations and airfields. Baghdad had finally decided to invade.

Even after the incursion, however, the reaction was not excessively alarmist. A CIA estimate predicted that Iran would last only three weeks against the Iraqi assault.[6] Captains of a fleet of oil supertankers seemed to agree; they decided to drop anchor and wait until the war ended. "Given the limited military capabilities of the combatants, the war did not appear likely to be a prolonged one," concluded *Time*'s cover story.[7]

The assessment applied particularly to Iran, which was more vulnerable than at any time since British and Soviet troops withdrew after World War II. The regular military had been crippled in 1979 by the exodus of monarchists and the detention or execution of ranking officers. "I inherited an army that didn't have a single soldier in Tehran," commented the newly appointed army chief of staff a month after the revolution.[8] Shortly before Iraq's invasion, the defense minister revealed that seventy-five hundred officers had been removed in another two-month purge.[9] The military was then drained by mass arrests linked to three coup attempts within the military in the summer preceding the war. By September 1980, the army's strength was estimated to be less than half what it was on the day the shah left twenty months earlier. At least one-third of the officer corps above the rank of major had been removed or replaced.

The remaining army, navy and air force troops were also ill equipped. A year earlier, the Islamic Republic had cancelled a $9 billion arms deal with the United States, while purchases already in the system from the shah's era had been frozen, along with other Iranian assets in the United States, after the American embassy seizure. Iran had even sought to return eighty F-14 warplanes and the stock of Phoenix missiles to the United States. Other equipment was in sad repair from simple neglect or as a result of the government's decision to cut off military supplies to avoid another internal challenge. One estimate claimed that only 30 percent of Iran's British-made Chieftain tanks were operational and that virtually the entire helicopter force had been grounded.

Since the revolution, the mullahs had focused on building up the Revolutionary Guards as a more reliable alternative to the army. Their disdain and distrust of the military were evident when they cut conscription to only one year and slashed the defense budget by a third. Meanwhile, the Pasdaran had quadrupled in size, but they were poorly organized and their training was limited. Their experience had so far been confined to putting down uprisings among poorly armed and untrained ethnic minorities, such as the Kurds in the west and the Baluchis in the southeast. The Pasdaran knew little about artillery and nothing about conventional warfare. Although the shah's four-hundred-thousand-strong military had been deemed the most powerful in the Middle East, revolutionary Iran had, by its own hand, become ill prepared even to defend itself.

Indeed, Tehran had been able to muster only parts of two divisions in response to the Iraqi attack.[10]

Most early projections suggested that Iraq would thrust as deep as possible, then sue for peace. The terms, depending on Iraqi positions, would be territorial. Some pundits went so far as to predict that the war would lead to the final disintegration of Iran's military and, possibly, the collapse of the Islamic regime. But virtually everyone was wrong. The war would turn out to be the new wind that the revolution needed, almost desperately. It would also become the longest and bloodiest conflict in modern Middle East history.

•

The 730-mile demarcation line between Iran and Iraq is an erratic frontier that wiggles down from the bleak mountain ranges of northern Kurdistan to the desert scrub and swampland in the oil-rich south. Dividing the ancient Mesopotamian plain from the Persian plateau, it is one of the few international borders to have remained relatively consistent for almost four centuries. Politically and physically, however, it has long been an unfriendly border.

In theory, the Iran-Iraq war erupted primarily over rights to the Shatt al-Arab, the strategic waterway where three of the regions' great rivers, the Euphrates and the Tigris in Iraq and the Karun in Iran, merge and flow into the Persian Gulf. The last, swampy leg of the Shatt is also the border, and access to it has been an issue for more than three centuries. Otherwise landlocked, Iraq needs the waterway as its only outlet to the Gulf sea-lanes. Iran needs the estuary to export oil from its Abadan refinery, the largest in the Middle East and one of the biggest in the world. Iran's most vital port, at Khorramshahr, is also more than thirty miles up the Shatt.

Since both Iran and Iraq have rivers flowing into the Shatt, both nations claimed a right to its use. After Iraq was carved into a nation by the British following the collapse of the Ottoman Empire, however, Baghdad claimed that it had inherited the Ottoman's control over the estuary. In a formal treaty between the two nations, Iran's Reza Shah reluctantly granted Iraq that right in 1937. But after the socialist Baath Party seized power in 1968, the new regime in Baghdad tried to charge Iranian ships for its use. Tehran refused to pay for use of a waterway to which its own river contributed, and Mohammad Reza Shah abrogated the agreement. Border tension flared sporadically until 1975, when Baghdad was finally forced to cede partial control of the Shatt to Tehran. The new border was based on the *thalweg,* or median line of the deepest channel.

Control of the Shatt al-Arab was, however, only the symbolic cover for a broader conflict in 1980. Also at stake were deepening ideological differences and a personal feud between two men: Ayatollah Khomeini and President Hussein. Both had come to power in 1979, and both had great plans for the region.

Khomeini, almost an octogenarian, was the oldest leader in the Middle East. His dream was the revival of Islam to replace the failed modern ideologies of capitalism and communism—especially in countries, such as Iraq, where injustice reined. To the ayatollah, the Iraqi Shi'a were victims of Baathist rule. Although the Shi'a constituted the majority, they were largely excluded from the political system and their incomes and standards of living were generally the lowest. And although the Shi'a lived over and worked many of Iraq's prime oil fields, they received few benefits from oil wealth. Khomeini's vendetta against the Iraq regime was also personal. Baghdad's expulsion of the ayatollah in 1978 had been ordered by then vice president Saddam Hussein; Khomeini never forgave Saddam for selling out to the shah.

At forty-three, Saddam, as he was popularly known, was then one of the two youngest chiefs of state in the Middle East. His pan-Arab socialism was avowedly secular, and his agenda was to modernize Iraq, particularly its military. After his elevation to the presidency in 1979, the new Iraqi president aspired to become the new regional leader. The shah's ouster had left open the role of dominant power in the strategic and oil-rich Gulf. And with Egypt isolated in the aftermath of the 1978 Camp David accord with Israel, a void in leadership of the entire twenty-two-nation Arab world also needed to be filled.

The main obstacle was Iran's zealous Islamic ideology. Since Iraq's population was 60 percent Shi'ite, Saddam, a Sunni Muslim, was concerned about the possible overspill on his own restive Shi'ite community. *Al Dawa al-Islamiya,* or the Call of Islam, Iraq's most extreme Shi'ite party, had clearly been encouraged by Khomeini's revolution. The late 1970s witnessed a series of sporadic disturbances tied largely to Al Dawa: demonstrations organized during religious commemorations; small attacks launched against government symbols, such as police stations and local Baath Party offices; and assaults or assassination attempts on officials. Khomeini had once said that creating another Islamic republic in Iraq would be the first step, after which all Muslims would fall in line. But Saddam's antipathy toward Iran also had a personal side. In his capacity as vice president, he had been forced to sign the 1975 accord ceding partial control of the Shatt al-Arab to Iran.

The fundamental differences between the two men were played out on the battlefield. Iraq's advanced armor and aircraft led the initial, punishing assaults. Saddam had invested in the latest military technology in order to keep casualties low and to prevent an internal backlash, particularly among the Shi'a, who made up the majority of troops. The main Iranian targets were economic, then military. Iraqi tanks and artillery quickly closed in on four key cities in Iran's southern oil province of Khuzistan or, as the Iraqis called it, Arabistan: the oil-refining center of Abadan; the port city of Khorramshahr; the provincial capital and industrial center of Ahvaz; and the military and transportation center at Dezful.

Iraqi tactics initially appeared to work. Reports from the front described the flight of tens of thousands of Iranian refugees. The impact on oil installations was widely visible: In several oil centers, gushing clouds of heavy black smoke billowed into the skies for days. The initial panic in cities farther from the fighting, where the atmosphere was heightened by the regular blare of air-raid sirens and power blackouts, led to hoarding of virtually all basic necessities and an overnight doubling of the black market rate. During the war's opening burst, Saddam's goals seemed to be within reach.

In contrast, Iran's two main weapons were human resources and commitment. Tehran did order the remnants of its air force out to try to cripple Iraqi oil installations and to destroy military positions. But the Islamic Republic was reckless, for it quickly expended a large percentage of its air fleet. Within the first five days, Baghdad military communiqués announced that Iraq had shot down 158 Iranian warplanes, about all Tehran had in the air.[11] The claim was clearly excessive, as would become typical of military communiqués from both sides throughout the war. But it underscored how the Islamic Republic, after a devastating early loss, had little to fall back on but manpower—and willpower.

With three times Iraq's population, Tehran could afford higher losses. In fact, according to Khomeini, casualties were not a loss but an asset. Death was honorable, even desirable, when fighting injustice. "We should sacrifice all our loved ones for the sake of Islam," Khomeini urged. "If we are killed, we have performed our duty."[12] As in the fight against the shah, the mullahs invoked Hosain's martyrdom in the name of the faith. The Iraqi president was compared with Yazid, the seventh-century caliph whose troops had slain the Shi'ite martyr. Iranian tactics did have an impact. Iraqi troops conceded that, after the initial Iranian flight, they came up against some surprising resistance from Iranian troops with only small or vintage weapons fighting on streets and from rooftops.[13]

For Saddam, the war was a territorial dispute with regional political repercussions. For Khomeini, it was a war against Islam. "It is not a question of a fight between one government and another," the imam declared. "This is a rebellion by blasphemy against Islam."[14] His pledge that Iran would fight until "the government of heathens in Iraq topples" was not rhetoric. This was God's war against the infidels.

•

Politically, the invasion could not have come at a worse time for Iran. Tehran had spent the previous nine months bogged down in implementing the constitution. The procedure involved three steps: electing a president, voting on 270 members for the new parliament, and selecting a cabinet. This turbulent period foreshadowed many of the political problems that were to trouble the Islamic Republic throughout its first decade. The process also offered insight into the radical clergy's ultimate goals.

The presidential campaign of January 1980 began with zeal—and some confusion. One of the most interesting facets of the election was Khomeini's declaration that no mullahs could run for the office—further proof almost a year after his return that he still did *not* intend to establish a theocracy. But, even without the mullahs, there was no shortage of candidates. More than 120 candidates from virtually every segment of society, including some associated with the monarchy, initially entered the race.

The number was clearly unmanageable, so the Revolutionary Council employed official and unofficial means to whittle down the list. The imam publicly charged that some candidates were "brainless" or "perverts," while a ranking mullah blasted the list as "an American-inspired plot . . . intended to subvert Iran's revolutionary dignity." The newly powerful Students Following the Imam's Line, who increasingly used their hold over the American hostages as a mechanism to promote their own views, charged that the flood of candidates represented a scheme "to destroy the nation from within."[15] Many candidates were effectively ridiculed into withdrawing; others were found by a government panel to have inadequate credentials.

Among the well-known candidates to withdraw for other reasons was Masoud Rajavi, leader of the Mojahedin-e Khalq, or People's Holy Warriors. Formed in 1965, the Mojahedin had a well-established record of opposing the shah; it had joined the mullahs in the street demonstrations that had forced the monarch's ouster. The alliance, however, had been short-lived. The Mojahedin has always been avowedly Islamic, but it is also socialist. Its boycott of the constitutional referendum had formalized the split. In a move directed largely at Rajavi, Khomeini rejected the candidacy of anyone who had voted against the constitution. By election day on January 25, 1980, the list had been narrowed to eight men.

In light of the state's past intervention on candidates, the campaign was surprisingly open and even lively. Debate was largely limited to competition over who was the best Islamic revolutionary and who was the most committed to Khomeini's vision. But the personal rivalry was intense, evident in television speeches, mass rallies, public posters and bids for support from public interest groups, including women's organizations. Khomeini did not intervene to endorse any of the eight, despite the fact that two had been his personal advisors.* "Compared with previous Iranian elections, the campaign came closer to Western democratic practice" than any during the shah's era, concluded one Western analysis. It also compared election day, despite disturbances among minorities in Azerbaijan and Kurdistan, to "a festival." [16]

The election was not, however, much of a contest. Abolhassan Bani-Sadr, a French-educated economist and son of an ayatollah, won 76 percent of the vote. The new president's revolutionary credentials were solid and included a brief stint in jail for his criticism of the monarchy in the 1960s. Like Khomeini, he also went into exile, although his was by choice. Moving to Paris, Bani-Sadr began a doctorate at the Sorbonne; he later wrote on Islamic economics as an alternative to capitalism and communism. Bani-Sadr had long admired Khomeini, but the two men had not joined forces until the imam arrived in Paris for what turned out to be, for both, their final months in exile. They differed on specifics, but at that stage they agreed on the two fundamental issues: The shah had to go, and Islam was the alternative.

The new president was clearly ambitious. He later claimed to have told French philosopher Jean-Paul Sartre years earlier that he would be the first president of Iran.[17] In some ways, however, Bani-Sadr did not fit in with the mullahs; his years in the West seemed to have rubbed off on him. A tall, lean figure, he was clean-shaven except for a neat little mustache. His coiffed haircut was distinctly

---

* Both Khomeini's brother and grandson did, however, reveal that they intended to vote for Bani-Sadr, although their statements were reportedly not made at the ayatollah's urging.

European and, although his first language was Farsi, he often preferred to speak in French. His personal style did not seem to matter
at first for, after nine divisive months of Bazargan's rule, the Islamic
Republic finally appeared to have an effective and fairly popular
chief of state.

Iran spent the next five months organizing its first parliament, or
majlis. This process made the presidential contest look simple; an
estimated two thousand candidates from more than a hundred parties announced their plans to run for 270 seats. The campaign period was a particularly anxious time for Iran, not only because of
the ongoing international furor and pressure over the American
hostages. In mid-January, Khomeini was hospitalized after a heart
attack. He was not released for seven weeks, not until a few days
before the March elections.

Although the constitution had provisions for selection of a new
Supreme Jurisprudent, there was as yet no obvious heir apparent.
Indeed, among the six grand ayatollahs, there was not one who
totally agreed with Khomeini on key issues—including on the
power or even the need for a supreme spiritual guide. The divisions
were so deep that some ranking clerics charged the imam's inner
circle with "confiscating the revolution." Clashes in December 1979
and January 1980, which pitted Khomeini's backers against supporters of rival ayatollahs, were so fierce that many Iranians feared
the outbreak of full-scale civil strife. The strained atmosphere was
not conducive to free and fair elections.

Some of the same politicians who made a run for the presidency
tried again for the unicameral legislature, including the Mojahedin's
Rajavi and several of his colleagues. The communist Tudeh Party
also put forward more than a hundred candidates. Former Prime
Minister Mehdi Bazargan, forced aside over the hostage ordeal, led
the slate from the Freedom Movement. But, most important, the
majlis election marked the emergence of the Islamic Republic Party
(IRP), a political grouping of mullahs and militant technocrats
founded by members of the Revolutionary Council. Although Khomeini never formally endorsed the IRP, its leadership thought it
spoke for the imam's interests. The IRP had made its first solid
showing in elections to the Assembly of Experts and its first imprint
in shaping the constitution, but the ban on clergy running for the
presidency had effectively left the IRP on the sidelines. Now the
party wanted to ensure a place within the new government.

In the end, Iran elected a diverse parliament that included busi-
nessmen, farmers, workers and even three women. Bazargan also

won a seat. But in a signal of things to come, the Mojahedin, the Tudeh and other leftists won nothing. The IRP or its sympathizers won almost half the seats; more than 45 percent of the new *majlis* members were mullahs.[18] As important as the result was the turn-out. Only half the electorate voted in the first round in March. Despite the failed U.S. military mission to rescue the hostages in April and President Carter's imposition of economic sanctions—which might have rallied public fervor—even fewer voted in May during a second polling to decide between the top two candidates in districts where no one won a majority. Public enthusiasm had again begun to wane.

The final step was the selection of a prime minister and cabinet. Bani-Sadr had hoped to form a cabinet before the *majlis* elections. But at each turn his nominees for the premiership had been rejected by the Revolutionary Council, which should have alerted him to the trouble ahead. He ended up having to wait an agonizing eight months and losing, in the process, his hold on the reins of power. Not until August 1980 did parliament begin to move on the selection of a prime minister. From the outset, however, the president and the IRP had different ideas about the powers and leadership of the executive branch. They were divided on familiar grounds: The president sought technocrats experienced in managing the various sectors of government; the IRP preferred ideologues committed to Islam. Although he had won a popular vote, Bani-Sadr had no independent power base to give him leverage within government. In the end, the IRP's radical clergy put forward a name, which parliament approved—and Bani-Sadr was forced to accept.

The new prime minister was Mohammad Ali Raja'i, a former street vendor who worked his way through school to become a math teacher. His life epitomized the struggle of the *mostazafin,* or oppressed, in whose name Khomeini had led the revolution. Like Bani-Sadr, he had been imprisoned during the shah's era, but there the similarity ended. While Bani-Sadr was comparatively pragmatic about the troubles Iran faced, Raja'i was an IRP hard-liner prepared to endure further national hardships to promote Islam.

The obstinacy of both men over the last phase, selecting a cabinet, created even deeper divisions and further defined the shape of new factions. The two men had once been allies; almost overnight they became rivals. As had now become a pattern in Iran, each time one layer of politicians was removed, the next layer broke into new factions. Finally, on September 11, 1980—a year and eight months after the revolution and only eleven days before the Iraqi invasion

—the Islamic Republic's first government was formed and presented to the imam.

•

With the lengthy transition over, Bani-Sadr hoped, finally, to get down to business. The Islamic Republic had made virtually no progress in the interim on its promises to address economic and social ills. Unemployment and inflation had begun to soar. The mass exodus of educated or skilled Iranians and the flight of capital had crippled many industries and businesses—a situation not alleviated by the isolation brought on by the continuing hostage affair. Growing public disillusionment was evident between May and July 1980, when three coup attempts were uncovered.

In fact, however, Bani-Sadr's presidency was almost over on the day he was formally sworn in by parliament. In effect, he found himself in the same position that had crippled Bazargan. Like the prime minister he had helped to oust, Bani-Sadr wrongly assumed that his powers exceeded those of the clerics. He, too, had hoped gradually to eliminate the komitehs and to weaken the power of the Revolutionary Guards in favor of the regular military. He also, naively, assumed that the IRP would become just one of many parties in a democratic system. He maintained good relations with the Mojahedin and other parties; he also tried to address the minorities' demands for local rights. Bani-Sadr agreed that government actions had to be in accordance with Islamic tenets, but he considered the state supreme—and separate from the mosque. He acknowledged that Khomeini was the supreme guide, but the imam's illness led him to predict that "he will oversee things, but will not be deeply involved."[19] With some daring, he said publicly that his views might occasionally differ from the ayatollah's.

After the radical mullahs' strong showing in the *majlis* elections, however, they were not afraid to challenge the increasingly independent president. The proclergy press began to attack him. One editorial described the president as a leader "who is blinded by vanity, egocentrism and thirst for power."[20] Bani-Sadr was specifically criticized for failing to purge the government of civil servants who had backed the monarchy, for coddling the ethnic minorities, and for not moving fast enough to Islamicize state institutions. Even Khomeini joined in. He charged that Iran was "still a monarchy," right down to the stationery that still bore the shah's insignia. Unless all traces of the Pahlavi dynasty were eliminated within ten days, he warned, "I will urge the nation to do the same thing with you as they did with the shah. . . . Resign if you are unable."[21]

For Bani-Sadr, the war was almost a blessing. The political infighting initially moved to the sidelines as Iran rallied for war. Nationalism temporarily bonded Iranians even more tightly than during the uprising against the shah. Thousands of young men volunteered to fight. Disgruntled military quarters mobilized behind the government. The reversal was reflected in the comment of a retired military officer. "The soldiers were humiliated by the revolution and then by the revolutionaries. What the hell are they fighting so ferociously for?" he asked.[22] The level of chauvinism was evident when Reza Pahlavi, the shah's heir, offered to return from exile to serve as a fighter pilot.[23] He pledged his "life's blood" to defeat Iraq—an offer the mullahs never bothered to answer.

Beleaguered Iran did manage to hold out, although barely. The first month was chaotic, as anyone with even marginal training— the Pasdaran, the gendarmerie, the border police, the komitehs, the hizbollahis, and even cadets in training—arrived at the front. More than a thousand officers detained during the military purges were also freed. The imam called for every threatened town to be turned into a Stalingrad[24]—which his supporters and opponents together often managed to do. The street battles and hand-to-hand fighting around the port city of Khorramshahr led to so many casualties, estimated as high as fourteen thousand, that it was renamed Khunishahr, or "the city of blood."[25] Poorly improvised strategy and weaponry shortages led to major territorial losses, including Khorramshahr and control of the Shatt, but the Iranians surprised the Iraqis—and the world. A war that Saddam had hoped to end after only a month, before the Muslim feast of Eid al Adha, or Festival of Sacrifice, instead deteriorated into a stalemate within the first weeks.

After Khomeini appointed him commander-in-chief, Bani-Sadr tried to use the war to improve his standing and his powers. The president began in early October to spend the majority of his time on the war front. His strategy, however, quickly backfired. As the conflict settled down to a war of attrition limited largely to long-distance artillery exchanges, the power struggle began to play out over war tactics and management. The controversy boiled down to professionalism versus piety.[26] Bani-Sadr wanted the American-trained army to direct the war; the militant mullahs favored using the then ragtag Revolutionary Guards.

The dispute was not limited to the politicians. From the war's onset, the army and the Revolutionary Guards displayed open hostility toward each other. One account claimed that infantry units were forced into direct contact with the Iraqi troops at dangerously close quarters. Behind them were the Pasdaran, "with orders to shoot any regulars attempting to withdraw or desert, which they did on several occasions."[27]

Interference in managing the war reached the point that Bani-Sadr pleaded with Khomeini to discharge the Raja'i government. He called it "a greater calamity for the country than the war."[28] Almost one-third of the *majlis* deputies then countered by introducing a motion to dismiss the president as commander-in-chief. The strain grew sufficiently severe that Bani-Sadr decided to prove his and the military's mettle by organizing Iran's first counteroffensive in January 1981.

Bani-Sadr was, however, not a military strategist, and the strike on five Iraqi positions was a debacle. Almost everything that could go wrong did. The winter rains bogged down Iranian tanks, costing valuable time and the element of surprise. Iraq had sufficient warning from reconnaissance that it organized its own surprises. Near the southern Iranian city of Susangerd, the Iraqis set a trap for the Iranians, luring their tanks into battle, then surrounding them. Iran lost most of an armored division deployed along the front.[29] Iran had not been ready for the offensive, but internal politics had made waiting until spring too dangerous for the president. Now Iran's losses were so great that it could not soon afford another major attack. It would take another full year—and resolution of the latest power struggle—before Iran could again challenge Iraq.

•

The conclusion of the Islamic Republic's time-consuming elections finally began to reap benefits for the hostages. On the day after the cabinet was presented to Khomeini, the imam announced his four conditions for the Americans' release. Tehran also notified Washington through the Germans that it was genuinely ready to settle. "The hostages are like a fruit from which all the juice has been squeezed out," Iran's top negotiator later explained.[30] The costs had begun to outweigh the benefits of keeping them any longer. Meanwhile, the shah had died an ignominious death of cancer in Cairo in July 1980, eliminating a key point of dispute. The outbreak of war in September 1980 and the election of Ronald Reagan in November accelerated the delicate mediation process. To pay for replenishing its arsenal, Iran wanted to retrieve the assets frozen in the United States by the Carter administration. Tehran also did not look forward to facing the unpredictable Reagan after he took office.

The hostages were all too aware of the war; Tehran had been a sporadic target of Iraqi warplanes since it erupted. Most were also aware that Reagan had been elected president. But, until the very end, they had no inkling of the scramble in Algiers to finish negotiations before President Carter left office. One group, pessimistic about their imminent prospects for release, began speculating about whether they would be held longer than the siege of Leningrad, which had lasted 999 days. Another group continued to plan an escape. Others, however, began to have an inkling that something was in the works when the food improved and when the guards brought them old Super Bowl films from the embassy to watch.

The end was as cruel for many as the beginning. Ordered to pack up, one group was appalled to find their small bundles of letters, books and tidbits tossed aside. They left with nothing but what they wore on their backs or stuffed in their pockets. They did, however, get their shoes back. One hostage recalled being taken into a room with hundreds of pairs of shoes on the floor—all the shoes the hostages had worn plus what had been confiscated from their homes. He saw five pairs of his own shoes. He picked out his favorite; the other four pairs were left behind.

One hostage almost did not make it. As the blindfolded captives were led toward buses for transport to the airport, a guard told them, in English, to shut up. He then muttered aloud in Farsi, "Goddamned Americans." Mike Metrinko, the embassy's political officer, was infuriated by this final insult. He turned angrily to the guard and said in Farsi, "Shut up yourself, you son of a whore."[31] Metrinko was hauled aside and badly beaten—as the buses drove away. He was later taken to the airport by car.

But all the hostages then had one final delay. The captors were waiting for the signal that the inauguration was over and that Jimmy Carter was no longer president. When they were finally told to board, the young militants put on one last display of hatred. A large group assembled around the aircraft ramp to shout *Marg bar Amrika*, or "Death to America," as the hostages went up the steps. Although the excitement was palpable as the plane took off, the hostages did not fully express themselves until the Algerian pilot, an hour into the flight, announced that they had cleared Iranian airspace. A cheer went up throughout the plane, and the stewards cracked champagne.[32]

•

Ironically, the end to the hostage affair deepened the crisis for Bani-Sadr, even though he had earlier and genuinely sought resolution of the crisis. He had appealed to Khomeini to transfer custody of the diplomats from the militant students to the government, but his bid had been rejected. The president had also accused the students of forming "a state within a state." His efforts had led the IRP clerics to charge him with being a pawn of the Great Satan. But after the deal was finally struck, the president criticized the clerics for accepting terms that were far less than they could have gotten earlier. He pointed out that Iran had obtained neither an American apology for its past meddling, nor the shah's wealth, nor, most importantly, the military equipment and spare parts purchased during the shah's reign. The last two, he charged, had hurt Iran's war effort.

With the war at an impasse, Bani-Sadr had to find other means to survive. He was obviously on the defensive. In public rallies and in his rather unusual column, entitled the "President's Diary," in the *Islamic Revolution* newspaper, he openly aired his problems. He condemned corruption and criticized his unnamed but obvious rivals for creating a climate of fear that led thousands of the nation's most able people to flee. He equated the IRP with the single party of the shah's era, the *Rastakhiz,* and their tactics with Stalinism. He won some public sympathy, but his actions only hardened the resolve of the IRP to get rid of him.[33]

By March 1981, he was in trouble. The *majlis* began to restrict his powers and to cut the budget for his office. The radical mullahs' supporters also launched disturbances at Bani-Sadr's rallies, as the in-house squabbling spilled over into the public arena. The Students Following the Imam's Line further undermined his position in April by revealing cables and documents pieced together from the American embassy. They showed that the CIA had made contact with Bani-Sadr in Paris and in Tehran in an attempt to "cultivate and recruit" him as an informer. The CIA had code-named him "SDLure-1." The students had no proof that the then future president had either taken money from or provided intelligence to the U.S. intelligence agency, but the revelations were in themselves sufficiently damning.[34]

Khomeini established a panel to mediate differences between the president and the IRP. The truce, however, was short-lived. Bani-Sadr still felt he could no longer carry out his duties against unchecked opposition. He called for a national referendum to decide the issue of government control, a move that finally began costing him Khomeini's support. "The nation is hostile to the cult of personality," the ayatollah warned in May.[35] In June, Bani-Sadr's paper, the *Islamic Revolution,* was ordered to close. Iran's first president made one last try. He sent a letter to Khomeini warning that the imam's trust in the IRP amounted to "committing suicide"; publicly, he called for "continued resistance to tyranny."[36] Tension mounted as all public demonstrations were banned and as Revolutionary Guard and komiteh forces deployed around key government installations.

On June 10, 1981, Khomeini began the process of removing Bani-Sadr by stripping him of the title of commander-in-chief. A formal signal that the president no longer had the imam's backing, it opened the way for more drastic action. On June 20, two dozen Iranians were killed in clashes between supporters and opponents of the president. The next day, the *majlis* declared the president "politically incompetent" to hold office. The vote was 177 to 1; the rest abstained or were absent from the chamber. The order was immediately issued to arrest Iran's first president.

But Bani-Sadr had finally recognized what was coming, and he had already gone underground. He briefly attempted to rally followers from his secret base. But the pointed silence by old allies and friends, the declaration of support for his dismissal by the army, and the nationwide manhunt that netted his wife, his brother and several aides finally made Bani-Sadr abandon the effort.

Meanwhile, having eliminated their last main opponent, the mullahs of the Islamic Republic Party finally achieved their goal. The last of the secular centrists had been purged, leaving only the radical clergy that formed Khomeini's inner circle in command. They had wrested total control of the state, a victory that many openly referred to as "the third revolution."[37] Until a new president could be elected, Khomeini invested power in a three-man committee that included Prime Minister Raja'i, *Majlis* Speaker Ali Akbar Hashemi Rafsanjani and Supreme Court Chief Justice Mohammad Beheshti. All three had led the campaign against Bani-Sadr; all three represented the radicals within the Islamic Republican Party. Their appointments symbolized the fact that Iran had become, in effect, a theocracy.

•

The power struggle, however, was not yet over. On June 28, exactly a week after Bani-Sadr's arrest was ordered, the IRP called an urgent meeting at its southeast Tehran headquarters to decide on a party presidential candidate and to debate the issue of political parties in Iran. The meeting was chaired by IRP secretary and Supreme Court Chief Justice Mohammad Beheshti, the party's chief ideologue and tactician who engineered the mullahs' rise to power.

His maneuvering had been pivotal to Bani-Sadr's demise. He was also one of the three men designated to oversee the presidency until a new election. More than ninety of the IRP's leading figures attended, including the two other members of the temporary presidential council.

Shortly before 9:00 P.M., as Beheshti spoke, a massive explosion ripped the conference hall apart. The whole area was rocked by the aftershock as doors imploded and windows smashed in dozens of nearby buildings. Accounts differed on where the explosion originated. One report claimed that there were two bombs, one planted in the rostrum, the second in the audience. Another claimed that the bomb was planted in a school next door to the conference center. Either way, the death toll was staggering. Seventy-four leading IRP officials were dead.* Among them were Beheshti, ten cabinet ministers and deputies, and twenty-seven members of parliament. The scheme was clearly intended to wipe out the three figures who took Bani-Sadr's place and as many of those who supported them as possible.†

The attack at IRP headquarters represented the toughest challenge that the Islamic Republic had ever faced. Even the war and the outside pressure during the hostage ordeal paled in comparison with the elimination of so many of the revolution's key players. And the incident was not isolated. Earlier that week, eight had been killed and twenty-three injured when a bomb exploded at the railway depot in the theological center at Qom. In a separate attack, Ali Khamenei, a member of the Supreme Defense Council that oversaw the war effort, had been seriously wounded in the midst of his Friday prayer service in Tehran. A bomb had been planted in a tape recorder on the dais.

The attacks marked the opening round in a campaign of revenge against the government by Mojahedin networks and other dissident cells that had gone underground. Since the government would no longer share power, the leftist groups attempted to weaken the regime to the point that they could overthrow it. It was not surprising when, two days after the bombing, the government revealed that a plan to blow up parliament had been foiled. The Mojahedin never claimed credit for these early attacks, but the mullahs held them responsible.

---

* The death toll was later adjusted to seventy-two to match the figure killed with the martyr Hosain at Karbala.

† Prime Minister Raja'i was only slightly injured, and *Majlis* Speaker Rafsanjani had left the hall just moments before the bombing.

The radical clergy's response was to escalate the crackdown that had begun after Bani-Sadr's escape. Many of those who had been detained were hanged or put before firing squads; hundreds more were picked up in new Revolutionary Guard raids. Many times the only way families knew what happened to loved ones was by reading newspaper columns listing the latest executions, although not all names were revealed.[38] The subsequent crackdown was so brutal that it quickly became known as the reign of terror, a term adapted from similar eras under Robespierre in France and Stalin in the Soviet Union. The campaign against Iran's own infidels dominated domestic policy for the next eighteen months.

In the midst of the bloodletting on both sides, Iran carried through with new elections on July 24 for a president and for twenty-seven members of parliament to replace those who had died in the June attack. From their hiding place inside Iran, Bani-Sadr and Rajavi called for a boycott of the vote. The former president claimed that he remained Iran's legitimate leader. On that basis, he appointed Rajavi to be his prime minister. The Mojahedin also tried to disrupt the election. Attempts were made on the lives of two candidates running for parliament and one of the four men running for the presidency. But the opposition was unable to intimidate the mullahs; the turnout was almost 70 percent, almost as high as the poll that had brought Bani-Sadr to power.* At that juncture, Bani-Sadr and Rajavi decided to leave Iran altogether; they were secretly flown out of Iran by the same pilot who had carried the shah and his family into exile.[39]

The new president-elect was Prime Minister Raja'i, the former math teacher and Bani-Sadr's old foe. As prime minister, Raja'i selected Mohammad Javad Bahonar, another former Khomeini student twice imprisoned by the shah. The new government accelerated the offensive against the Mojahedin and other leftist cells. The few remaining political freedoms evaporated during a ruthless series of arrests and street clashes. Prisons overflowed with men and women ranging in age from twelve and thirteen to seventy-five. The Justice Ministry announced that seven hundred executions had been ordered since Bani-Sadr's departure.

But still it was not enough. Assaults continued internally, while the opposition began new campaigns overseas. Among the targets were several Khomeini associates, judges, komiteh officials, Friday

* The turnout was boosted by the fact that the government lowered the voting age for the presidential contest, although not the *majlis* election, from sixteen to fifteen. That added an estimated eight-hundred-thousand voters to the polls.

prayer leaders and IRP members. The Mojahedin even dared a bold
raid on the headquarters of the Revolutionary Guards, who were
conducting the clampdown of the Mojahedin. It failed, but the inability of the government to end the attacks underscored its vulnerability. Overseas, Iranian diplomatic facilities in Washington, the
Hague, Oslo, and Brussels were attacked or seized by opposition
groups in August. The summer of 1981 became the bloodiest since
the uprising against the shah.

On August 30, just five weeks after the presidential election, new
President Raja'i and Prime Minister Bahonar called a secret summit
of national security officials at the premier's office to deliberate
strategy against the opposition. Two hundred government officials
had been killed since Bani-Sadr's ouster. The latest victim, murdered just a week earlier, was the revolutionary prosecutor; somehow a bomb had been smuggled into his office. Even more ominous,
a bomb without a detonator had been planted in the complex where
the Khomeini entourage lived. Attached to it was a note suggesting
that the imam "surrender."[40]

Security was tight at the premier's office, a converted villa ringed
with Revolutionary Guards and police. No one but high-level officials was admitted. As the secret meeting came to order, one of
Raja'i's most trusted national security aides placed a briefcase full
of classified documents on the table, then left. The briefcase also
contained a bomb. When the explosive went off, the Islamic Republic's new president and prime minister and three top security officials were dead. Their bodies were so badly burned by the
incendiary device that they could only be identified by dental rec-
ords.

Khomeini blamed "American mercenaries," but this time the Mojahedin did claim credit. The man who had left the bomb behind
turned out to be among the highest-level Mojahedin members to
penetrate the government. Tension once again reached the point
that Iranians feared the outbreak of civil war. From Paris, Bani-
Sadr called on Iranians to "rise and resist. Overthrow this regime
which has proven more bloodthirsty than the monarchy."[41]
Clandestine activities began to come out in the open. Protestors
boldly took to the streets to distribute leaflets, to urge others to
demonstrate and, increasingly, to take on Revolutionary Guards
and komiteh units. The government responded in kind and
with little discrimination. Thousands were detained and hundreds
executed. On one day alone, September 19, 1981, 149 people
were hanged or put before a firing squad; the following week, 110

were executed in a single day.[42] The reign of terror was in full swing.

In this anxious atmosphere, Khomeini's inner circle once again, for the third time in two months, had to pick new leaders to direct the beleaguered nation. On October 2, it held yet another round of presidential elections. The turnout, roughly 80 percent, was the highest of any poll to date. Iran's newest president was Ali Khamenei, another former Khomeini *talabeh,* or student, who was still recovering from the June bombing at his Friday prayer service. Although not initially among the more visible public figures, he had been a key link in the network during the ayatollah's exile, for which he was arrested six times. He was also a member of the secret Revolutionary Council, one of the six founders of the IRP, and one of the select few on the Supreme Defense Council.

What made Khamenei's election even more important than the two earlier rounds was that he was the first mullah to win the presidency—which represented a major reversal in Khomeini's thinking. In each earlier contest, the imam had intervened to prevent the mullahs from running for the top job. Now, it appeared, he no longer trusted secular allies; his actions suggested that he believed only a full-fledged theocracy would ensure fulfillment of his dream. The radical clergy had gained de facto control of all state institutions after Bani-Sadr's ouster. But Khamenei's election meant that they now headed all four branches of government.* Despite the wave of attacks and assassinations, Iran was moving ever closer to entrenching the government of God.

•

As the clerics moved even more ferociously against their internal opposition, they also began to counterattack against Iran's external threat on the war front. Unlike the situation in January 1980, they were ready this time. Two limited battles in September and November 1981 were particularly important. In the first, Iran's military created a diversionary front to draw Iraqi troops away from Abadan, the vital oil center in southwest Khuzistan. The Iranians then surprised the forces laying siege to Abadan by attacking from the rear and the flanks.[43] Within two days, Iran managed to break the year-old siege.

---

* Besides the executive, legislative, and judicial branches of government, the Iranian constitution also called for a Council of Guardians to ensure that government, particularly the *majlis,* never took any action incompatible with Islamic tenets. Six of its twelve members were appointed by Khomeini, the other half by parliament. The constitution stipulated that it had to be headed by a cleric.

The second battle in late November was code-named *Tariq al-Qods,* or Path to Jerusalem; Iranian offensives usually had religious names. It reflected Iran's goal of retrieving the city where the Prophet Mohammad had, according to legend, ascended on his stallion to heaven. After Mecca and Medina, Qods is the third holiest city in Islamic history. Pledges to "March all the way to Jerusalem" were popular revolutionary catchphrases. Operation Path to Jerusalem also took place in the southern sector near Bostan. Iran was again victorious, recapturing the town in only thirty-six hours.

What made this small offensive so important, however, was the strategy used—almost by accident. Basij volunteers and Revolutionary Guards ignored the battle plan that called for a heavy artillery barrage followed by a land assault. In their enthusiasm, the Basij and Pasdaran charged ahead without the advantage of "softening" the enemy first. It marked the first human-wave assault, and it worked in overwhelming the better-trained and well-armed Iraqis.[44] The Iranian strategy was almost primitive, but it was so effective that it changed the nature of the warfare for the next seven years.

The new tactic was simple: Leading the attack were thousands of Basij, or "the mobilized," the poorly trained troops who ranged in age from their young teens to their mid-fifties. The teenage and geriatric warriors volunteered for temporary duty in-between school terms or to pick up extra pay at a time of serious economic shortfalls. Most came from the rural areas or from the most devout Shi'ite families. They were little more than cannon fodder or human minesweepers sent in advance of Iran's other military forces to clear the fields, desert scrublands and marshes. Their best weapons were often those they managed to pick up from among Iraqi casualties. The Basij were distinguishable from the regular forces by their tacky, leftover uniforms, mismatched boots, and the colorful red or yellow headbands that declared God's or Khomeini's greatness. Many also wore keys around their necks, a symbol of their automatic entry into heaven upon martyrdom. At the battle for Bostan, a hundred young Basij walked across a minefield to clear it for advancing Pasdaran troops.[45]

Behind the Basij were the Revolutionary Guards, whose fanaticism also made them fight boldly, even recklessly. The rearguard was reserved for the army and artillery. In earlier campaigns, the army had been in front with the Pasdaran at the rear—to ensure that the regulars did not drop back or give up. The Pasdaran pressure was a main reason for past tensions between Iran's two rival military forces. The new tactic was costly in human lives, but the shortage of equipment and warplanes left Iran few alternatives. Now, having found a formula that worked, Iran began planning its biggest offensive to date.

Operation *Fath,* which means "conquest" or "victory," was launched on March 22, 1982. The delay after a series of small campaigns in late 1981 was due to two factors: the need to repair as much of its deteriorating or damaged equipment as possible and the weather. With arms sources limited and the economy in dire condition, Iranian technicians were forced to patch and repatch whatever artillery, tanks and aircraft Iran still had.[46] The weather was also no small factor in terms of both the Gulf climate and Iranian strategy. Clashes in the summer months were usually limited to the northern front due to the smothering heat in the southern deserts that made troops wilt and artillery simply too hot to handle for very long. The fall and spring rainy seasons were usually advantageous times for Iran's mobile foot soldiers, while the same rains often led Iraq's high-tech armor to get mired in the mud.

Moonlight was also an important factor. Compared with Iraq, Iran's reconnaissance was almost negligible, so the Islamic Republic was forced to initiate strikes in the cover of night if it sought an element of surprise. Too much moonlight, however, might reveal the Iranians' presence, while too little could make them lose their way. An army officer, surrounded by tanks and cannons, was asked in 1982 what had accounted for a particular war-front success. "The moon," he responded seriously, "was just right."[47]

Roughly a hundred thousand Iranian troops—thirty thousand Basij, thirty thousand regular army, and forty thousand Revolutionary Guards—were committed to Operation *Fath.*[48] At 4:30 A.M. on March 22, they moved in six columns along a fifty-mile front in oil-rich southern Khuzistan, near Dezful and Shush. Wave after wave of Iranian troops drove at the Iraqis, hoping to wear out the troops and use up their ammunition. After one column of Basij and Revolutionary Guards dropped, it was followed by another group of frenzied troops, usually urged on by mullahs attached to each unit. Some mullahs even ran alongside them across the frontlines.

The role of the Iranian clergy was another unusual side of Iran's war effort. During a press tour of the front at Dezful a week after Operation *Fath,* mullahs clad in their flowing robes and turbans were everywhere in evidence—with troops moving to new front lines, chanting with them as Iraqi MiGs strafed the area, and inspecting seized territory. At the site of a captured battery of Soviet-made surface-to-air missiles, foreign reporters joked that this was the first place where the clerics were not in sight. Then three mullahs, deep in conversation about the sophisticated weapons that had earlier brought down so many Iranian warplanes, walked from behind the missiles' launcher.[49] By the end of the war, hundreds of clergymen were among Iran's war dead.

Fighting was intense for the first three days. The Iranian goal was to surround the Iraqis, estimated at up to forty thousand, and to cut off either a retreat or reinforcements. While the Iranians were tenacious, they were also occasionally lucky. Scores of new Soviet-made T-54 and T-62 tanks were simply made immobile by the weather. At another site, a unit of Iraqi troops was surrounded under cover of darkness at midnight. They had let down their guard, in part because they never believed that anyone would penetrate the surrounding fields. The "minefield martyrs," or combined columns of Basij and Revolutionary Guards, had defied the statistical odds that favored Iraq. Virtually the whole Iraqi unit, including the commander, had been forced to surrender without much of a fight.[50]

By the end of eight days, Iran had recaptured more than a thousand square miles of its oil lands. At one point, it was within fifteen miles of its own border. Iran also had acquired an estimated four hundred tanks or armored vehicles as well as about sixteen thousand prisoners of war, not all of them Iraqi. Roughly two hundred prisoners came from Yemen, Somalia, Sudan, Lebanon, and Tunisia; several told woeful tales of taking jobs in Iraq only to be, literally, pressed into service. Several asked reporters to alert their respective embassies to their plights.[51]

The Islamic Republic was clearly pleased, and even somewhat surprised, by the dimensions of its overwhelming victory in a war that it was supposed to have lost, quickly and decisively, eighteen months earlier. Officers went to great pains to point out that victory had been achieved without outside help. "The only foreign presence at the war front is you," the commander of an Iranian infantry division told foreign reporters. "The party of God does not accept advisers."[52] Boasted the overall ground commander, "We are going to write our own military manuals from now on with absolutely new tactics that Americans, British, and French can study at *their* staff colleges."[53]

A month later, another major offensive using similar tactics retrieved the vital port of Khorramshahr. It was equally devastating. In the end, Iraqi troops at the Iranian port were forced back across the Shatt al-Arab; their position was so desperate that many of them were forced to swim. Together, the two offensives recovered more than thirty-three hundred square miles of Iranian territory and netted over twenty-five thousand prisoners of war.[54] By May 1982, Iran had finally turned the tide of the war in its favor. It had retrieved vast tracks of lost territory. And Iraq was on the run.

•

The war victories coincided with the Islamic Republic's third anniversary of Khomeini's pronouncement of the government of God. It was celebrated by tens of thousands at parades and demonstrations. While those still loyal to the revolution had much to celebrate, they faced mounting problems. Shortages necessitated by a wartime economy and political isolation had led to rationing of basic foodstuffs, including gasoline, meat, rice, tea, sugar and cooking oil. Alongside rationing, a black market boomed—in currency, goods and even exit permits. The lower classes still showered adoration on Khomeini, but signs of disillusionment among the middle classes grew constantly in response to the Islamic dress code, high unemployment and increasing noises about imposing further restrictions on the private sector.

The undercurrent of constant fear from the ongoing reign of terror was present at the April commemoration. A cabbie was one of many who joined the crowd after being stopped by Revolutionary Guards who asked why they were working instead of celebrating.[55] The crackdown was not over, and anyone not rallying to the Islamic cause was suspect. The atmosphere was described in an open letter in the fall of 1982 from former Prime Minister Mehdi Bazargan, the only ranking former official to remain in Iran. In this case, "open" meant circulation among private channels in Iran and in the overseas press; it never appeared in Iranian papers. Bazargan accused the government of creating "an atmosphere of terror, fear, revenge and national disintegration." He charged, "What has the ruling elite done besides bring death and destruction, pack the prisons and cemeteries in every city, create long queues, shortages, high prices, unemployment, poverty, homeless people, repetitious slogans and a dark future?"[56] The government never responded.

More ominous for the mullahs, however, was the uncovering in April of a plot by Sadeq Qotbzadeh, the former foreign minister under Bani-Sadr and a former Khomeini aide and confidant. He had earlier incurred the wrath of the radical clergy when, as foreign minister, he had sought to resolve the American hostage ordeal— before the mullahs were ready. He was widely suspected of having a pro-American bias. This time, Qotbzadeh was charged with scheming to assassinate the imam and, along with sympathetic military officers and mullahs, to overthrow the regime. The plot was particularly traumatic for Iran because Qotbzadeh implicated one of the nation's six grand ayatollahs, Kazem Shariatmadari, in the plot.

Shariatmadari had long represented a major problem for Khomeini's inner circle, for he did not support the concept of a Supreme Jurisprudent. Indeed, he differed with Khomeini on most interpretations of Shi'a Islam, which made him potentially more dangerous than the Mojahedin. The Islamic Republic could not tolerate opposition from one of its greatest authorities. An enlightened mullah, Shariatmadari advocated greater individual freedoms and a lower profile for the clergy. He had earlier criticized the new constitution and condemned the revolution's judicial excesses. Because of his strong and independent base of support in Azerbaijan, which often demonstrated and rioted in his support, Shariatmadari was ultimately Khomeini's highest-ranking religious rival. And since no successor had yet been officially selected, this was no small threat.

In the angry atmosphere that countenanced no opposition, the government's response to the Qotbzadeh plot was again emphatic. Hundreds of military officers were arrested. Forced to confess on nationwide television, Qotbzadeh was put on trial, where he admitted plotting to eliminate key government clerics, but denied planning to kill the imam. On September 15, 1982, he was executed by a firing squad, as were seventy officers. In a move unprecedented in Shi'ite religious history, Shariatmadari was stripped of his title as grand ayatollah and placed under house arrest. It was the most sweeping indication to date of just how far the radical clergy was prepared to go to silence dissent, even among its own ranks.

By December 1982, Amnesty International listed more than three thousand executions in the eighteen months since Bani-Sadr's demise. The Mojahedin claimed it was almost seven thousand. The vast majority were Mojahedin guerrillas or supporters; about 10 percent of the victims were from other leftist cells, tribes, ethnic groups, notably the Kurds, and the constantly persecuted Baha'is.* But the punishment of Qotbzadeh and Shariatmadari in September had marked the last threat of any magnitude and the last grand

---

* The Baha'is were considered heretics of Shi'ite Islam. Since many had been put in key posts by the shah, their political loyalties were also suspect. Unlike other religious minorities, they were pointedly excluded from any constitutional rights or representation in parliament. Dozens were executed in the early years of the revolution.

strike of retribution. While the reign of terror continued until the end of the year, the leftist opposition had largely been either decimated or discouraged from continuing their campaign at any serious level.

Aware of the toll the past eighteen months had taken on national morale as well as on his base of support, Khomeini moved, on December 15, 1982, to put an end to the terror. In an unusual display of public pique, he criticized the government for "deviating" from Islamic behavior and exceeding their mandates. Accordingly, he issued an eight-point edict that served, in effect, as a new bill of rights. Among its most important clauses: No arrests or confiscation of property could be carried out without a court order. No homes could be entered without the owner's permission, nor any "inhuman actions" carried out against citizens. Bugging telephones or spying on individuals was prohibited, even for the purpose of uncovering a crime or a sin. And any judicial action had to be taken in a way that ensured that people felt "their lives, property and dignity are safe." [57]

The edict was particularly pointed at the Revolutionary Guards and komitehs, both of which were placed under the control of government ministries to monitor their activities. In an attempt to prove the regime's sincerity, Iranians were encouraged to submit complaints. During the first month, an estimated eleven thousand grievances were filed. Dozens of komiteh leaders were later purged or moved to other positions. Several civil servants who had lost their jobs because of suspected opposition were rehired. In limited cases, even property was returned.

Thousands of complaints were not redressed or compensated, but Khomeini's eight-point declaration nonetheless represented a major turning point for the revolution. By intimidation, detention or execution, the theocrats had weakened, even obliterated the main opposition forces. Entrenchment of the government of God was now secured. And by an enormous expenditure in human lives, Iran had driven Iraq from almost all Iranian soil. In control at home and dominant on the battlefield, the threat to the Islamic Republic's survival was, for the time being, over. God's will had prevailed over the infidels. Iran was now ready to move on to tackle others standing in His path.

CHAPTER FOUR

The Islamic Crusade

✥

"All Muslims shall be considered as one single nation and the Islamic Republic of Iran shall make its general policy on the basis of coalition and unity of all Muslim people and shall constantly make every endeavor to realize the political, economic and cultural unity of the world of Islam."

—Iranian Constitution

"We shall export our revolution to the whole world. Until the cry 'There is no God but God' resounds over the whole world, there will be struggle."

—Ayatollah Khomeini [1]

On June 12, 1982, a thousand elite troops of the Revolutionary Guards, dressed in their unmarked olive fatigues, boarded planes at the military section of Tehran's Mehrabad Airport and flew to Damascus. From the Syrian capital, the Pasdaran split into two groups. The first set up a staging post in an old youth camp in the Syria border town of Zebdani, where, according to local legend, Noah's Ark and Adam's tomb are located. Using an old dirt track traveled mainly by smugglers of hashish and stolen cars, the second contingent moved into eastern Lebanon's Bekaa Valley. In the ancient city of Baalbeck, the Guards entrenched themselves in an old Lebanese army barracks, a tatty local hotel and a clinic, which was promptly renamed Hospital Khomeini.

The Bekaa Valley, an expansive and lush plateau some nine hundred miles from Tehran as the crow flies, had for centuries been famous for its summer resorts, Roman ruins and some of the Middle East's finest vineyards. Enclosed between the Lebanon mountains that rise up dramatically from the Mediterranean and the Anti-Lebanon range that runs along the Lebanon-Syria border, the plain is three thousand feet above sea level and a hospitable reprieve from the humidity of the coast and the dryness of the south. In Baalbeck, the colossal columns from the Great Temple of Jupiter, the religious center begun under Julius Caesar and finished during the reign of Augustus, attests to the region's great part in history. In 1982, the Bekaa again became a religious center, this time during a more controversial turning point in history. Baalbeck became the Iranian revolution's forward outpost.

Little fanfare surrounded the deployment, even though the group was led by Mohsen Rafiqdoost, the small but wiry-tough commander who had been a leading figure in the 1979 revolution. Trained secretly in Palestine Liberation Organization (PLO) camps in Lebanon during the shah's era, he was later a key coordinator of the demonstrations and strikes that paralyzed the monarchy. He had secured, hidden and eventually distributed weapons that played a vital part in overthrowing the remnants of the regime in the fateful eleven days after Khomeini's return.[2] Rafiqdoost's presence in Lebanon, at a time of intense fighting in the Gulf war, should have indicated the importance of the deployment. Yet the Islamic Republic's first military expedition beyond its own borders gained little attention. The Beirut press and other Middle East papers only mentioned it in passing. At the time, even Western intelligence agencies missed the magnitude of what turned out to be the biggest and boldest attempt yet to export Iran's revolution.

Lebanon was, at that moment, consumed by other events. A week earlier, Israel had invaded Lebanon, sweeping hard and fast across the south. The goal of the fifth modern Arab-Israeli war was to push Palestinian guerrillas beyond penetration range of the volatile southern border and out of artillery range of Israel's vulnerable Galilee. But the Israelis were even more successful than they had hoped. They quickly reached and passed the Awali River, the stream marking the southern third of Lebanon where all parties, including the PLO and the United States, had assumed Israel would stop. By the end of the invasion's first week, as the Iranians were arriving in the Bekaa Valley, the Israeli Defense Force was closing in on West Beirut, the predominantly Muslim half of the Lebanese capital where the PLO had its headquarters. It was the beginning of what would be a ten-week siege, ending only after the PLO agreed to abandon Beirut and southern Lebanon altogether and to disperse its forces to eight, more remote camps in the Middle East.

Iran's deployment in Lebanon reflected the sweeping shift in Tehran's foreign policy. The shah had been little more than a distant observer of the four other Arab-Israeli wars since 1948. Defying pressure from OPEC colleagues, he had sold oil to Israel and maintained low-level diplomatic ties, which included an Israeli mission in Tehran. In contrast, the mullahs actively sought a role in the fifth conflict. Unlike the Arab world, which ranted with fury and threats, Tehran followed through on pledges of support by dispatching the Pasdaran.

The motive was in part solidarity. Before the revolution, dozens of Iranians opposed to the monarchy had trained in the PLO's camps in Lebanon. After the shah's ouster and the subsequent purge of SAVAK, Iran had relied on the PLO's efficient intelligence network throughout the Middle East for information about the activities of Iranian exiles and opposition groups. The relationship was still warm in 1979 when, in one of its first diplomatic acts, the Islamic Republic turned over the Israeli mission in Tehran to PLO chairman Yasir Arafat.

But loyalty to the Palestinians was not Iran's main motive. Indeed, in the intervening three and a half years, Tehran's relationship with the PLO had cooled into ambivalence. The radical mullahs were infuriated when they discovered that the PLO had also been training the Mojahedin. The Iran-Iraq war added to the distance. Although Arafat tried to remain neutral in his mediation efforts between the two Gulf nations, his long ties with Baghdad and his Arab loyalties made him suspect in Tehran. And while the Islamic Republic shared the Arab world's passion about retrieving Jerusalem, its primary interest was in the city's Islamic heritage. A Palestinian homeland was a secondary issue. For the mullahs, the Israeli invasion finally offered the pretext to fulfill their own agenda: penetration of the Arab world.

•

The venture into Lebanon was not Iran's first attempt. In its first year, the Islamic Republic had opened training camps for hundreds of young Islamic zealots from the Gulf states, the Arab heartland known as the Fertile Crescent, and North Africa, as well as from nations outside the Middle East, such as the Philippines. Most, but far from all, were Shi'a. They received rudimentary training from the Pasdaran on small arms, rocket launchers, grenades, sabotage techniques and explosive devices. They also spent long hours in classrooms where, sitting at the feet of clerics or listening to translations through walkman headsets, they were indoctrinated in Khomeini's thoughts. More than a dozen opposition groups, such as the Islamic Front for the Liberation of Bahrain and Iraq's Al-Dawa, were given office space and financial aid for their campaigns. The activist clergy from nearby nations were allotted broadcast time on Tehran Radio's Arabic shortwave service to preach subversion and Islamic revolution to their constituencies back home.

But the Islamic Republic's efforts had little impact, and the mullahs always paid a price. Attempts to foment a revolt in Iraq were met with a security clampdown that squelched dissent against the Baghdad regime and that contributed to the Gulf war. Aid to factions of Afghanistan's Mojahedin—a group that had no relation to the Iranian Mojahedin—made a tangible, albeit small, contribution to the group's ability to fight the Soviet occupation. But the aid antagonized Moscow, Iran's most powerful neighbor. Support of the minority Shi'ite communty in Saudi Arabia's oil-rich Hasa Province during limited uprisings in 1979 and 1980 had created further tension along the Persian Gulf. Fears of Iranian intentions in the Arabian Peninsula eventually led to the formation of the Gulf Cooperation Council (GCC), an alliance of the six most powerful and wealthy sheikhdoms to pool their military resources.

During the first three years of Iran's revolution, its Arab neighbors were more angered than intimidated by the revolutionary bravado and boasts. The reaction, however, began to change in December 1981 when an airport official in Dubai became suspicious of a group of youths waiting for a flight to Manama, the tropical, rather sleepy Bahraini capital. When they passed up an earlier flight, the official decided to check their passports. He found several "irregularities" and immediately alerted Manama. The youths turned out to be an advance team for a network of saboteurs. News flashed through the Gulf that a coup was being plotted against the tiny sheikhdom of Bahrain.

Although it was uncovered at an early stage, Bahraini officials later conceded that the plot could have been one of the greatest threats to national security since the island-state off the Saudi coast gained independence from Britain in 1971. As Bahraini officials later revealed, at least 150 men were to infiltrate Bahrain through nearby Kuwait, Dubai in the United Arab Emirates, and possibly elsewhere. They also discovered submachine guns, grenades and ammunition smuggled across the Gulf by dhows, presumably from Iran, and buried at night along the coastal strip. And they learned that communication equipment had been dispatched in the diplomatic pouch to the Iranian embassy in Manama.

The goal, Bahraini officials surmised, was to seize strategic installations during celebrations marking the tenth anniversary of Bahrain's independence and to overthrow the monarchy in favor of an Islamic Republic. The perpetrators were linked to the Islamic Front for the Liberation of Bahrain, one of the groups headquartered in Tehran—just one of several reasons why Bahrain ultimately blamed Iran.

Although no Iranians were found among the saboteurs, the Bahraini premier accused the Islamic Republic of "training hundreds of nationals from Gulf states in special camps under the supervision of experts on sabotage and demolition."[3] Added Bahrain's information minister, "Tehran denies it sponsored the plot, then it beams radio programs over here telling people to rise up and how to make petrol bombs. Who are they trying to fool?"[4] The threat of an overspill from the Iranian revolution was suddenly a reality that the desert sheikhdoms had to take seriously. But the implications of the Bahrain plot were not limited to the archipelago of thirty-three islands. The seventy-three youths later tried included youths from Saudi Arabia, Kuwait and Oman, three of Bahrain's closest allies.

The Islamic Republic was unrepentant about being implicated in the somewhat clumsy and transparent plot. It was also undeterred. Indeed, it was almost keen to spurn regional condemnation of its foreign policy. For the mullahs, monarchies were anathema to Islam; they represented the most unjust system of rule. That position was even more intense in sheikhdoms, such as Bahrain, where the Sunni minority dominated over a Shi'ite majority.* But, having

* The Twelver branch of Shi'ism, dominant in Iran, accounts for about 70 percent of the population in Bahrain. In the other five GCC states, Kuwait is second with about 25 percent; the United Arab Emirates and Qatar tie for third with between 16 and 18 percent; Saudi Arabia is fourth with about 8 percent; Oman has the smallest, with only 4 percent. Unrest among the Shi'a in nations such as Saudi Arabia, Iraq and Kuwait is potentially more troublesome than their population strengths might indicate, however, because they live over and work at major oil fields. Unrest in the late 1970s and early 1980s was often

failed in Bahrain, Iran did begin to alter its strategy and focus, which became clear within months of the foiled coup attempt in December 1981.

The scope and direction of Tehran's ambitions came together in the spring of 1982, when the Islamic Republic summoned leading clergymen throughout the Muslim world, from Indonesia to Morocco, to a seminar in Tehran. The theme was "the ideal Islamic government." The real subject was, in fact, the Islamic revolution. Newly secure at home after purging rivals and after gaining dominance on the war front, the Islamic Republic was now ready to go on the offensive with its ideology. "The turning point was the ability of Iran to break the back of internal armed opposition and to maintain power during two years of war and to run the economy," explained an Iraqi Shi'ite. "People became more certain that the revolution was a successful enterprise. They were willing to commit themselves and, more actively, to inspire others to follow suit."[5]

The seminar symbolized a turning point. Some 380 Islamic clerics from throughout the seventy nations in Dar al-Islam, or House of Islam, issued a declaration that formed the basis for a new stage of action. First, they concluded, religion should not be separated from politics; Islam should be a primary idiom of political opposition throughout the Muslim world. Second, religious activism was the only pure and effective means of purging foreign influence from their societies. Third and most important, the faithful should be deployed more actively to rid the region of foreign infidels. Iran's parliamentary speaker called exporting the revolution "our duty" to "oppressed people of the world."[6]

For the Iranians, the seminar reflected a new strength. "We have aided the liberation movements in the best possible manner, and no government has had the right or power to tell us that we have intervened in their internal affairs," President Ali Khamenei boasted at the time. "No one can tell us to stop publicizing our version of Islam or stop us from describing our revolution to the world."[7] Arab neighbors, however, preferred to view the summit as a sign of weakness. A Bahraini cabinet minister later described the conference as a "change of tactics, not policy. It had to take into account the failure of the revolution to pick up support [outside Iran] on its own steam. The rising masses did not rise. There were

related to Shi'ite grievances that they did not reap the benefits of their respective nations' oil wealth, which was channeled largely to Sunni leaders and communities.

no calls to prayer from the roofs of government buildings. It did not happen as they expected. That left one option, to become much more militant than before."[8]

Unable to rally Shi'ite zealots in rival Iraq or nearby Bahrain, the theocrats turned to Lebanon, where the situation was ripe for exploitation. Over the previous forty years, a demographic explosion had led the Shi'ite community to emerge as the largest of the nation's seventeen religious sects. Lebanon's Shi'ite clergy also had long-standing ties to Iran, and the Israeli invasion created regional turmoil and diverted attention. Lebanon thus became the test case for the export of Iran's revolution in an experiment that would last for more than eight years.

•

Soon after the Iranians arrived, the Lebanese started calling Baalbeck "Little Tehran" because of the changed look and feel of the historic city. Lebanese women were urged and, in some cases, intimidated into donning the black chador. Banners exulting Khomeini and posters proclaiming Koranic verses covered streets, fences and mosques. Bars were closed down, and liquor became available only in somewhat dangerous, behind-the-counter sales. The Pasdaran ran ideological "seminars" at local mosques. A radio station transmitted eight hours of daily sermons, religious programming and interviews on *Voice of the Iranian Revolution.* A network to provide welfare and social services was established for Iran's Lebanese brethren.

Militarily, the Iranian troops kept a low profile. Although they were deployed only thirty-five miles from Israeli frontlines at the southern end of Lebanon's Bekaa Valley, the Pasdaran never engaged in combat, nor did they attempt to sabotage Israeli facilities during the summer invasion. They acted as missionaries more than fighters during this early stage, systematically mobilizing the local Shi'ite community and establishing small cells of activists under the leadership of radical local clergy for later action. At that stage, the Iranians were in no hurry; time was on their side.

Iran's recruitment process was evident in the cultivation of Hussein Musawi, a bearded former chemistry teacher and a prominent figure in Amal, Lebanon's dominant Shi'ite militia. Musawi had become disillusioned with Amal leader Nabih Berri's political moderation and his willingness to play along with U.S. mediation to end the invasion. After all, Musawi argued, the United States' closest ally in the region had, in the process of pushing Palestinian guerrillas out of southern Lebanon, also rampaged through the land and holdings of the predominantly Shi'ite south. Hundreds of Shi'a had been killed by Israeli artillery and bombs. Berri's ambivalence about the revolution in Iran, where Musawi had received military training, also heightened the tension between the two men. Musawi finally broke away in disgust after his failure to convince Berri to take a tougher position on Israel and the United States and a softer line on Iran.

Musawi was then in a distinct minority, however, for most Shi'a, once allies of the PLO, were now tired of the Palestinians, who had created a state-within-a-state in south Lebanon. Thousands of southern residents had virtually embraced the advancing Israelis, throwing rose water and rice at the invading troops as a sign of welcome. They initially thought that the invasion meant regaining political and physical control of their lands. So Musawi defected to the Bekaa Valley, where he was embraced by the Iranians. Together, they formed the new Islamic Amal movement, a forerunner of the broader Hizbollah, or Party of God, that was soon to become a major force in Lebanese politics and the biggest threat to foreign influence and personnel in the Levant.

The quiet early days of Iran's presence in Lebanon were disturbed by only one, little-noticed event. But it was a mishap that would ultimately change the nature and tactics of violence in the region. On July 4, 1982, only three weeks after Iran's deployment, a car carrying four Iranians—three members of Iran's embassy in Lebanon and one journalist—headed toward Christian-controlled east Beirut. At a checkpoint run by the Lebanese Forces, the Israeli-backed Christian militia, the car was stopped even though it had diplomatic plates and, according to the Iranians, a police escort. Diplomatic immunity has rarely been honored by Lebanese gunmen of any political persuasion. The four Iranians disappeared.

When the car did not arrive at its destination, Tehran expressed outrage that regional governments and American mediators in Lebanon, all preoccupied by the Israeli invasion, ignored its entreaties to trace the four Iranian hostages. Even the local press gave the news scant coverage. The four Iranians were quickly forgotten, which turned out to be a costly oversight.

Fifteen days later, David Dodge, the tall, friendly acting president of the American University of Beirut (AUB), was walking home across the seafront campus at dusk when two gunmen emerged from a red Renault station wagon and jumped him. After a brief struggle, Dodge was hit with a pistol butt and shoved inside. The car then sped off the campus grounds with the highest-ranking

American civilian left in west Beirut. Moments after Lebanon's state radio broke the story, the Lebanese prime minister ordered police to "redouble" efforts to find the four Iranians. The connection had apparently immediately been assumed, even though no formal communiqué or set of demands was ever received. But it was too late.

The four Iranians were never heard from again. U.S. intelligence officials later said that they learned "authoritatively" from Christian sources within two months that the four were interrogated and then killed by the militia, which publicly and repeatedly denied any involvement in the episode. Through intermediaries, the United States passed word to Iran that the four were dead, in part to point out that a swap for Dodge was not an option. There was, initially, no response. Dodge languished in captivity—first in Lebanon, then in Tehran—for a full year.*

The two rounds of abductions launched the opening phase of the hostage phenomenon that would eventually affect more than 130 foreigners from more than twenty nations. Iran's original deployment had been tied to regional ambitions. The hostage seizures, however, suggested the international potential of Tehran's campaign. The next three years marked the most aggressive stage of the Iranian revolution.

•

In late August 1982, the United States, France and Italy dispatched troops to Lebanon to oversee the withdrawal of the PLO, the basic condition for ending Israel's siege of west Beirut and, theoretically, the invasion. The withdrawal went so smoothly that the Multi-National Force (MNF) was able to leave two weeks early, which turned out to be premature. Within days, Lebanon's new Christian president-elect, Bashir Gemayel of the Lebanese Forces militia, was assassinated. Israel invaded West Beirut. An estimated eight hundred Palestinian men, women and children in the Sabra and Shatilla refugee camps on the perimeter of Beirut were massacred —by axes, by firing squads, and by artillery—by Lebanese Forces gunmen. The United States, France and Italy quickly sent their MNF contingents back to Lebanon to try to restore the peace and, this time, to oversee the Israeli withdrawal from west Beirut.

But the situation soon turned into a stalemate. By the spring of 1983, eight months after the United States forces "temporarily"

* Dodge was freed through Syrian mediation after a tip from U.S. intelligence that he had secretly been taken through Damascus to Tehran.

returned to Lebanon, American mediation appeared to be on the threshold of a broad peace agreement between Lebanon and Israel, which was Jerusalem's precondition for pulling out of Lebanon completely. The pact, however, became a catalyst for new domestic strife. Because of Israel's long-standing support for the Christian minority, many Muslims and their Iranian and Syrian backers viewed the agreement as a means of further entrenching Christian domination in Lebanon. The proposed treaty provided a new opportunity for Iran and its Lebanese allies to exploit. Like the original invasion, the pact offered the pretext to promote Islamic unity and militant action in righting obvious injustices.

At 1:05 P.M. on April 18, 1983, a dark delivery van turned abruptly into the guarded cobblestone driveway of the United States embassy in west Beirut. It then exploded, sucking away the entire front facade of the concrete high-rise and enveloping the building in fire and massive clouds of black fumes. After a week of digging, rescuers retrieved parts of sixty-three American and Lebanese bodies, including nine CIA officers assembled for a high-level meeting with a senior analyst from Washington and a member of the ultrasecret American Delta Force, who operated under the cover of the regional security office. Of all the terrorist attacks ever perpetrated against the United States, the embassy bombing then ranked as the bloodiest.

An anonymous male voice later called Western news agencies to claim credit for the attack in the name of Islamic Jihad. Islamic Holy War, as it translated, was an enigmatic underground group believed to be made up of Shi'ite extremists loosely or formally tied to Hizbollah, the Party of God. Western intelligence suspected that Islamic Jihad's roots were in the Bekaa Valley and that it was aided by the Revolutionary Guards deployed there as well as by Iranian diplomats in nearby Damascus. Evidence was largely circumstantial, however, because of the small cell's tightly knit, impenetrable structure. The caller offered little further insight. After threatening even greater bloodshed unless the Americans pulled out of Lebanon completely, he hung up.

In the eight months between the MNF's redeployment and the embassy bombing, Lebanon's political landscape had been reshaped by the emergence of Islamic extremism. The Pasdaran and its local allies had successfully indoctrinated hundreds of young and poor Shi'ite peasants in eastern Lebanon. Long treated as second-class citizens both politically and economically by Maronite Christians and Sunni Muslims, the Shi'a were ripe for mobilization. In the mid-

1970s, the first Shi'ite organization, Amal, was founded by Musa Sadr, a leading Iranian cleric with Lebanese roots. Sadr had disappeared, however, during a 1978 trip to Libya, for which many Lebanese held Colonel Moammar Qaddafi responsible. Berri, a lawyer with an American green card, later took over, but he had neither the charisma nor the authority so important to Shi'ite tradition. The Iranian mission was to reenergize Shi'ite activism in a new organization that, it hoped, would eventually replace Amal and ultimately assert Islamic supremacy in a state where Muslims had become the majority.* The Revolutionary Guards in the Bekaa, with help from Iranian diplomats in nearby Damascus, began by creating Hizbollah cells.

The word *hizbollah* comes from a Koranic verse promising triumph for those who join the party of God. In the seventh century, the Prophet Mohammad used the phrase to spread the new faith; thirteen centuries later, it was again employed by the Iranians as a means of spreading the revolution. Tehran provided the idea, the promotion and the funding, up to a $100 million a year in cash along with other material support, according to American intelligence. Various local clerics then built up cells around their mosques. Unlike other militias in Lebanon, however, Hizbollah was not a formal party. A comparatively small movement, it lacked traditional structure and membership lists; unlike other political groups, it issued no cards providing free passage through its strongholds. Followers were largely self-designated. "If you are a believer," a young Shi'i once explained, "then you are a member of Hizbollah." [9]

For the Iranians and their militant Lebanese allies, the U.S. presence in Lebanon mirrored its intrusion in Iran during the shah's era —symbolized by the peace pact between Israel and Lebanon signed on May 17, 1983, a month after the embassy bombing. "We cannot consider Lebanese society to be sound and clean when it is tied to an agreement with Israel and subject to American designs in the region," explained a leading Lebanese cleric associated with Hizbollah. [10] The elimination of the peace pact and the Western military presence in Lebanon became a potent rallying cry that helped the

---

* Christians had the presidency and an edge in all government positions over Muslims in a six-to-five ratio as the result of a 1943 gentlemen's agreement among Lebanon's seventeen recognized sects. The so-called National Pact, orchestrated by France, was based on the Christians' demographic edge at the time. But by the 1970s, the Maronites had lost the demographic race as the Muslims outnumbered them. Among the Muslim sects, the Shi'a also soon outnumbered the Sunni, who held the premiership. The Shi'ite community thus sought higher political standing for Muslims as well as for itself.

movement gain wider legitimacy—and helped it expand from the fringe of society to center stage.

During the summer of 1983, Hizbollah quietly began moving some of its operatives and operations from the Bekaa into the labyrinth of poor Shi'ite suburbs in west Beirut. Then, in September 1983, a second catalyst conveniently intensified the increasingly bitter climate. The trouble started when Israel decided to pull back from the idyllic Chouf Mountains that overlook Beirut to a more defensible position twenty-two miles south—ironically to the Awali River, where so many had originally thought the Israeli invasion would stop. The withdrawal created a vacuum that led rival Christian and Druze* militias to renew fighting for control of the area considered to be Lebanon's heartland.

The Druze quickly managed to push the main Christian militia out of more than 80 percent of the picturesque region. By September 19, the Christian-led Lebanese Army was panicking about a Druze attack on the gateway to Christian east Beirut. The Lebanese army commander appealed to the United States for help. The United States, which had so far used its guns only in self-defense, agreed to go on the offensive at a time when the American Marines were not under fire nor their lives endangered. Within an hour of the request, the USS *Virginia* opened fire on the Druze positions. With that act, the United States immediately lost its neutrality and its credibility as a mediator in Lebanon.† The Marines quickly became known as the "international militia" in Lebanon. By pushing the peace pact with Israel, the United States had been perceived by militant Muslims to be using diplomatic muscle to entrench Christian domination; now it was seen to be deploying military might to the same end. And that had to be stopped.

On October 23, 1983, just thirty-four days after the USS *Virginia* opened fire, another suicide bomber struck. Ten minutes before reveille on a balmy Sunday, the one day of the week when the Marines were allowed to sleep in an extra half hour, a young Shi'ite extremist drove a Mercedes truck into the main airport compound where most of the American troops were housed. The explosion, estimated to contain the equivalent of nine tons of dynamite, was

* The Druze are a breakaway branch of Islam with a secret set of religious beliefs that are in some ways sufficiently different from Muslim tenets that they do not consider themselves Muslims. In Lebanon, however, they were generally aligned politically with the major Muslim factions.

† Tragically, the Marine commander realized the implications of the use of American warships and pleaded with superiors not to force him to carry out the order. He correctly predicted that his contingent would become enmeshed in domestic strife as a new target.

later judged by FBI forensic specialists to be the largest non-nuclear explosion since World War II.

Under the debris of the four-story, concrete-reinforced building, 241 American Marine and Navy personnel were buried.* Never before had so many Americans died in a single terrorist attack, and not since Iwo Jima in 1945 had so many Marines died at one time. Once again, the anonymous voice of Islamic Jihad claimed credit. "We said after that [embassy bombing] that we would strike more violently still. Now they understand with what they are dealing. Violence will remain our only way." The Americans were warned once again to go home.

"In Lebanon, we trained the people who drove a bomb into the American Marine barracks, but we didn't tell them to do such an act," admitted Mohsen Rafiqdoost, the Revolutionary Guard Minister, five years later. "We only trained the Lebanese to defend their country. When we heard about the bomb, we were happy. But we didn't plan it. It was their right. Ask yourself, Why were the Americans in Lebanon?"[11] Not, he implied, to help the Muslim community.

Although he denied his involvement in the bombing, Islamic Amal's Musawi later explained, "If America kills my people, then my people must kill Americans. We have already said that if self-defense and if the stand against American, Israeli and French oppression constitute terrorism, then we are terrorists in that context. This path is the path of blood, the path of martyrdom. For us, death is easier than smoking a cigarette if it comes while fighting for the cause of God and while defending the oppressed."[12] The Marine bombing and the attacks on other American targets were seen as acts of self-defense; the suicide bombers were merely following in the tradition of the martyr Hosain in fighting injustice— and, in the process, changing the nature of warfare in the Middle East.

•

The attacks on the embassy and Marine barracks marked a heady new stage in the Islamic revolution. Iran had proven that it was able to cultivate and unleash extremists in other nations against their mutual foes—not only the United States. In early November 1983, only ten days after the Marine bombing, a truck laden with explo-

---

* Within seconds of the attack on the Marines, another suicide bomber drove into a French MNF barracks, killing fifty-eight. The motive, while not as straightforward, appeared to be in part related to historic French support for Lebanon's Christians as well as its recent increased support for and arms sales to Iraq in the Gulf war.

sives plowed into a plain, two-story building in Tyre, the southern Lebanese port city that was once the seat of ancient Phoenicia. The facility had become a strategic installation after the occupying Israeli Defense Forces converted its upper floors into a headquarters and its lower floor into a prison. A suicide driver managed to penetrate the perimeter security and, in a massive explosion, kill twenty-nine Israelis and more than thirty Lebanese and Palestinian prisoners. It was the most devastating attack on Israeli troops since the occupation had begun seventeen months earlier. Islamic Jihad again claimed credit.

"We have never directly, or even indirectly, supported the arguments of those opposition groups outside Iran," claimed Ali Akbar Mohtashami, Iran's ambassador to neighboring Syria at the time, in an interview five years later. Mohtashami was alleged by Western intelligence to be deeply involved in the misadventures of Lebanon's Shi'ite extremists. "This, of course, does not mean that if a nation has been crushed by a foreign power and if it stands up and fights a foreign power we don't support this right. For example, a man in Lebanon bombed Israeli soldiers in Tyre. His name was Ahmed Ghasir. Before we make a judgment about this, we have to look at the situation. He lost all his relations under Israeli boots and bombardment. We believe it is the right of other nations to defend themselves."[13] Revealing the name of the bomber was interesting in itself. Neither Israel nor the United States had ever been able to identify him; the bomber, like his earlier counterparts, had been blown to dust.

The violence was not limited to anarchic Lebanon. On December 12, 1983, just five weeks after the Tyre bombing, six bombs went off over a ninety-minute period in the tiny city-state of Kuwait on the Persian Gulf. Among the targets were the American and French embassies, a power station, the Kuwaiti airport control tower, an oil depot and the residential compound of an American defense contracting company. The attacks were believed to be motivated mainly by opposition to American meddling in the Middle East and U.S. arms sales to Kuwait; France's arms sales to Iraq; and Kuwait's economic and overall political support of Baghdad. Six were killed and more than eighty injured.

The casualties could have been much higher. Only a quarter of the forty-five gas cylinders on the truck that rammed into the American embassy compound went off. At the oil refinery, a faulty connection among the two hundred large cylinders rigged in the back of a yellow truck without license plates prevented a complete catastrophe. American and Kuwaiti investigators later said that, if the bombs had gone off as planned, the entire American compound would have been leveled into "a parking lot"; the oil complex, which also included the country's main water-desalination plant, would have burned for months and the nation been left "almost totally dry."[14] The bombings were the biggest terrorist threat Kuwait had ever faced.

Based on the thumb of the suicide bomber dismembered at the U.S. embassy site and the trail of accomplices the fingerprint led to, twenty-one men were subsequently arrested and tried for the bombing spree; four others were tried in absentia. Again, no Iranians were among the accused. They were all Kuwaitis, Iraqis or Lebanese. All were Shi'a. Islamic Jihad had once again claimed credit in anonymous calls to news agencies in Beirut. The claim was particularly credible as the voice said that seven bombs had been planted; a seventh, unexploded device was later found by Kuwaiti security forces near the Immigration Bureau. Yet the men on trial admitted their membership in Al-Dawa, the Shi'ite Iraqi dissident group that had offices throughout the region but whose headquarters were in Tehran.

The overlapping organizational links and claims of credit made it difficult to determine the line of command. But the multiple ties revealed the loose network that led back to Iran, but which could also function independently of the theocracy. While Iran openly boasted of the direction it provided the soldiers of God, the concatenation of cells often acted independently of each other—and even of their Iranian sponsors.

The trail unraveled after the Marine bombing was instructional. The only piece of evidence left behind was a piece of the axle from the Mercedes truck. After three years of painstaking investigations, the FBI determined that it had come from an assembly plant in Iran. The explosive was found to have originated in Bulgaria, having made its way to Baalbeck and then Beirut via Syria. Investigators even discovered the identity of the suicide driver, nicknamed "Smiling Death" by the Marines because of the chilling expression locked on his face as he raced his truck toward the building full of sleeping Marines. The youth was a devout Shi'ite Lebanese from a poor religious family, according to American intelligence. Trained by the Revolutionary Guards deployed in Baalbeck, he was handpicked for martyrdom by his Lebanese colleagues. The largest loss of American military life since the Vietnam War was carried out, according to U.S. intelligence, by a "young nobody" with no earlier criminal record.

The description was again telling, for Iran's crusade to export the revolution was specifically addressed to a category of people described by the world's governments and intelligence organizations as "nobodies." The theocrats called them the *mostazafin*, the "disinherited" or "downtrodden"—the Iranian equivalent of the French revolution's *citoyens* and the Russian revolution's *proletariat*. As the sign on the former American embassy in Tehran declared, "God willing, this will be the century of victory by the oppressed over the oppressors."

The world viewed Iran's campaign primarily in terms of violence, which was, in fact, only a small part of the Islamic Republic's message. For the disinherited, Iran symbolized the reawakening of an activist faith that is, because of the legend of the martyr Hosain, theoretically in a constant state of rebellion against injustice. On a broader level, the Iranian-directed crusade's utopian priorities were greater political representation for the downtrodden, more equitable distribution of economic resources and restoration of social dignity and independence. For the nobodies of the Shi'ite world, that initially had great appeal.

"The Western media is trying to frighten the world about the export of the Islamic revolution of Iran," said the angered speaker of Iran's parliament, Ali Akbar Hashemi Rafsanjani. "We have announced that we are for the export of the revolution and have explained what we mean by this. We have launched an Islamic movement and Islam must prevail in the region." The theocrats claimed that their emphasis was on cultural, ideological and spiritual adaptation of the revolution elsewhere and that it did *not* seek military conquest of other Muslim nations. Rafsanjani vowed, "We will never conquer a country through the use of our army, unless that country commits an act of aggression against us." [15] But few in the outside world believed him.

•

The theocracy's period of expansion was not limited to the outside Muslim world. As Iran championed its Islamic message abroad, it also aggressively pushed Islamization back home. More clerics were appointed as advisors and aides in government ministries and bureaus. Western words were officially abolished from Farsi. Television and newspapers were told to devote more time to background pieces on Islamic history and on the faith's vital contemporary role in society. Legislation made interest payments, considered usury in Islam, illegal at banks, which replaced the traditional system with a fluctuating dividend.[16] In big ways and small, the mullahs had begun to deepen and to institutionalize their hold on Iranian society.

The mullahs also used their growing strength to eliminate the last nonclerical group, the communist Tudeh Party. Long an irritant to the theocracy, the Tudeh had claimed a right to participate in the revolutionary regime because of its role in ousting the shah. But unlike the outspoken Mojahedin, Tudeh leaders kowtowed to the mullahs, despite the often hostile response. They quietly accepted restrictions banning them from running for the presidency, and they chose not to publicly criticize electoral conduct when their candidates failed to win seats in parliament. But subservience was not sufficient to survive in the Islamic Republic.

Two events precipitated the Tudeh's fall. First, Moscow resumed arms sales to Iraq, which infuriated the mullahs and made them fear the loss of their advantage on the battlefield. Second, a list of agents used by the Soviet Union in Iran was passed along to the mullahs from an unlikely source. In 1982, Vladimir Kuzichkin, a Soviet diplomat stationed in Tehran, had defected to Britain. During the debriefing, he had provided names of Soviet spies and their Iranian agents, which the British, in turn, shared with their American counterparts. Fearful that Moscow had made new inroads in Iran during its absence, the United States made the list available to Tehran in 1983.

Iran reacted swiftly: eighteen Soviet diplomats were expelled on charges of espionage, and hundreds of Tudeh members were arrested. The crackdown, begun in the spring, lasted until the fall of 1983. Throughout this period, Tudeh leaders were put on nationwide television to confess their crimes, ranging from subversion to espionage, and to disclose the malevolent intentions of the Soviet Union in Iran. Unlike earlier crackdowns, there was little public reaction to the elimination of the last serious rival to the Islamic regime. The purge of the Tudeh was the final step in consolidating the clergy's rule.

With their newfound self-confidence, the mullahs began to relieve the domestic tension, based on the imam's eight-point declaration on individual rights of December 1982. Exit visas required for visits abroad, which had been tightly restricted, were made available to tens of thousands of Iranians. In 1982, universities that had been closed down to adapt curricula to Islamic tenets were gradually reopened. A campaign was also launched to convince exiled Iranian professionals, especially doctors, engineers and academics, to return. By 1984, Khomeini was admonishing the clergy not to press "too hard" and "to refrain from extremism." [17]

The strongest indicator of the revolution's new sense of security was the decision to begin the long-awaited process of selecting Khomeini's heir. The succession issue was particularly sensitive because most of the imam's peers, a half dozen grand ayatollahs, opposed in differing degrees the Islamic system that Khomeini had established as well as many of the tactics used by the lower-ranking clergy. To preempt potential opposition, the theocrats turned to the electorate to select eighty-three mullahs for a permanent Assembly of Experts. The Assembly would, in turn, pick the heir apparent and, eventually, oversee the transition. Although they did not select an heir for more than two years, the opening of their deliberations in 1983 fostered a greater sense of assurance that, should the aged and ailing leader suddenly die, a mechanism was in place for the transition of power.

Parliamentary elections in the spring of 1984, the second round since the revolution, also went comparatively smoothly, free of the violence that had marked the 1980 campaign. The mullahs' tightening control on the state apparatus was evident in formal bans on opposition groups such as the Mojahedin-e Khalq and the Tudeh Party. To protest the lack of democratic freedoms, former Prime Minister Bazargan, who had held a seat in the first *majlis*, and his Freedom Movement opted against running again. Yet the dominant Islamic Republic Party felt sufficiently secure to encourage many nonclerics, including women, to run, one of several steps designed to widen the clergy's following.

•

Even the war effort was consolidated during this period of expansion. Although Operation Sunrise, Iran's first, widely heralded "final offensive" in February 1983, failed to cut the oil and shipping center of Basra off from Baghdad, each of Iran's sporadic offensives further eroded Iraq's position. Baghdad was increasingly on the defensive, not only militarily. The regime of President Saddam Hussein, having exhausted its massive financial reserves, was also becoming dependent on aid from his Gulf allies for economic survival.

The fighting remained bloody, but the major Iranian cities and rural centers were still little-touched by the Gulf conflict, which was becoming a war of attrition. Tehran stuck adamantly to its ultimatum for a truce. "There are no conditions," Khomeini said. "The only condition is that the regime in Baghdad must fall and must be replaced by an Islamic Republic."[18] Bravado on the war front and aggression in the Muslim world fed each other; Iran appeared to be unstoppable.

Baghdad tried. One of its deadly new tactics, in violation of all international agreements, was the use of chemical warfare. In February 1984, the Iranian military probed deeply into the one area that Iraq considered impenetrable—the thick marshes at the head of the Shatt al-Arab, near the confluence of the Euphrates and Tigris rivers. Scraping together an amphibious unit, the Iranians stunned Baghdad by crossing the Tigris. They also took Majnun Islands, or "Mad" Islands, which consisted of little more than a floating labyrinth of oil installations. The two victories were important because the Tigris crossing demonstrated how deeply Iran was capable of penetrating inside Iraq and because Majnun is among the richest of Iraq's oil fields.[19]

The surprise thrust panicked Baghdad. The first indication of Iraq's response came from the unusual injuries—the blistering burns and the pained breathing indicating lung damage—among Iranian troops. Red Cross doctors later confirmed that the injuries had been caused by chemical weapons. Since 1981, Tehran had charged Iraq with use of mustard gas, a substance banned from modern warfare by the 1925 Geneva Protocol. But Baghdad had never used the toxic chemical on such a massive scale. The tactic, designed psychologically and militarily to intimidate the Iranians into withdrawing, partially worked. Iran retreated across the Tigris. Revolutionary Guards did, however, manage to hold on to part of Majnun. In the end, Iraq remained on the defensive.

In an attempt to reverse its losses, Baghdad also took the war from land to the strategic Gulf sea-lanes. At the time of Iran's February 1984 offensive, the Baghdad regime declared that Kharg Island, Iran's main terminal in the Gulf, would henceforth be under siege. Throughout the spring, Iraq also used its new French-made Super Etendard warplanes to escalate aerial attacks on Iranian tankers and on ships doing business with Iran. The goal was to economically cripple Iran into suing for peace. But this tactic also backfired.

On May 13, 1984, the twenty-seven-man Bulgarian crew of the *Umm Casbah* had left Kuwait, bound for Britain with 765,000 tons of crude oil. Shortly after 9:00 A.M., the crew noticed a small spotter plane flying low over the ship. A few minutes later, a fighter suddenly soared down from the sky and unleashed two rockets, forcing the sailors to scramble for cover. The rockets hit the deck and ended up overboard, creating limited damage. The crew was confused, for they had thought they were safe. The ship had not done business with Iran nor was it sailing in the "exclusion zone" that Baghdad had declared around Kharg Island. American and Saudi intelligence monitoring Gulf traffic from AWAC radar planes realized what had happened, but they initially kept the cause of the stunning development to themselves.[20]

The next day, a Kuwaiti tanker, the *Bahrah,* was returning empty from a trip to Egypt. In mid-afternoon, five rockets rained down on the *Bahrah,* ripping a massive hole in the starboard side and starting a fire that raged for eight hours. Two days later, news of a third attack, this time on a Saudi supertanker, the *Yanbu Pride,* sent shock waves through the Gulf as diplomats, shippers and oilmen called one another frantically in search of an explanation. Because it fired at shipping targets from up to eighteen miles away, Iraq had occasionally mistakenly hit friendly targets.* But these attacks were daring, not distant; the warplanes flew low over the ships before dropping their bombs.

Iran had not responded to six Iraqi attacks earlier that spring on tankers doing business with Tehran; the mullahs had always in the past focused primarily on the land war as the most effective means of pressuring Baghdad. Besides, Iraq had at least a three-to-one advantage in warplanes. Iraqi ships also did not use the Gulf for export since it had been cut off from the Shatt al-Arab in the conflict's early stages.

But the mullahs changed tactics. As Parliamentary Speaker Rafsanjani pronounced, "Either the Persian Gulf will be safe for all or for no one." Tehran had decided to challenge Iraq in the sea-lanes —by going after the tankers of Iraq's allies, such as the *Umm Casbah,* the *Bahrah* and the *Yanbu Pride.* The shift opened the first round in the "tanker war" that brought the entire Gulf region into the war. The emboldened Islamic Republic was now prepared to face off not only Iraq but also its powerful sponsors. Eventually, the tanker war would also internationalize the war by drawing in both superpowers.

•

In Lebanon, 1984 opened with a visible victory for Iran. In the aftermath of the Marine bombing in October 1983, the United States had ordered its troops to move underground. Living in subterranean shipping containers, the Marines became preoccupied

* Among the friendly targets hit by Iraq in 1987 was the USS *Stark,* an attack that killed thirty-seven American sailors.

with rumors of imminent attacks. Reports claimed that suicide pilots flying out of the Bekaa would bomb the now tightly cordoned area and that bomb-laden dogs would penetrate the perimeter and be detonated by remote control.

In February 1984, eighteen months after their arrival, the Reagan administration finally decided to "redeploy" the troops onto ships positioned off the Mediterranean coast. Admonitions that the move was not a retreat were a sham; since the bombing, the American troops had effectively been forced to abandon their mission in order to preserve their own lives. It was not surprising when, a few months later, they were told to sail home. The French, Italians and a small unit of British troops who belatedly joined the MNF followed suit. The Islamic extremists had won the first round.

But the crusade against the American infidels was not over. Islamic extremists began turning on individuals. In separate incidents between February and May 1984, four Americans were plucked from the unruly streets of Beirut by masked gunmen. They were usually bundled in the trunk of an unlicensed car and whisked off to indefinite captivity. Among the hostages were an American University of Beirut professor, a journalist, a missionary and, most valuable to the extremists, CIA station chief William Buckley.

Islamic Jihad again claimed credit as "confirmation" of its warning after the Marine bombing "that we will not leave any American on Lebanese soil." The captors also sought freedom for the four Iranian hostages abducted in 1982 and the release of the seventeen Al-Dawa prisoners detained in Kuwait for the 1983 bombing spree. The American panic deepened after a report in May 1984 claimed that the extremists planned to abduct a hundred Americans, mainly embassy and American University of Beirut personnel, by June 1. The same week, the U.S. embassy in west Beirut announced that it was moving to a hastily prepared building in east Beirut. Other European embassies soon followed suit.

Moving out of anarchic west Beirut to a quiet hillside suburb in the Christian east was, however, not enough. On September 20, 1984, a beige Chevrolet van, the same kind used by American embassy guards, veered past a security gate and accelerated toward the new embassy annex. A quick-thinking British bodyguard, on duty in the parking lot as the British ambassador paid a courtesy call on his American counterpart, fired five rounds at the vehicle. The driver slumped over the steering wheel as the van rammed into a car parked next to the annex, just a few feet short of its target. Then it exploded. Fourteen Americans and Lebanese were killed and dozens, including the two ambassadors, were injured. Once again, Western news agencies received anonymous calls from Islamic Jihad claiming credit.

Despite pledges that the United States would not succumb to terrorism, the Reagan administration moved more American diplomats out of Beirut—by helicopter convoys to Cyprus because Beirut International Airport in west Beirut was deemed too dangerous. From a high of 190 envoys stationed in Lebanon a year earlier, the United States had only 6 in place by the day of President Reagan's reelection in November 1984. Antiaircraft guns were installed atop the ambassador's residence, which became the latest "temporary" embassy. The few Americans left behind were even banned from going out at night.

After the third devastating suicide bombing in Beirut, President Reagan pledged that the United States would not "crawl in a hole someplace and stop performing." But the impact of Iran's campaign to export its revolution was felt far beyond Lebanon. Embassies throughout the Middle East were fortified, and strategic facilities at home, including the White House, the Pentagon and the State Department, were secured behind massive concrete blocks to prevent another suicide attack. Anything seemed possible.

Meanwhile, the scenic Bekaa Valley gained a reputation as one of the most dangerous places on earth. Even journalists and diplomats willing to travel to Tehran were unprepared to tempt fate by visiting Baalbeck. The momentum behind the Islamic extremists seemed out of control, their force almost omnipotent. The revolution had reached its pinnacle.

CHAPTER FIVE

The Road To Tehran

ↄ৴৹২

"The world is determined on the diplomatic
scene. If we are not present, it will be determined
without us."

—Iranian Foreign Minister
Ali Akbar Velayati [1]

"It is not easy to sleep next to an elephant that
you have wounded."

—Iranian official to Oliver
North [2]

On June 14, 1985, a steamy Mediterranean summer day, TWA Flight 847 took off from Athens
en route to Rome, the transfer point for flights to New York. But
the red-and-white Boeing 727 never arrived in Italy. As soon as the
seat-belt signs were turned off, two young Lebanese, wielding a
pearl-handled pistol and handfuls of live grenades, commandeered
the aircraft. For the next three days, the plane virtually shuttled
between Beirut and Algiers on an 8,300-mile odyssey. Along the
way, a young American Navy diver named Robert Dean Stetham
was brutally beaten and shot through the head; his body was
dumped on the Beirut airport tarmac. For the next two weeks, the
trauma of the thirty-nine Americans who were finally taken off the

130

plane and transferred to hiding places in the slums of west Beirut by Shi'ite militiamen mesmerized the world.

The hijackers' demands centered on the release of 766 mainly Shi'ite Lebanese who were being held by Israel's occupying army. Eight days before the hijacking, the Israelis had withdrawn from all but a narrow enclave inside the Lebanese border—exactly three years to the day since their 1982 invasion. They had taken the prisoners with them. For the Reagan administration, the TWA ordeal was more than just a hijacking crisis. Three Americans seized in 1984 were still being held, and four other U.S. citizens living in Lebanon had been kidnapped in 1985. One had been abducted just five days before the TWA skyjacking. After his campaign pledge to fight terrorism and his first-term promises of retribution, Ronald Reagan was finding his presidential watch even more muddied by terrorism than the Carter years had been—and not just because of Middle East violence.

During the first week of the TWA hijacking, an attack in El Salvador killed 6 Americans, including 4 Marines; a bomb aboard an Air India flight killed 329 over the North Atlantic; a bombing at Frankfurt's airport killed 3 and injured 42; and five bombs near government facilities in Nepal killed 7 and wounded 240. The United States needed, urgently, to prevent another prolonged mass-hostage episode, and Reagan had to be *seen* to be responding to this scourge.

In a series of precarious deliberations, Washington eventually managed to work out the famous "no-deal deal" in which the Americans, followed in stages by the release of the 766 prisoners in Israel, would go free—all under the pretext that the United States had made no concessions. On July 1, 1985, seventeen days after the TWA seizure, the thirty-nine Americans were freed. The deal appeared to have been struck with the help of Amal leader Nabih Berri and Syrian president Hafez al-Assad. But neither had any leverage over the feistily independent extremists to persuade them. Behind the scenes, the most crucial role was, in fact, played by Iran.

In secret meetings in Syria, *Majlis* Speaker Ali Akbar Hashemi Rafsanjani ultimately convinced—some say ordered—the Hizbollah hijackers to end the ordeal. Iran was not prepared to endure a repeat of the 1979–81 hostage episode. "Iran had no connection whatsoever with this incident and, had it known, would have prevented it," Rafsanjani said in Damascus. Several U.S. officials tended to believe him; the Reagan administration later publicly acknowledged Iran's "helpful" role.[3] Rafsanjani's actions represented a seeming reversal in Iranian tactics. The episode marked a turning point in Iran's foreign policy.

There had been hints of a shift. In mid-1984, a year earlier, German Foreign Minister Hans Dietrich Genscher became the first ranking Western official to visit Iran since the revolution. At the time, he said that Tehran would gradually open its doors to the West. Within a month, Iran's foreign minister declared that Tehran was taking a "more positive" approach to diplomacy. Ayatollah Khomeini even denounced Islamic Jihad's claims of mining the Red Sea, which had created an international panic in mid-1984. The Islamic Republic also probed détente with other rivals. In May 1985, a month before the TWA hijacking, the first high-level diplomatic exchange with Saudi Arabia, not coincidentally, overlapped with the release of a Saudi diplomat who had been held hostage in Lebanon for seventeen months.

Iran's intervention in the TWA crisis appeared to Washington to be the first solid indication of Iran's interest in dealing again with the outside world. It coincided, however, with an interagency review of Iran policy that included a CIA assessment outlining what was mistakenly perceived as the Soviet Union's growing influence in Iran. The document set off alarm bells in the National Security Council about where Iran's openness might lead. To counter Moscow's initiative, the five-page memorandum outlined eight options, including a suggestion that Washington allow its allies to sell American weapons to Tehran.[4]

The unfolding of the TWA hijacking also taught the Reagan administration an important lesson: Tehran, not Damascus, was the key to freedom for the final seven American captives—an argument that Israeli officials had been making for almost a year. Just two days after the hijacking ended, a ranking Israeli foreign ministry official met with National Security Advisor Robert McFarlane, who had conducted the sensitive TWA negotiations, to discuss an American initiative toward Iran.[5]

•

At the time of the TWA hijacking, Iran's revolution was in trouble. Whatever the spiritual rewards of Islamic rule, the physical situation of the *mostazafin* "dispossessed" had deteriorated since the shah's ouster. A black-market economy charged prices three to ten times higher than the official costs of rationed goods, such as meat, butter, rice and cooking oil. Shortages of rationed foods meant that the poor occasionally went hungry. Young women, who traditionally provide a dowry as well as a new home's furnishings and appliances, postponed marriages their families could not afford. Housing shortages, a population explosion and the migration of hundreds of thousands of war refugees forced two and even three generations to live in the same cramped quarters. Slum shanties sprang up around most major towns.

The *mostazafin*'s problems were made all the more conspicuous by the construction of new yellow-brick or whitewashed villas in the wealthier suburbs and by the profiteering of entrepreneurs with foreign currency to exploit the black market. In the neighborhood groceries of wealthy northern Tehran, virtually any import was available, from Pampers diapers and Toblerone chocolates from Switzerland to L'Air du Temps bath oil from France. Prices were exorbitant, but business indicated that some quarters were thriving during these hard times. The gap between the rich and the poor had, in fact, grown wider rather than been narrowed since the shah's ouster. The cost of the war, combined with a world oil glut, had prevented development of the theocracy's social welfare programs. And the discrepancies between the revolution's grand promises and the harsh realities of living under its rule were beginning to be aired in the Iranian press and in parliament.

Meanwhile, the war dragged on. The 1982 breakthroughs had heightened Iranian expectations, but the major winter and spring offensives of the next three years failed to end the costly stalemate. In March 1985, Iran launched Operation Badr, named after the Prophet Mohammad's first military triumph in Mecca. As in 1984, the goal was to cross the Tigris River and to cut off Basra. But Iran's campaign fizzled within ten days.

The Islamic Republic had taken steps to improve its military performance. Although the emphasis remained on human-wave assaults, the Pasdaran and the Basij volunteer units had been reorganized along more conventional military lines. But Tehran had two increasing problems: Iraq's ever-expanding chemical-weapons capability and the U.S.-orchestrated arms embargo. Launched in 1983 and code-named Operation Staunch, the embargo had begun to affect Tehran's arsenal. When it could get American arms, the theocracy had to pay at least twice the going price.[6]

Fears in Baghdad about Operation Badr led Iraq to launch a series of devastating air raids against civilian areas in Iran. The so-called "war of the cities" brought the war to major towns, including Isfahan, Shiraz, Tabriz and even Tehran, previously beyond the range of Iraqi guns. Its air force depleted, Iran could only respond with missile barrages on Basra. Tehran still had the edge on the ground, but it was clearly losing momentum. The problem was evident in the diminishing numbers of volunteers for the Revolutionary Guards and Basij and in government warnings to draft dodgers. Iran's boasts of a "final offensive" began to be replaced by talk of a "defensive jihad."[7] By the summer of 1985, the Islamic Republic needed to break the cycle that had diverted its attention and resources from the social purposes of the revolution.

•

Within two months of the TWA episode, Israel responded to the perceived opening in Iran. In two highly secret operations between August 30 and September 14, 1985, Israel shipped badly needed arms supplies to Iran.[8] The deal included 508 American-made TOW antitank missiles, the weapon Iran wanted to improve its ground war against better-armed Iraq. The second installment on September 14 coincided with the release in Beirut of the Reverend Benjamin Weir, a Presbyterian missionary who had been held in captivity by Islamic Jihad for fourteen months.

Encouraged by the hostage release, Reagan administration officials had decided to probe an overture toward Iran. A rather bizarre combination of middlemen—an exiled Iranian named Manuchehr Ghorbanifar, a Saudi businessman, and various Israeli arms dealers and counterterrorism specialists—became central figures in the initiative. Ghorbanifar, a portly entrepreneur with a Vandyke mustache and goatee, lived in Europe but maintained contacts in Tehran. He became the centerpiece of the effort. The Saudi billionaire Adnan Khashoggi was used mainly for arranging and transferring funds. The Israelis served as advisors and intermediaries.

The Islamic Republic had made no secret of its interest in American weapons. The primary issue, however, was not Tehran's willingness to buy American arms but, rather, its long-term diplomatic intent: Was Iran genuinely willing to come to terms with the Great Satan? Or was it manipulating a massive sting operation to gain legal access to arms at the minimal price of a handful of American hostages? The answer was as complex as the political spectrum in Iran at the time.

For two years before the first arms shipment, Rafsanjani had been open about the potential of renewed relations with the United States. Directly addressing "the Americans" in a 1983 Friday prayer sermon, he had said that the Islamic Republic would recognize any country that "honored" the revolution. At the time of the 1985 TWA hijacking, he had suggested that Washington could move to restore relations with Tehran. The shrewd politician, whose Mongolian roots had left his face hairless and rather cheru-bic-looking, was clearly signaling a change—although not a com-plete reversal.

The initial arms-for-hostages swap was not the first time that the theocracy had been prepared to compromise to achieve greater ends. Despite some threatening noises, Iran had never closed the Strait of Hormuz, the global chokepoint for Western oil supplies from the Middle East. It had also shown restraint during the tanker war in responding to Iraqi air attacks, striking only tit-for-tat and never initiating an escalation. The Islamic Republic's position on Israel was another example of ambiguity. Officially, Iran hated Is-rael. Yet one of the worst-kept secrets in Iran was that, dating back to the early stages of the war, Tehran had quietly purchased Amer-ican arms from Israel and Israeli arms dealers. Even troops on the front talked openly about it.[9]

By mid-1985, the time of the TWA hijacking; the shift in Tehran was being explored or exploited by such disparate former Iranian rivals as the Soviet Union and Saudi Arabia. Both nations were almost as controversial in Iran as they were in the United States. Moscow openly sold arms to Iraq. It was also then in its sixth year of occupying Afghanistan, Iran's neighbor, and of trying to elimi-nate the Mojahedin holy warriors, with whom Iran sided. Riyadh, the Gulf monarchy most criticized by Tehran and its main rival in leading the Islamic world, had just a year earlier shot down an Iranian warplane. So the United States was not beyond reach—under certain conditions. In a speech at Tehran University, Kha-menei said, "We are not enemies of the U.S. nation. We bear no hostility towards that geographic region and that land. We are hos-tile towards domineering policies."[10]

Renewed relations with the United States might provide access to arms as well as possibly end the flow of American military intel-ligence, mainly from satellites and AWAC radar planes, to Bagh-dad. Also, after six years of self-imposed isolation, some Iranian leaders felt that it was time to reenter the world community. As Foreign Minister Ali Akbar Velayati had told the Iranian parliament in mid-1984, "The world is determined on the diplomatic stage. If we are not present, it will be determined without us."

The Reverend Weir's release in September 1985 had led to opti-mism within the Reagan administration that an approach was worth exploring. A second arms shipment from Israel, this time with direct American involvement, was organized in November. It was, how-ever, a disaster. The Iranians expected eighty HAWK antiaircraft missiles, which they wanted in part to protect oil installations. In return, they would pay $250,000 apiece—and arrange for a further hostage release.

But, at the last minute, Washington could not get clearance from Lisbon for a cargo plane to transit via Portugal. A smaller aircraft was sent to Israel to pick up the weapons, but it could only carry eighteen missiles. The few HAWKs that eventually arrived in Iran were not only an older version than had been promised, they were marked with Israel's Star of David insignia. The Iranians were livid. They demanded that their funds be returned and that the eighteen weapons systems be picked up. Through middlemen, they charged that the United States had acted dishonorably and had tried to cheat them. And no hostages were released.[11] It initially appeared that an arms-for-hostages deal had collapsed in bad faith.

Less than a month later, the special task force on terrorism headed by Vice President George Bush completed the first major U.S. study of a problem that was considered by most Americans to be a more serious national security threat than communism. The report pledged "total war" on terrorism, whatever its origins. Meanwhile, Washington pushed its allies, again, not to sell arms to Tehran.[12]

•

The fall of 1985 was a particularly acrimonious time in Iran. Cracks had developed within the ruling circle; the mullahs had begun to fight among themselves. The brewing storm was most visible during a dispute over the appointment of a prime minister and a new cabinet following the August 1985 reelection of President Khamenei to his second term. For both personal and political reasons, the president was intent on replacing Prime Minister Mir Hussein Musavi, the tall, bearded, former engineer who was the ranking noncleric in government, and other cabinet ministers. Khamenei sought to strengthen the presidency, which had become a secondary, even a minor position compared with the premiership. He also disagreed with Musavi on key political and economic issues.

During this period, the shades in the theocracy's political spectrum began to be defined. No major Iranian theologian or politician in the Islamic Republican Party disagreed about the revolution's ends. But a debate, which had simmered behind the scenes since 1979, now came to the forefront over the means.

At one end of the spectrum were those who argued that the Islamic Republic should be a "redeemer state," championing the cause of the world's oppressed, restoring Islamic purity and rule throughout the seventy-nation Haven of Islam, and creating and leading a new power bloc capable of defying both East and West. Their ambitious agenda endorsed fundamentalist extremism to purge the region and eventually the world. They also favored strong government control of the economy at the expense of the private sector, particularly the bazaar merchants, who had been a mainstay of the revolution. Their goal was to redistribute Iran's wealth in the name of "social justice." They promoted perpetual revolution led by theologians.

At the other end were those who argued that Iran should seek legitimacy by creating a model Islamic government, or by institutionalizing the revolution—but always within a realistic framework. Their immediate goals were also lofty: a new political system that attended to indigenous goals rather than priorities imposed by foreign powers, and a new social order that restored dignity and independence from outside intervention and ideologies. But that did not preclude relations with foreign powers or dealing with alien ideologies. They also opposed such dramatic steps as nationalization of all foreign trade, which would, effectively, put most bazaaris out of business. A new economic structure, like the new political system, had to take into account strong Iranian traditions and all sectors that supported the revolution. Their agenda envisioned Tehran winning converts and supporters both inside and outside Iran by example, not by force.

The difference boiled down to a choice: whether to give priority to the revolution or to the new state. This was not the first time that this issue led to a conflict. The forced resignation of former Prime Minister Bazargan in 1979 and the purge of former President Bani-Sadr in 1981 were both ultimately produced by the same dispute.[13] Both men had futilely attempted to exert the supremacy of the state. At both junctures, however, the revolution was still too fresh and too energetic; the mullahs were unwilling for it to be compromised. Since the clergy had consolidated power, however, at least some of them had had to face up to the hard realities of running a complex bureaucracy, of managing a troubled economy, and of directing a war in which the odds, at least on paper, were often against them.

The autumn 1985 debate over the premiership—and the broader division it represented—finally led 135 members of parliament to seek counsel from the imam. Solving disputes, always in response to formal letters of inquiry, was exactly the role the Supreme Jurisprudent was designed to play. But as had been the case so often in the past, Khomeini refused to issue a ruling. Unwilling yet to make the crucial decision between the state and the revolution, he played to both sides. While failing to give unqualified support to the prime minister, he said Musavi had been "faithful and loyal."[14] He also pointedly appealed for unity among government officials. Musavi kept his job, but the underlying tension within the regime went unresolved.

In the context of mounting factional rivalries and public discontent, the need grew to finally select Khomeini's heir apparent, a need both the state and the revolution shared. A succession struggle had to be avoided. There was, however, never much of a choice. In November 1985, more than two years after the Assembly of Experts first met, the eighty-three elected mullahs picked Ayatollah Ali Montazeri, one of Khomeini's earliest students and a lifelong protégé. They had taught at the same Qom seminary before the imam's expulsion. Montazeri had also participated in the 1963 demonstrations that brought Khomeini to prominence. And, for his antishah activities, he had been imprisoned between 1974 and 1978. After the shah's ouster, he was a member of the Revolutionary Council, and he later headed the Assembly that wrote the new constitution.

Initially secret, the choice was not unanimous.[15] Montazeri, a plump, bespectacled figure with a long, trim white beard, had neither an independent following nor charisma. His white turban was that of an ordinary mullah who had not descended from the Prophet's family. Any special status had to be earned, and he was not among the most noted theological scholars. Indeed, of the half dozen grand ayatollahs eligible for selection, Montazeri was in many ways the least prominent. In his early sixties, he was also the youngest. He was, however, the only one who totally endorsed Khomeini's vision. Loyalty was his chief qualification.

Iran's constitution provided for a Council of Leadership of three to five clerics as an alternative to a lone Supreme Jurisprudent. At this time, however, it seemed impractical. First, the revolution still needed a single symbol around which to rally support. Second, for most of the previous twenty-five hundred years, Iran had had a single leader, whether monarchical or religious; a council might be less comfortable or less acceptable to Iranians. And third, finding three to five men acceptable to the majority of mullahs might have been difficult. The danger was too great that all factions would have to be included to win compromise.

One of the reasons for the two-year selection delay was due to a division among the clergy over Montazeri's qualifications; his nomination could not muster the requisite votes. In the interim, Montazeri's backers used the time to groom and to popularize him so that his selection would be seen as the choice of the people, not just the mullahs. He had been named a grand ayatollah only since the revolution; before his selection, he had to be made more prominent than others who had held the title for decades. Montazeri's position as head of the Friday prayer leaders, whose weekly sermons at mosques and universities nationwide were among the most closely watched political events in the Islamic Republic, improved his exposure. His picture slowly began appearing alongside Khomeini's giant portraits at government buildings and public places throughout Iran. Montazeri also began speaking out and appearing at ceremonial functions with which the ayatollah no longer bothered. Both also meant that he more frequently appeared on national television.

Montazeri's political position at the time of his selection explained much about Iran's unusual political spectrum. On domestic issues, the new heir apparent appeared "moderate." He frequently and firmly reminded the komitehs and the Revolutionary Guards that excesses and abusive treatment of the public were now forbidden. Not even suspicion of a plot against the government warranted arrests without court orders or violations of private property, he said.[16] He was among the first to advocate actively encouraging exiles to return home, implying that all but the gravest crimes, such as serving in the shah's cabinet, might be forgiven. He also warned that extremism reflected badly on the revolution.

At the same time, however, Montazeri's foreign policy actions gave him the appearance of being, by outside standards, a hardliner. He lent his name to the group most active in exporting the revolution. After his son, Mohammad, who trained with the PLO in Lebanon, died in the massive 1981 bombing that killed dozens of government officials, Montazeri continued to shelter his followers. Among them was a youth named Mehdi Hashemi who headed the World Islamic Movement, a front for Iranian-backed extremist groups throughout the Middle East. Like so many of the Shi'ite political groups in Iran and elsewhere, there were also family connections. Hashemi was the brother of Montazeri's son-in-law. In theory, the role of patron of the export campaign suited Montazeri. He could gain recognition for doing in the Muslim world what Khomeini had done for Iran. But Montazeri lacked judgment in monitoring the groups using his good offices and spending the funds under his supervision. And that was to cost him—and the Reagan administration.

•

In December 1985, less than a month after Montazeri's selection as heir apparent, Lieutenant Colonel Oliver North wrote a White House memo suggesting another arms deal with Iran, despite the November debacle. "They have been 'scammed' so many times in the past that the attitude of distrust is very high on their part," North wrote. "I find the idea of bartering over the lives of these poor men [hostages] repugnant. Nonetheless . . . if we do not at least make one more try at this point, we stand a good chance of condemning some or all to death and a renewed wave of Islamic Jihad terrorism. While the risks of proceeding are significant, the risks of not trying one last time are even greater." [17] The threat of hostage deaths had been made all the more real by reports of the death in captivity of CIA station chief Buckley. Islamic Jihad had announced his "execution" in October 1985, but based on freed-hostage accounts, he was in fact believed to have died of illness complicated by earlier beatings in June, even before the TWA hijacking.

At a White House strategy session in early December 1985, the Reagan administration assessed its position. Different officials later had different recollections of the meeting, but in the end Robert McFarlane, who had resigned a few days earlier as National Security Advisor, was dispatched to London with a message for Ghorbanifar and the Israeli intermediaries: The United States wanted both better relations with the Islamic Republic and the release of the hostages, but it was unwilling to barter in arms. At the London meeting, the intermediaries, particularly the Israelis, argued that Washington was passing up an opportunity. [18] The effort appeared to have reached another impasse—but only briefly.

Shortly before the holidays, President Reagan invited hostage families to the White House. At the emotional meeting, he told them that efforts to free the hostages before Christmas had collapsed and that the short-term prognosis was not good. Clearly moved by the families' trauma, he later ordered his staff to "redouble" attempts to gain the hostages' freedom. [19] North turned to Amiram Nir, a former journalist and a counterterrorism adviser to Israeli officials who had earlier advised the Israeli prime minister's office as well as Vice President Bush's task force on terrorism. Nir also urged a second try. Within President Reagan's inner circle, there were only two dissenting voices. Secretary of State George Shultz and Secretary of Defense Caspar Weinberger vehemently opposed any further dealings as a contradiction in the administration's terrorism policy. The risks of failure and of being exposed were also too high.

Two factors convinced the president to go ahead: concern about the hostages and fear that Iran would fall into the Soviet camp, especially after Khomeini's death, which was then, again, being widely prophesied. On January 17, 1986, President Reagan signed a secret finding:

The United States Government will act to facilitate efforts of third parties and third countries to establish contacts with moderate elements within and outside the government of Iran by providing these elements with arms, equipment and related material in order to enhance the credibility of these elements in their effort to achieve a more pro-U.S. government in Iran by demonstrating their ability to obtain required resources to defend their country against Iraq and intervention by the Soviet Union.

Plans for a new round in the arms-for-hostages deal were under way.

Once steps were undertaken for the transfer of a new round of TOW antitank missiles, North drew up a secret schedule for the plan, which had been code-named Operation Recovery, based largely on information from Ghorbanifar's communications with Iran. It called for the delivery of a thousand TOW missiles to Iran via Israel over a three-week period in February 1986. The next day the five American hostages and Buckley's remains would be turned over to the United States. Three thousand additional missiles would then be shipped to Iran, followed by the release of British and Italian hostages. Most incredibly, North's schedule said that on February 11, the Islamic Republic's seventh anniversary, Ayatollah Khomeini would step down.[20]

From the beginning, nothing went as planned. A bit later than North had scheduled, an Israeli 707 registered under a false flag flew the first thousand missiles in two installments to the Iranian port city of Bandar Abbas. (The planes also picked up the eighteen, vintage HAWKs that Iran had been sent earlier.) North's schedule now called for a hostage release. But no one was freed.

At a secret meeting in Europe, North discovered in December that the two nations had vastly different understandings of the arms delivery. The blunt revelation was made by Mohsen Kangarlou, a poorly educated former cobbler who had risen to the post of deputy to the prime minister as a result of his brutal actions against the shah's officials during the early days of the revolution. Kangarlou explained that the Islamic Republic viewed this shipment as only a sign of good faith after the mishap over the HAWKs. Tehran had never agreed to intervene over the hostages at this stage; the TOW missile delivery was only the starting point for serious negotiations. The discrepancy was probably the fault of neither side. According to one American participant, Ghorbanifar had "lied to both sides to get them to the table, and then sat back and watched us fight it out. It was a real slugging match. It was awful."[21] The misinformation and duplicity should have been a signal, but it was ignored.

The United States should also have been alerted by events on February 11, 1986. Instead of an announcement that Khomeini was stepping down, the Islamic Republic's seventh anniversary was marked by one of the most stunning moments of the entire war. In a surprise attack on the eve of national celebrations, more than a hundred thousand Iranian troops captured Faw Peninsula, Iraq's swampy but strategic southern oil port jutting out into the Shatt al-Arab. Faw was also a major acquisition because it is only fifty miles from Basra; the Iranians were now within easy artillery range of Iraq's second most populous city. The campaign's importance, psychologically as much as militarily, was unmatched since Iran's recapture of Khorramshahr in 1982. In Khorramshahr, however, Iran was only taking back what it had lost. At Faw, Iran was on the offensive, aggressively moving into Iraq.

The surprise nighttime amphibious assault, largely by Revolutionary Guards and Basij volunteers, proved Iran's ingenuity while underscoring Iraq's inability to use its technical superiority—either on land or by air. Iran took thousands of casualties but, this time, so did Iraq. Once again, weather was a factor. The seasonal rains had created cover—both from Iraqi reconnaissance and from American satellite intelligence. Baghdad later blamed the United States for its setback, basically because of faulty intelligence. One credible account later reported that U.S. intelligence had provided Iraq with an assessment suggesting that the most likely Iranian push would be north of Basra; it failed to point out, however, that cloud cover of the south had precluded satellite photos.[22] The Faw victory was sufficiently crucial that, for the first time, Western analysts began seriously considering the possibility that Iran might actually win the war.

•

Throughout the winter and spring of 1986, the U.S.-Iran initiative was on-again, off-again. The Reagan administration held out for release of all hostages before a final arms transfer, while the Iranians kept upping their demands for new weapons systems. But for every setback in the initiative, there was a spark to revive the effort. A major factor was the killing of American hostage Peter Kilburn, the ailing librarian from American University of Beirut, as well as two British hostages. Their bodies were dumped on a Beirut street on April 17 in retaliation for the United States air strike on Libya. The raid had been prompted by intelligence linking Tripoli with the bombing of a German disco in which an American soldier had been killed. Although Washington was aware that Kilburn was not held by Islamic Jihad, the three deaths underscored the dangers to any captive.

The persistent Ghorbanifar and the Israelis also pressed the Reagan administration to move—as did the Iranians. Rafsanjani said publicly that Tehran was prepared to consider formal diplomatic ties with Washington "based on equality and justice." [23] During one impasse that looked permanent, Mohsen Kangarlou, the official from the Iranian prime minister's office who had met North in Europe, made the first use of a telephone number in Maryland set up for secret communications. He "asked why we had not been in contact and urged that we proceed expeditiously since the situation in Beirut was deteriorating rapidly." [24] After their successful but costly Faw offensive, the Iranians clearly wanted the arms. That factor, combined with North's energy, Israel's prodding and Ghorbanifar's duplicity in mediating between the United States and his former homeland, again brought the deal back on track.

In the wee hours of May 25, 1986, a white Israeli Boeing 707 with a temporary Irish registration landed at Tehran's Mehrabad International Airport. Among the six passengers, all carrying Irish passports, were former National Security Advisor Robert McFarlane, Oliver North, National Security Council official Howard Teicher, CIA Iran specialist George Cave to act as interpreter, a CIA communications expert, and Amiram Nir. Also on board were three sets of chrome-plated Magnum pistols in presentation boxes, a chocolate cake with a skeleton key on it,* and a pallet of HAWK

---

* While the guns were genuine gifts, the cake was the result of a query from North to Ghorbanifar about anything else he might usefully take to Tehran. According to others present, Ghorbanifar jokingly replied, in a poor allusion to Marie Antoinette and the French

missile spare parts. Almost a year after the TWA hijacking, the United States had finally traveled the road to Tehran.

The long-delayed meeting between American and Iranian officials, however, was another disaster. Enormous expectations collapsed in three days; neither side got what it wanted because of four basic problems. Like the meetings between North and Kangarlou in Europe, the biggest problem was the advance misinformation. Ghorbanifar had repeatedly made two promises before the Reagan administration agreed to let McFarlane make the trip: first, that the four remaining American hostages would be freed upon McFarlane's arrival and, second, that the Iranian delegation would include President Khamenei, Prime Minister Musavi and Parliamentary Speaker Rafsanjani.[25] But, as McFarlane concluded after the first day of meetings, Ghorbanifar had engaged in "considerable hyperbole, occasional lies and dissembling" to bring the two sides together.[26] No hostages were freed during the three-day visit. And none of the ranking officials ever appeared. The highest-level interlocutor was Hadi Najafabadi, the well-educated and eloquent deputy chairman of the *Majlis* Foreign Affairs Committee, who was aided by Kangarlou and other junior officials.

The Iranians also appeared to have been duped. At one point, when McFarlane pointed out that the delay in the hostage release was a clear violation of the prearranged terms of agreement, Najafabadi expressed surprise. "He stated that these were not the terms as he understood them. The basic difference was that they expected all [arms] deliveries to occur before any release took place," McFarlane later reported. "He was obviously concerned over the real possibility that his people"—Ghorbanifar and Kangarlou—"had misled him and asked for a break to confer with his colleagues. . . . Ollie, Cave and Nir are all confident of their ground but understand the probability that [Ghorbanifar or Kangarlou] or both oversold their accomplishment."[27] Meanwhile, both sides waited futilely for the other to fulfill what had been promised in advance.

The second problem was mutual suspicion and fears of the consequences of negotiations. As McFarlane reported to the White House on the first day of the meetings,

> In the course of the four-hour meeting, it became evident that the three Iranian leaders—Rafsanjani, Musavi and Khamenei—are each

---

Revolution, "Bring a cake." North bought the cake at a kosher bakery in Israel. It was eaten by Revolutionary Guards at the Tehran airport.

traumatized by the recollection that after [former Premier Mehdi] Bazargan met with [President Carter's National Security Advisor Zbigniew] Brzezinski in the spring of 1980, he was deposed (so strong was the sentiment against doing business with the Great Satan). Today the force of events and self-interest has brought them to the point of realizing that we do have some common interests. . . . But they still cannot overcome their more immediate problem of how to talk to us and stay alive.[28]

The fears were not unfounded. Unknown to the Americans in Tehran, they came close to being detained by a Revolutionary Guards unit angered by dealings with the Great Satan. A group of Pasdaran arrived at the former Hilton intending to arrest the McFarlane team; in the parking lot, other Iranian guards fought them off—in a scene reminiscent of the first U.S. embassy seizure in 1979.[29]

A subsequent exchange between North and Najafabadi, after both sides explained the need for the other to fulfill its half of the swap first, was also telling. "We have tried for months to come to a point where we could talk government-to-government," North told the Iranians. "Some in our government opposed [it]." Najafabadi later replied, "We have the same problem that you have. Some here oppose relations with the U.S. . . . It is not easy to sleep next to an elephant that you have wounded."[30]

The third problem centered on the question of Iran's ability to control the Lebanese captors. When the Iranians recognized that nothing would happen without action on the hostages, they returned on the final day of the increasingly fruitless talks with a grim report. The Lebanese hostage holders had made stiff new demands: Israel had to withdraw from the Golan Heights and southern Lebanon; Kuwait had to free the seventeen Shi'ite prisoners held for the six 1983 bombings; Iran had to provide a substantial payoff for expenses incurred while holding the hostages; and the head of the pro-Israeli Christian militia in southern Lebanon had to abandon the enclave along the Israeli border. McFarlane reported that even the Iranians appeared astonished, and a bit angered, by the scope of the demands and realized that they were unacceptable.

Later that day, the Iranians informed the McFarlane team that, under pressure, the captors had reduced their terms to a payoff, which Tehran would cover, and the release of the Al-Dawa prisoners in Kuwait, for which Iran would need Washington's intervention. Cave, the CIA Iran specialist, noted a more fundamental doubt. "The serious problem we must address is whether the Iranians can gain control of the hostages. The French don't think they can. This could be our real problem. The Iranian side may be most willing, but unable to gain control."[31]

In fact, the enigmatic but committed extremist who led Islamic Jihad, Imad Mughniyah, was obsessed with the fate of the Al-Dawa prisoners. Among them was his closest friend and brother-in-law, who was also one of the three prisoners sentenced to death. As the United States learned, this Islamic Jihad cell, originally formed to terrorize Americans in Lebanon, had refocused its campaign on freeing the seventeen. And Mughniyah's attachment to his relative was unyielding. Tehran would have to pull out all stops to get him to change his mind on the hostages—and even then he would almost surely try to keep some in reserve.[32]

Finally, the discussions failed because they never got beyond the subject of arms-for-hostages. As the record of the talks show, every time the issue of a long-term relationship arose, it broke down over the requisite signs of good faith from the other side. Arms was the wrong barometer of the United States long-term intentions, especially since Washington's goal was an end to the war rather than an escalation. And the obsessive preoccupation with American hostages sent the wrong signals about the depth or sincerity of the Reagan administration's interests. What should have been the final step of a broader agenda was, in the end, lost because it came first.

The combination—mischievous intermediaries, mutual suspicion, misrepresented terms, Iran's brewing power struggle, Tehran's limitations on the hostages, and the vehicle for discussions—made failure most inevitable. On the final morning, the Iranians made one last plea. Najafabadi said that mediators in Lebanon thought they might get two hostages freed immediately, while the other two would require "joint action." McFarlane responded that this was the fourth time that Iran had failed to honor an agreement. "The lack of trust will endure for a long time. An important opportunity was lost."[33] The Americans flew home. Yet still the Reagan administration did not fully perceive the fundamental flaws in the effort —nor did it give up.

•

On July 26, 1986, two months after the failed mission to Tehran, Father Lawrence Martin Jenco, the sweet-faced director of Catholic Relief Services who had barely arrived in Lebanon when he was abducted, was secretly driven from the Shi'ite slums of west Beirut to the Bekaa Valley. After more than sixteen months in captivity, he was freed. Although the Reagan administration had begun reexamining military options to free the hostages, key players, including Ghorbanifar and North, had refused to drop the possibility of dealing with Iran. Ghorbanifar particularly maintained contacts with Iran in an attempt to win a hostage release by July 4, the Statue of Liberty's centennial.

Earlier, in July, Iran sent two signals. The first came through a third country that had earlier mediated between the United States and Iran. In discussions with Parliamentary Speaker Rafsanjani, two envoys were pointedly told that "the U.S. government knows what it should do" to better relations.[34] He had even gone public at a Friday prayer service: "We have never been determined to cut off relations with the West. For many reasons we prefer to have ties. But what we do not want is Western hegemony. . . . We seek cordial and friendly relations, and we are endeavoring to establish better relations."[35]

The second, again through a neutral third country, came from Iran's deputy foreign minister, Mohammad Javad Larijani, a philosopher and mathematician who had studied for his doctorate at the University of California at Berkeley. "Despite Iran's rhetorical invective against the USA, Iran wanted an easing of relations on substantive matters with [the] USA," the third party quoted him as saying in a message he requested be transmitted to Washington.[36] Despite the earlier disarray at the Tehran talks, the Islamic Republic apparently maintained an interest in the new connection. Then Father Jenco was freed. For once, the United States was initially uncertain what actually had happened. But to no one's surprise, the Iranians began asking for the next arms delivery. In early August, the United States delivered, as before on false-flagged Israeli aircraft, twelve pallets of HAWK missiles. Yet again, the arms-for-hostages swap had been revived.

In fact, it had been revived with some gusto. The Reagan administration suddenly found it had four channels to Tehran. Two came from third countries, including Japan, which regularly relayed messages between both sides about ways of improving relations. Another was the Ghorbanifar link, which the Reagan administration was increasingly trying to close out because of his misinformation and financial manipulations.

A new fourth channel, however, appeared to offer the most interesting new prospects. A private American arms dealer with long experience in Iran, retired Air Force General Richard Secord, made contact in Europe with Ali Hashemi Bahramani, a nephew of Parliamentary Speaker Rafsanjani whom the CIA considered "the most influential and pragmatic political figure in Iran."[37] In a series of lengthy meetings, Bahramani revealed an intimate knowledge of the previous dealings between Tehran and Washington. He outlined a "specific mandate from Rafsanjani to meet with U.S.G. officials seeking a means for 'getting beyond the hostage issue'."[38] The youth also broached more substantive issues, such as assistance with Iran's two million homeless refugees and repair of war-damaged oil installations, in outlining what Iran wanted from the United States. North actually began speculating about a second trip to the Islamic Republic.

In September 1986, however, planning was complicated by three events. First, an eleven-minute broadcast by the late shah's son, Reza Pahlavi, was clandestinely transmitted on Iranian national television. The tape called for Iranians to rise up against Khomeini in favor of a constitutional monarchy led by the new self-crowned king. Whatever the truth, Tehran believed that the CIA had helped to pirate the broadcast frequency on behalf of the young monarch, whose main base of operations in exile was just outside Washington. In one of several secret telephone exchanges that fall, an obviously irate Kangarlou demanded to know how the United States "could profess to 'accept the Iranian revolution as fact' and still sponsor such an event."[39]

Second, Nick Daniloff, a *U.S. News & World Report* correspondent, was detained in Moscow, apparently in retaliation for the arrest of a suspected KGB agent in New York. Although the Reagan administration again denied any deal, both men were returned within three weeks to their respective countries. If nothing else, the swap reinforced perceptions both at home and abroad that the United States was prepared, at least occasionally, to do deals. Most ominous, however, was the third event. On September 9, 1986, Frank Herbert Reed, director of the Lebanese International School, was kidnapped in Beirut. Three days later, Joseph Cicippio, a controller at the American University of Beirut, was also seized off the streets of west Beirut. Washington, again, had four Americans to get out.

Despite the setbacks, North arranged for three meetings with the new channel in the fall of 1986. The first was in Washington in September. Bahramani, whose youth was offset by his connections as well as his intelligence, was flown on a chartered plane from Istanbul for two days of talks. During the sessions on September 19 and 20, North took him on a late-night tour of the White House grounds. The main issues, again, were the "obstacle" of hostages and Tehran's need for military and intelligence assistance.[40] But, as in the initial contacts, discussions were also more substantive. The youth put forward the idea of a joint American-Iranian committee to meet in Portugal or Turkey to resolve other issues of mutual concern. Talks ranged from Afghanistan and the Soviet Union to Iran's recent attempts to better relations with the Gulf sheikhdoms.

The Americans were impressed with Bahramani's candor about the difficulty that Tehran had in winning freedom for all the captives. In all previous exchanges with other Iranians, the United States had been told that all problems could be resolved—which Washington doubted. His standing had also risen after Reed's abduction, when he initiated a call to Washington to say that Islamic Jihad did not have the newest hostage and that Tehran would do whatever was possible to trace his location.[41] Independent U.S. intelligence reports had earlier come to the same initial conclusion about Reed's captors. Finally, Rafsanjani's nephew offered his Washington hosts a titillating tidbit that had long been the source of speculation: Ayatollah Khomeini had been briefed "in great detail" by Ahmad, his son and chief of staff, about negotiations with the Americans.

The second meeting between October 5 and 7 was held in Frankfurt and included, for the first time, a Revolutionary Guard intelligence official. As a gift to Bahramani, North had brought a Bible with a handwritten passage from Galatians inscribed by President Reagan. North's explanation reflected to what degree he was growing out of control:

> We inside our government had an enormous debate, a very angry debate inside our government over whether or not my president should authorize me to say "We accept the Islamic Revolution of Iran as fact." He went off one whole weekend and prayed about what the answer should be and he came back almost a year ago with that passage I gave you that he wrote in front of the Bible I gave you. And he said to me, "This is a promise that God gave to Abraham. Who am I to say that we should not do this?"[42]

In fact, President Reagan later said that he wrote the passage because he had been told it was a favorite of one of the Iranians with whom the United States was dealing. North also reported to the Iranian delegation that the president personally told him, first, that he favored an end to the Gulf war on terms "acceptable" to Iran and, second, that the neighboring sheikhdoms should be convinced

that Iraqi President Saddam Hussein was "causing the problem."
North elaborated, after questioning by the Iranians, that "We also
recognize that Saddam Hussein must go."[43]

Both were untrue. Building relations with Baghdad, in an attempt
to moderate the radicalism of the seventeen-year break in relations
between the two nations, had become a mainstay of American foreign policy since formal ties had been reestablished in 1984. And
after Iran's Faw victory, the United States more than ever feared
the possibility of an Iranian victory—and the potential boost to
Islamic extremism throughout the Middle East.

At the second session, North and Bahramani worked further on
details for a new swap. The Iranians warned the Americans that
they had immediate access to only the two original Islamic Jihad
hostages and that they might be able to free only one. The Pasdaran
official claimed that the group holding the two new hostages was
"not responsive" to Iran; he "begged" the Americans to let Iran
find out where Reed was held, after which the United States "can
rescue him and not ruin us with Hizbollah."[44]

During the final meeting on October 26, again in Frankfurt, Bahramani's delegation was more forthcoming than ever before, promising action on two hostages, offering to obtain a copy of the
four-hundred-page transcript of Buckley's interrogation by Islamic
Jihad, and proposing to give the United States one of the advanced
Soviet T-72 tanks captured from Iraq—an offer readily accepted.
In turn, North was more generous than his mandate authorized,
promising the Reagan administration's help in freeing the seventeen
Al-Dawa prisoners in Kuwait.[45] A new deal had been struck.

Between October 26 and 29, two shipments, each containing five
hundred TOW missiles, were flown to Iran. On November 2, David
Jacobsen, an American University of Beirut hospital administrator,
was freed in Lebanon. But that was to be the final trade. Before the
swap, "the relative" had called Washington to warn that the situation in Tehran and Iran's influence over the Lebanese Hizbollah
were both "deteriorating."[46]

·

In mid-October, crude leaflets began appearing on university campuses and in Tehran's southern suburbs, the revolution's stronghold. Their allusion to secret talks between ranking mullahs and the
Great Satan set off the capital's always lively rumor mill about the
implications of clandestine visits by American officials. As is usually
true of even the revolution's most closely held information, the
secret had gotten out. During the fourteen-month escapade, ever-

increasing numbers of Iranians had to be brought in. The Revolutionary Guards at the airport when McFarlane's plane landed almost two hours early and the staff at the former Hilton where the Americans stayed tripped on obvious clues. And news spreads fast on Tehran's intelligence grapevine.

Among those who learned of the initiative was Mehdi Hashemi, a religious front man for the World Islamic Movement who had risen to power through his brother's marriage into Ayatollah Montazeri's family. Tehran's instructions to halt terrorist attacks against American targets, as well as information gleaned through his links with Lebanon's Hizbollah had sparked his fury. Ironically, U.S. intelligence officials also believed that he may have been tipped off by an embittered Ghorbanifar, who had been excluded from the deal since Washington had turned to Bahramani.[47] For Hashemi and other determined proponents of the revolution's export, the secret initiative was nothing less than a betrayal of the revolution. For him, the needs of the state, even in wartime, never transcended allegiance to the revolution's glorious goals. He set out to sabotage the initiative.

Hashemi represented a growing problem not only for those implicated in talks with the United States. Iran's heady successes in promoting its ideology in Lebanon, Kuwait and elsewhere had led to excesses with which many government officials no longer wanted the Islamic Republic associated. They were not giving up the revolution's export, but at least two recent hijackings by Shi'ite extremists linked to Tehran had proven embarrassing and costly for Iran. New hostage seizures by groups over which the Islamic Republic had little control complicated its economic, military and diplomatic initiatives.

Hashemi wanted to give the extemists free rein. A few months earlier, he had attempted to sneak weapons into Saudi Arabia to distribute to Iranians and other Shi'a during the annual Haj pilgrimage—at the same time that Tehran was trying to gain Riyadh's support for joint action to counter plummeting oil prices. Hashemi had become a force unto himself and he had to be checked. To prevent a deterioration with Riyadh, certain quarters in Tehran tipped off the Saudis, who picked up Hashemi as he entered the country.[48] But the same quarters did not move fast enough the next time.

As the dialogue between North and the new Iranian channel began to take root, Hashemi was arrested on October 12. The charges against the cleric, who theoretically was protected by his connections with Khomeini's heir apparent, included treason, murder, sabotage and a host of lesser crimes. Some four dozen of his associates were also detained. Iranian officials never aired all the specifics of his misadventures, but the subsequent indictment was scathing—and telling. Never before had a mullah from within the ruling circle been so publicly condemned.

But the arrest of Hashemi and his crowd was, again, not enough. In mid-October, a small Hizbollah newspaper in Baalbeck, Lebanon, published a story based on the leaflets and mentioning McFarlane by name. On October 21, Edward Austin Tracy, an American writer, was abducted in Beirut. This time the hand of Hizbollah elements was visible. There were also indications that while Reed may have been taken by a group beyond Iran's control, Cicippio was also in the hands of those broadly classified as pro-Iranian. Finally, on November 3, the day after Jacobsen's release, a Lebanese weekly, *As Shiraa,* published a story that the United States was secretly selling arms to Iran. It also mentioned the McFarlane visit to Tehran. Not surprisingly, the magazine's editor later disclosed that his sources were allies of Mehdi Hashemi.

The disclosure was particularly well timed, just one day before November 4, the always volatile anniversary of both the hostage seizure at the American embassy and Khomeini's 1963 arrest. In an anniversary address, Rafsanjani tried to preempt domestic fallout by conceding the arms purchases, which were necessary for the war effort. He admitted that, "After the issue of the TWA aircraft, they [the Americans] started begging us to help them in Lebanon through scores of channels." In reply to a formal request conveyed in a letter from Japanese Prime Minister Nakasone, Rafsanjani said, "I told him that if we were sure that America was sincere, then we would take steps to help. Our great suspicion was that the Americans were engaged in deceit."

Of contacts in Tehran with the Great Satan, he told chanting crowds that McFarlane had come uninvited. "Their purpose was basically to come along, as they put it, and melt the cold ice separating Iran and the United States, to melt the frozen ocean! Their immediate aim was to turn us into interceders in Lebanon, and their distant goal was to create the amicable relations and the golden vision that they had in mind! They begged, pleaded and sent messages requesting that one of our country's responsible officials receive them." Instead, he alleged that the McFarlane team had been detained and held in a hotel for five days. "How could we meet and talk to you! Have we forgotten that [former National Security Advisor Zbigniew] Brezezinski met our ad interim government in Algiers and our ad interim government has been swept aside and now you have come inside our house, our country, intending to meet us? Could our nation be asleep in such matters?"[49]

Somewhat surprisingly, however, Rafsanjani still did not completely close the door. "If your governments prove to us in practice that they are not fighting against us, if they prove in practice that they do not engage in treason against us, if they prove in practice that they do not confiscate our assets through bullying tactics . . . then the Islamic Republic in a humane gesture is prepared to announce its views to its friends in Lebanon."[50]

But the preemptive strike was not sufficient to repair the damage. As in Washington, members of Iran's legislature demanded a full public inquiry to disclose the extent of the exchange and those involved. And Iran's fragile political environment could not then easily withstand an investigation; the revolution was already dangerously divided. In the end, the imam had to intervene in the crisis to prevent an open split. "Why do you wish to cause schism?" Khomeini pointedly asked of Rafsanjani's critics in a late November speech appealing for unity. "This is against Islam."[51]

For the time being, the inner circle was protected and at least one challenge eliminated. The cost of the ill-fated arms-for-hostages swap to both Iran and the United States, however, was high. By the end of November 1986, Washington had as many hostages languishing in captivity as it had before the initiative. And the proven effectiveness of winning concessions from the United States by nabbing its citizens would lead within the next fifteen months to the abduction of five more Americans in Lebanon. The initiative also cut deeply into United States relations with its closest allies in the Arab world, compensation for which would later lead to a risky naval venture in the Gulf and further confrontation with Tehran. For Iran, any effort to deal on any issue with the United States quickly became off-limits. More importantly, the episode turned out to mark the beginning of the Islamic Republic's retreat.

CHAPTER SIX

The Final Offensive

"The United States should conclude that military intervention in the Persian Gulf is not simply an experiment. It is a big step, a dangerous game."

—Ayatollah Khomeini [1]

"We have enough enemies in the world. It is, frankly, not fair to ignore those enemies and to fight among ourselves."

—Parliamentary
Speaker Rafsanjani [2]

On Christmas Eve 1986, a flotilla of rubber dinghies and small motorized seacraft snuck wave after wave of Iranian troops along the Shatt al-Arab's slow-moving current. Slipping across one of the waterway's widest passages in the dead of night, the column of sixty thousand Revolutionary Guards and Basij volunteers sailed straight toward the Iraqis' easiest line of fire. The timing and approach were calculated for surprise. The ambitious new thrust was designed to cut off the arid south from access to Baghdad. Isolating Basra, Iraq's vital port and its second largest city, was supposed to force Baghdad, finally, to capitulate.

Widely heralded in Tehran as the beginning of the Final Offen-

sive, the new campaign was the largest Iranian attack since the
seizure of Faw Peninsula. Its importance was underscored by the
infusion of religious symbolism. The operation was the fourth in a
series code-named Karbala, after the Iraqi city where the martyr
Hosain and his followers had died in the seventh century, and it
was led by the Division of the Prophet Mohammad.[3]

For all its daring, however, Karbala-4 was lost almost before it
began. Tactically, the offensive was a disaster. Iran reverted to the
poorly coordinated human-wave assaults of the war's early years.
Meanwhile, since it had been forced to go on the defensive four
years earlier, Iraq's forces had dug in deep inside the southern
border; a network of concrete bunkers equipped with heavy weapons and huge earthen berms provided a protective arc around
Basra. The defensive wall proved to be impenetrable. The fighting
dragged on for two days, but Iran's failure to break through was
clear within six hours.[4] After Iran's retreat, the Iraqis found their
shores littered with thousands of bodies.

Like the premature offensive organized under pressure by former
President Bani-Sadr in early 1980, Karbala-4 had a rushed, almost
suicidal quality to it; it lacked the scrappy, imaginative quality of
all other campaigns since 1984. In many ways, it appeared to be
aimed as much at diverting domestic attention from the revelations
of dealings with the Great Satan as at defeating Iraq.

Although Ayatollah Khomeini had quashed official debate, the
arms-for-hostages issue was still the focus of private discussions and
public displays. Ironically like the reaction within the Reagan administration, certain Iranian officials were aghast at the privatization of Tehran's foreign policy by an elite few. Others were
resentful about being excluded; the only explanation seemed to be
that they were not sufficiently trusted.[5] In early December, a mob
chanting "Death to compromisers! Death to America!" protested
the clandestine talks in front of the former American embassy in
Tehran.[6] Opposition to the discussions with the Americans was apparent in even unlikely places. "Rafsanjani must be punished for
McFarlane," proclaimed the lavatory graffiti at Tehran University.[7]

The fallout was uncomfortably visible in mid-December when the
full confession of Mehdi Hashemi, whose allies leaked news of the
McFarlane trip, was repeatedly aired on nationwide television and
radio. He admitted to murder and treason as well as to the broader
offense of "standing up against the Imam of the Islamic nation."[8]
His testimony was so controversial that Ayatollah Montazeri, the
heir apparent, took the unprecedented step of publicly disowning

Hashemi, a man linked by family, clerical profession, political affil-
iation and long-standing loyalty. In some ways, Montazeri was dis-
tancing himself from his lieutenant in the same way President Reagan distanced himself from Oliver North's actions.* The Hashemi
case indicated how the scandal, again as in the United States,
seemed to unravel endlessly. Iran had clearly been planning a winter offensive, but Karbala-4's Christmas Eve strike seemed also to
be politically expedient.

Although Karbala-4 was a disaster, Tehran did not give up. Two
weeks later, it tried again. Karbala-5 was far better coordinated.
Shortly after midnight on January 6, 1987, tens of thousands of
Pasdaran and Basij forces again moved toward the water defenses
surrounding Basra. Besides the swampy Shatt al-Arab, Iraq had
constructed a virtual moat around Basra that ran into man-made
Fish Lake. Both water defenses were built to hold off zealous Iranian troops unintimidated by gunfire. For the next fifty days, during
one of the longest single campaigns of the war, the Islamic Republic
thrust hard and with fevered determination. This time, it broke
through.

By February 25, the Iranians had established a bridgehead along
the shores six miles inside Iraq. Despite their vastly superior air
power and the use of poison gas, Iraqi troops were forced back to
the outer perimeter of Basra.[9] Now within easy artillery range of
Iraq's second most important and populous city, Iran pounded
Basra. The bombardment was so heavy that, for the first time, Iraq
had to help residents flee. In the midst of Karbala-5, Khomeini
emerged, for the first time in almost three months, on his balcony
in northern Tehran and called for "war until victory."

To Iraq and the outside world, it appeared that Tehran had finally
made the strategic strike it needed. The Iranian victory stunned the
Gulf sheikhdoms, much of the Arab world, and Iraq's French and
Soviet suppliers; it also worried the United States. Karbala-5 had
been successful in part because of American intelligence provided
Tehran during Irangate. The military assessments passed through
the "second channel" included information on Iraq's defensive positions and troop strengths. The intelligence did not change Tehran's
strategy, but it did help determine in what strengths and directions
Iran deployed its troops and artillery.[10] Iran's use of the informa-

---

* Nor was Montazeri able to save Hashemi's life. After a bitter and much-publicized trial in
August 1987, Hashemi was executed on September 28.

tion, two months after the revelations and at a time when relations were once again openly hostile, alarmed Washington—and led to a new initiative that would later help to turn the tide of the war.

Little known at the time, however, was the toll of the Karbala offensives, which continued through Karbala-10 in brief and less successful assaults on both the northern and the southern fronts until the end of April. Losses, both human and military, were enormous. Iran expended much of its best war materiel, including the antitank missiles obtained from the United States during the arms-for-hostages swap.[11] With the U.S.-orchestrated Operation Staunch back in full swing, the equipment was not easily replaced.

Foreign military attachés in Tehran later estimated that up to half of the hundred thousand Basij deployed during the four-month campaign became casualties. Because of the Karbala-4 fiasco, Iran had mobilized its most experienced Pasdaran officers for Karbala-5; up to a quarter were reportedly killed or seriously injured during the winter and spring campaigns.[12] The impact of the war's heavy toll on public morale was evident during an antiwar demonstration in April. Several hundred, including Revolutionary Guard members, paraded boldly down Vali-e Asr, Tehran's main boulevard, to call for reconciliation with Iraq—a near heretical compromise.[13]

The toll was not, however, limited to the battlefront. To increase pressure on Iran, Iraq retaliated from the air and in the Gulf sea-lanes. From mid-January through mid-February, Iraqi warplanes bombed several major civilian areas including, for the first time in two years, Tehran. The Islamic Republic responded with missile barrages on Baghdad and elsewhere. Hussein's military command also ordered an escalation in the "tanker war." For every vessel, Iranian or those trading with Iran, that Iraq hit, the Islamic Republic retaliated against a tanker doing business with Iraq's allies in the Gulf. Within the first five weeks of 1987, sixteen Gulf ships were hit, raising the total since the war broke out to 284.[14] The toll had risen to the point that Tehran had to begin purchasing new tankers, another unplanned expense.

By April 1987, when the Karbala offensives ended, Iran had hit Iraq at its most vulnerable point, leaving Baghdad and its allies deeply worried that the next campaign might just do it. In truth, however, Iran's war costs appeared to outweigh the gains; it had lost many of its best people and much of its best materiel. Operation Karbala was not the first final offensive announced by Tehran, but it would prove to be the last.

•

On January 28, 1987 *Majlis* Speaker Rafsanjani held a news conference in Tehran for foreign correspondents summoned to view Iran's
gains in the Karbala offensives. Journalists, usually granted only
limited-entry visas, were actually invited to extend their stay to
attend the briefing. Rafsanjani conducted the session at parliament
with the disarming candor that had become his trademark; the
Cheshire-cat grin locked mischievously on his face made him seem,
to both Iranians and outsiders, more approachable than most of his
ever-serious colleagues.

Rafsanjani clearly had a purpose for this meeting, but the session
drifted until one of the speaker's aides quietly suggested to a journalist that he inquire about the Bible sent by President Reagan. Not
surprisingly, the Bible just happened to be in the room. When
asked, Rafsanjani produced the volume and held it open at the
flyleaf for all to read, in the President's own handwriting:

> And the scripture, forseeing that God would justify the Gentiles by
> faith, preached the gospel beforehand to Abraham, saying, "All na-
> tions shall be blessed in you." Galatians 3:8, Ronald Reagan, Octo-
> ber 3, 1986.

Would the foreign press, he inquired, also be interested in a copy
of McFarlane's forged Irish passport? Photocopies of the document,
made out in the name of Sean Devlin, were passed around.[15]

For a man so vulnerable, it was a curious thing to do. The master-
mind of Iran's deal with the Great Satan, however, apparently had
little choice. Going on the offense was his best, and perhaps only,
defense. Almost three months after the revelations, Irangate, as
even some Iranians called it, would still not go away. American,
European and Israeli press disclosures poured forth daily with further snippets of the scandal. On the pretext of his membership in
the Supreme Defense Council, Rafsanjani was highly visible at the
war front during Karbala-5,[16] perhaps to associate himself with a
victory or even to infer, unsubtly, that his role in the arms deal was
paying off with a victory.

But two developments had further tainted Rafsanjani: First, the
American and Israeli press disclosed that an Israeli terrorism advisor, Amiram Nir, had been among the delegation visiting Tehran.
His nationality had been concealed by an Irish passport identifying
him as "Miller." To deal with the Great Satan was bad enough; to
be caught talking to an Israeli was among the few sins even worse.

Rafsanjani had weathered all the earlier disclosures, but this one was more threatening.

Second, Secretary of State George Shultz disclosed in January that he had authorized one last meeting with the so-called second channel, Rafsanjani's nephew, in Europe in December—after the revelations. That appeared to make a mockery of Tehran's disowning of the affair; the revolution's credibility was more undermined now than after the original disclosures. The salvage operation was not over.

The messy internal dynamics of Irangate's aftermath were reflected on January 31, three days after Rafsanjani's press conference, when Gerald Seib, *The Wall Street Journal*'s Mideast correspondent, was jumped by four men in fatigue jackets in front of the former Hilton and shoved, facedown, inside a car. After a wild ride through Tehran, during which he was switched to a second car, Seib ended up in notorious Evin Prison at the foot of the Elburz Mountains.[17]

For the next four days, Seib was interrogated by two Iranian intelligence officials—in English. Both, it turned out, had been educated in the United States. Their only interest was in his Israeli connections. As Seib saw it, the two men clearly believed he was an Israeli spy posing as an American journalist, perhaps another infiltrator like Amiram Nir.* Neither expressed interest in his visit to the Iranian war front or his three earlier trips to Iraq, clearly indicated in his confiscated passport. On the fourth day, they let him go—without even organizing a flight or an extension for the visa that he still needed to leave the country, which took him another two days.[18]

Seib concluded that he was a victim of a power struggle produced in part by Irangate, a "division so deep that one ministry can invite a reporter to visit and another can arrest him. . . . It is plausible to conclude that I was detained by a faction within Iran's internal security and intelligence agencies that simply wanted to grab an American journalist to embarrass those who had invited us." And, he noted, "It is widely accepted in Tehran that we journalists were invited in by a faction in the government led by Parliament Speaker Rafsanjani."[19]

Seib's detention seemed all the more serious in light of events in Lebanon. On January 20, British hostage negotiator Terry Waite,

---

* Nir died under mysterious circumstances in a plane crash in December 1988 in Mexico. He was listed on the manifest under a false name; he was reportedly traveling on business involving produce trade.

nicknamed "the gentle giant" by the media and hostage families because of his hulking, bearded frame, disappeared in Beirut. The Archbishop of Canterbury's troubleshooter, who had earlier won hostage releases in Iran and Libya, told associates that he had arranged a rendezvous with Islamic Jihad; he asked his Druze militia bodyguards to let him go alone. Waite never returned. He, too, may have been a victim of fallout from the secret arms deal. In light of the arms-for-hostages revelations, Waite's earlier trips to Beirut on behalf of the American hostages suddenly appeared to be a sham. Despite his repeated denials, he was widely perceived in the Middle East, even by his Druze guards, to have been a front for the United States.[20]

Four days later, the Beirut University College faculty was summoned to a campus hall by uniformed men to discuss security measures to prevent further hostage seizures. Three American lecturers and an Indian professor with United States residency were escorted off the campus for further briefings; they also never returned. The next news their families heard was a claim from Islamic Jihad for the Liberation of Palestine,* a heretofore unknown group, that the four men had been taken hostage. During a two-week period in January, a French journalist, two Germans—a businessman and an engineer—and two Saudi citizens were also kidnapped off the unruly streets of Beirut. More people were seized in January 1987 than at any time since the abductions began in 1982. By the end of January, with the addition of nine new captives, a total of twenty-two hostages from nine nations languished in captivity.[21]

Most of the seizures were tied to local issues. The various cells under the Hizbollah umbrella usually issued demands associated with imprisoned relatives or colleagues. But the rash of kidnappings also happened in the context of developments in Iran. The restraints imposed on hostage seizures for fourteen months—between the June 1985 TWA hijacking through the internal rumblings in Tehran in September 1986—had been lifted. No Iranian power was prepared to endanger his position by attempting to rein in the increasingly independent Shi'ite clans and cells in Lebanon. There were even indications that certain Iranian intelligence officials and Revolutionary Guards, embittered by the sellout to the Great Satan and infuriated when the attempt to detain the McFarlane team in Tehran had been frustrated, encouraged the abduction of new hostages.[22]

* Although both groups were widely believed to have ties to the Hizbollah umbrella, Islamic Jihad and Islamic Jihad for the Liberation of Palestine were believed by U.S. intelligence to involve different individuals.

1

For Ayatollah Ruhollah Khomeini, the stakes of his 1979 return to Iran were high: "This time, either Islam triumphs or we disappear."

Frustrated by the mullahs' growing power, the Islamic Republic's first prime minister, Mehdi Bazargan, described himself in 1979 as "a knife without a blade."

After his 1980 election, President Abolhassan Bani-Sadr erroneously predicted that Khomeini "will oversee things but will not be deeply involved."

Recalling the Iranian mobs who seized the U.S. embassy in 1979, one hostage commented: "Most of them had probably never seen an American before. I think a lot of them were surprised to find out we didn't have horns."

Iran's tactics after
Iraq's 1980 invasion
were informed by
Khomeini's words:
"Victory is not
achieved by swords.
It can be achieved
only by blood.
Victory is not
achieved by large
populations; it is
achieved only by
strength of faith."

A slogan on the U.S.
embassy fence
reflected Iran's
foreign policy. "What
do you think Iran is,"
exclaimed an Iranian
official, "a lackey of
the superpowers?"

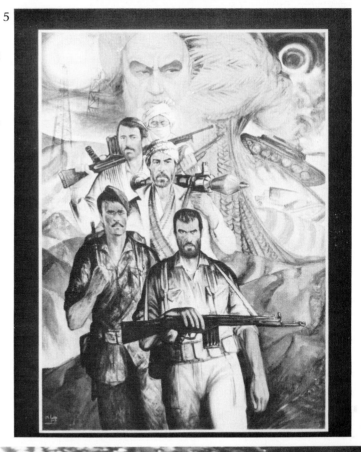

WE WILL MAKE AMERICA FACE A SEVERE DEFEAT

7

The Marine compound in Beirut was bombed in 1983, underlining Khomeini's pledge, "We shall export revolution to the whole world. Until the cry 'there is no God but God' resounds over the whole world, there will be struggle."

The abduction of American hostages in 1984–85 followed a vow from Islamic Jihad "to confirm our commitment of the statement made public after the bombing of the Marine headquarters that we will not leave any American on Lebanese soil."

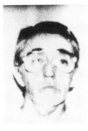 William Buckley: abducted March 16, 1984; died in captivity June 1985.

 Terry Anderson: abducted March 16, 1985.

 Rev. Benjamin Weir: abducted May 10, 1984; freed September 14, 1985.

 David Jacobsen: abducted May 28, 1985; freed November 2, 1985.

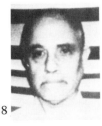 Father Laurence Martin Jenco: abducted January 8, 1985; freed July 26, 1986.

 Thomas Sutherland: abducted June 9, 1985.

8 ▶

9

Of the 1985 hijacking of TWA Flight 847, which paved the way for the arms-for-hostages swap, an Iranian leader claimed, "Iran had no connection whatsoever with the incident and, had it known, would have prevented it."

In 1987, Ali Akbar Hashemi Rafsanjani publicly revealed a Bible inscribed by President Reagan, underscoring an Iranian official's earlier words to the U.S. team in Iran: "It is not easy to sleep with an elephant you have wounded."

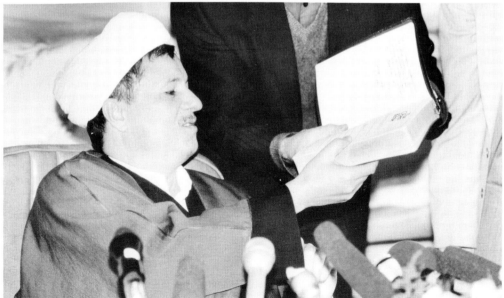

11   The 1988 U.S. naval strike on Iranian installations in the Gulf was interpreted in Teheran as an assault on Islam as much as on Iran: "The main problem of the revolution is that our enemies intend to create a barrier around the course of the revolution. This was true in the early Islamic era, too."

Before the 1987 Mecca riots that ended in more than 400 deaths, Khomeini had decreed, "Some ignorant people might say that the Haj is a place of worship, not a battlefield. [But] with all their might and faculties, Muslims should seriously fight for and defend divine

12   standards."

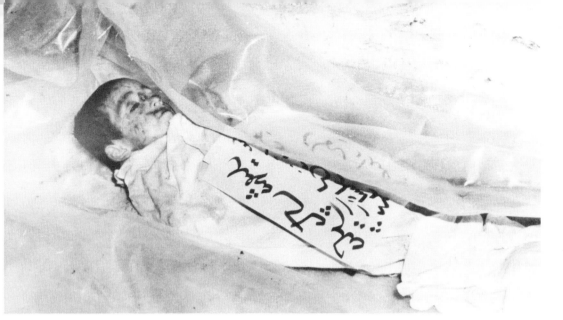

13   After the 1988 U.S. Navy downing of an Iranian airbus in which 66 children were among the 290 killed, Iran's leadership conceded, "Our main problem now is with the war."

14   International demonstrations in 1988 over Salman Rushdie's *The Satanic Verses* sparked Khomeini's edict: "The author of *The Satanic Verses* book, which is against Islam, the Prophet and the Koran, and all those involved in its publication who were aware of the content, are sentenced to death."

15

Of the internal power struggle in the late 1980s, Ali Akbar Hashemi Rafsanjani advised: "We have enough enemies in the world. It is, frankly, not fair to ignore those enemies and fight among ourselves."

After his selection as Khomeini's successor, President Ali Khamenei pledged: "Our path is the same as Imam Khomeini's and we will continue the path vigorously and decisively."

16

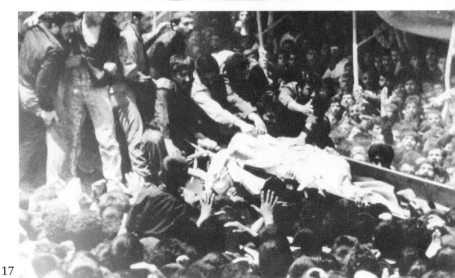

17

At his 1989 funeral, Khomeini's body was exposed, then dropped during a tumultuous outpouring of grief. *Time* wrote, "Rarely has so improbable a leader shaken the world."

After more than two years of a gradual and tempered relaxation of the Islamic Republic's firebrand foreign policy, the xenophobic and extremist tendencies reemerged supreme. After tentatively declaring its new openness in 1984, the Islamic Republic was, by mid-1987, slamming the door shut again—not for the last time.

The shift played out in direct confrontations with a host of nations through the spring and into the summer of 1987. The Iranians referred to the incidents as the "war of the embassies." In an act that would foreshadow a subsequent international incident between clashing cultures, Tehran protested to Bonn in February about an "insulting" German documentary on Iran. Two German diplomats were expelled and Iran's consulates in Hamburg and Frankfurt were closed. In March, Tunisia abruptly broke off relations, and new tension with Italy led to expulsions of Italian workers. In April, Tehran expelled two Australian diplomats to protest an Australian television satire on the Islamic Republic that "defamed" Islam.

In May, Tehran responded to the arrest of an Iranian diplomat on shoplifting charges in Britain by abducting and brutally beating a British diplomat in Tehran. The two nations then began a phased expulsion of each other's envoys until there were no British envoys left in Tehran. In June, the Iranian embassy in France refused to hand over an interpreter allegedly linked to a group responsible for a 1986 wave of Paris bombings. He claimed diplomatic immunity that France said he did not have. France cordoned off the embassy where he had taken asylum. The Islamic Republic retaliated by barricading France's Tehran mission and preventing French diplomats from leaving; one envoy was also charged with espionage. In mid-July, the two nations formally severed relations, although diplomats languished inside both embassies for months.

While Tehran was clearly in an aggressive mode, the Islamic Republic also viewed itself as the victim of a coordinated attempt to isolate it. Whatever the reality, the xenophobic revolutionaries perceived that they were the quarry forced into reacting for their own survival.

The theocracy was, in fact, deeply vulnerable, not only because of souring relations with the outside world and the increasingly unmanageable costs of the war. In June, in the midst of several foreign policy setbacks, at a juncture when Iran needed unity more than at any time since the early days of the revolution, the dominant Islamic Republic Party (IRP) was abruptly dissolved. Pooling the resources of the revolution's inner circle, the party had been its most vital organ. Its six founders had come from the hierarchy of the early Revolutionary Council. The clerics' party had also forced Prime Minister Bazargan's resignation, purged President Bani-Sadr, and eliminated the left and centrist opposition—each helping to pave the wave for the theocracy. Now it had turned on itself.

The formal announcement followed a letter submitted to Ayatollah Khomeini by President Khamenei and *Majlis* Speaker Rafsanjani. In an attempt to preempt a formal split, they reported that the party had fulfilled its role by mobilizing Iranians and by foiling counterrevolutionaries and foreign plots. The party, they said, no longer had any purpose. "Now, with the help of God, institutions of the Islamic Republic have been consolidated and the level of political awareness of the people has made the revolution invulnerable," the letter read. "Therefore, it is felt that the existence of the party no longer has the benefits of its early days and, on the contrary, party polarization under the present conditions may provide an excuse for discord and factionalism."

The ayatollah's published reply—and thinly veiled warning—reflected the depth of the problem. "I hope at this sensitive time you will strive united and unequivocally for spreading the sublime goals of Islam and the Islamic Republic," he said. "I point out that insulting any Muslim, whether member of the party or not, is against Islam and at this juncture in time, sowing discord is one of the worst sins."[23]

The IRP's problems were not a total surprise. Rafsanjani had admitted in 1986 that there were "two relatively powerful factions in our country with differences of view on how the country should be run. . . . They may, in fact, be regarded as two parties without names."[24] And in March 1987, just three months before the IRP was abolished, Khomeini had twice appealed for unity "particularly among those in charge." On March 21, the Persian new year as marked on the solar calendar, the imam warned that "big power conspiracies" sought to divide and weaken the revolution. "I beseech Almighty God to safeguard the unity among all organs, between the parliament and the government, between the judicial power and other people and among all strata of the nation," the imam said. "God forbid that they confront each other."[25]

The price of preventing a full-fledged confrontation, however, had been eliminating the forum for dispute—and the united front that the theocrats presented to Iran and the outside world. Rafsanjani called the decision to "freeze" the party "temporary. There is a possibility of reviving it if the consensus which led to its formation in 1979 is available again."[26] For the foreseeable future, however, the party was a dead issue. Iranian factionalism had deepened into a chasm.

•

The series of setbacks during the first half of 1987, however, turned out to be only a prelude to crisis. During eleven days in July, three events forced Iran into a corner.

The first occurred at the United Nations. On July 20, all fifteen members of the Security Council, assembled around the cavernous chamber's U-shaped table of blond Scandinavian wood, voted in favor of Resolution 598. A multifaceted formula to end the seven-year-old Gulf war, the resolution evolved largely under U.S. impetus and won support due to the international community's fear, after the Karbala offensives, that Iran could conceivably win the war. Even nations such as China, a leading source of Tehran's arms, did not welcome the implications of an Iranian victory.

The Reagan administration immediately followed up by calling for a second resolution imposing a worldwide arms embargo on either or both combatants if a ceasefire was not accepted. Since the government of President Saddam Hussein had all but publicly begged for peace, the pressure was clearly aimed at the Islamic Republic. Tehran's theocrats called the resolution "unjust" and wondered out loud why the international body had not passed a similar resolution during the war's early stages when Iran was losing. But they did not reject it outright. While the embargo motion had little hope of immediate passage, the future potential heightened the pressure on Tehran. The resolution led the theocrats to believe that the bilateral confrontations known as the "war of the embassies" had escalated into a coordinated international assault.

The second event happened in Kuwait. At a small ceremony on July 21, the morning after the United Nations vote, two Kuwaiti oil tankers were reflagged under an American mast. In order to qualify for U.S. naval protection as they passed through the Gulf's troubled waters, they were rechristened the USS *Gas Prince* and the USS *Bridgeton*. "This is a milestone," said U.S. Ambassador Anthony Quainton. "We are providing direct reassurance to one of the small countries in the Gulf that has found itself in danger from the Iran-Iraq war." [27] The two were the first of eleven Kuwaiti tankers—one-half of the sheikhdom's fleet—to come under American protection.

Direct American intervention in the Gulf evolved as much from fallout in the United States over the secret Iranian arms deal as from Washington's concern for freedom of navigation. The arms-for-hostages swap, a unilateral act that ignored the United States' other strategic goals and commitments in the Middle East, had cost Washington its credibility with Arab allies, such as Jordan, Egypt and Kuwait. Iran had received weapons that allies had been refused on the pretext that Congress would never approve the sale. For the Islamic Republic, however, the Reagan administration had been willing to simply circumvent Congress. The United States had also been prepared to bend laws and use questionable middlemen and financiers to expedite planeloads of weapons for belligerent Tehran while, at the same time, dragging its feet over help for economically strapped Egypt, the cornerstone of American peace efforts in the Arab-Israeli conflict.[28]

The distrust played out most visibly in Kuwait. When the tanker war heated up in December and January during the Karbala offensives, the tiny city-state had appealed for American flags and U.S. Coast Guard protection for its tankers. The Iraqi escalation of strikes on Iranian ships had, in turn, increasingly made Kuwaiti tankers retaliatory targets for Iran. Diverted by the unraveling Iran-Contra scandal at home, however, the Reagan administration did not initially respond—until it learned that the Soviet Union had offered to lease three tankers to Kuwait. The United States then suddenly saw new urgency in preventing a heightened Soviet presence in the Gulf sea-lanes. By March 1987, a deal had been struck with Kuwait to bring the U.S. Navy into the Gulf—at the cost of $20 million a month.[29]

Iran was angered and perplexed by the American decision. Tehran had neither initiated nor wanted the expensive tanker war; its actions thus far had been limited to retaliation for Iraqi bombardments. For the first three years of the war, Iran had not responded to Iraqi strikes; and in 1984, the year the tanker war erupted, Iraq had fired on almost three times more ships than Iran had hit.[30]

Indeed, to Iran, the folly of an increased U.S. naval presence had been evident when the USS *Stark* was hit—by Iraq, not Iran—in May. Thirty-seven American sailors had, by mistake, been killed in the high-seas drama. If the Reagan administration wanted to ensure freedom of navigation, Tehran argued, then it should pressure Saddam Hussein to end the tanker war. The puzzling inconsistency seemed only to prove to the theocrats that, after fourteen months of courting Iran, Washington now actively sought a confrontation.

As always when cornered, the Islamic Republic struck back. In May, for the first time since the tanker war began in 1981, Tehran hit more ships than Iraq. It also laid new minefields. Only two days after the four-hundred-thousand-ton USS *Bridgeton* began its inaugural voyage, surrounded by three American navy escort vessels, it hit a mine halfway down the Gulf. An escalation began to appear unavoidable.

The third incident triggering an Iranian reaction happened ten days after the reflagging ceremony. On July 31, two million Muslims from 120 countries assembled in Mecca, Saudi Arabia, for the annual Haj pilgrimage. Making the trip at least once in a Muslim's life is one of the five pillars of Islam. Since the Iranian revolution, however, the Haj had also become one of the most tense moments in the Middle East.

For Iran, Saudi Arabia symbolized the Sunni world's usurpation of the rightful leadership of the Prophet Mohammad's descendants. Riyadh's alliance with the United States further represented the compromise of Islamic dignity and independence. Because Shi'ism is centered around the fight against injustice, the holiest religious commemoration was viewed by the theocrats as a time to protest and to mobilize the world's Muslims against perceived wrongs. In one of the longest speeches of his life, Khomeini set the tone for the 1987 Haj with a call to militancy. He exhorted the pilgrims,

> Some ignorant people might even say that one should not dishonor the House of God and the Great Kaaba [stone around which pilgrims parade] with slogans, demonstrations, marches and disavowal. They might even say that the Haj is a place for worship, not a battlefield. . . . [But] with all their might and facilities, the Muslims should seriously fight for and defend divine standards and the interests of Muslims. . . . They must echo the crushing slogan of disavowing the pagan and apostates of world arrogance—headed by the criminal United States—in the house of monotheism and remember to express their hatred toward the enemies of God and mankind.[31]

Because of problems in years past, including the 1986 discovery of more than a hundred pounds of explosives in Iranian luggage, officials of the two nations worked out full details of a limited three-hour Iranian demonstration, right down to the slogans allowed on banners. Nervous Saudi officials, however, came back on the eve of the demonstration with new conditions: that the number of pilgrims must be restricted; that foreign pilgrims would be excluded; and that Saudi citizens could not join the demonstration. The Iranians balked, and the situation was primed for a showdown.

Hours before the march, Saudi security forces massed along the road to Mecca's Grand Mosque. At 4:30 P.M., in sweltering 115-degree desert heat, a hundred thousand pilgrims, including five hundred from Lebanon, Afghanistan, the Philippines, India, Pakistan, and Bangladesh, began their demonstration. For the first two hours, the crowd rallied noisily in place, listening to fiery speeches denouncing the United States, the Soviet Union and Israel and waving enormous sheet-banners of ayatollahs Khomeini and Montazeri. The demonstration climaxed, as agreed with the Saudis, with the burning of three American flags. At 6:30 P.M., led by women and war victims, the pilgrims began their short march—and the trouble began.

As a Pakistani participant in the 1987 Haj later reconstructed, edgy Saudi riot police halted the crowd about a quarter of a mile short of its destination. The Iranians, urged on by Revolutionary Guards directing the crowds from the sidelines, aggressively pushed ahead as the Saudi cordon tried to hold them back. Scuffling turned into a melee as stones, bricks and sticks, the latter pulled off banners, were hurled at the Saudis, who responded with tear gas. The confrontation turned into a stampede as the choking pilgrims began to flee—only to find the exits closed off.[32] In apparent panic, the Saudis opened fire—they claimed in the air, the Iranians said at the crowd. The whole thing was over in an hour. In the end, at least 407 were killed, another 649, including Khomeini's wife, Batoul, were injured. Some were trampled to death, others clearly were shot.[*]

Riyadh charged that the Iranians had planned to seize the Grand Mosque and declare Khomeini the leader of the Muslim world.[†] Tehran, in turn, claimed that the United States had put Saudi Arabia up to provoking a bloody clash with Iran.[33] An infuriated Khomeini blamed the riots on "the mercenaries of the Great Satan. . . . We hold America responsible for all these crimes. God willing, at an opportune time, we shall deal with her."[34] It was not an idle threat.

The violence did not end in Mecca. In Tehran the next morning, thousands of demonstrators shouting "Revenge! Revenge!" ran-

---

[*] The official Saudi death toll included 275 Iranians, 85 Saudis and 47 other pilgrims. Many of the Iranian bodies, shown to American and European reporters immediately upon their return to Tehran, had bullet punctures.

[†] The fate of the Mecca shrine was a partiticularly sensitive issue, since Saudi fundamentalists had seized it for two weeks in 1979; more than four hundred had been killed when the Saudis finally resorted to military force to retake it.

sacked and looted the Saudi and Kuwaiti embassies. Classified documents were thrown over balconies into the Saudi embassy courtyard; liquor bottles found in the Kuwaiti mission were lined up on window sills for the public to view.[35] A Saudi security officer subsequently died of injuries incurred when he tried to hold off the mob.

The Iranian reaction, however, was also telling about the damage since the Irangate revelations. Within hours of the Mecca riots, but long before news of the more than four hundred deaths was broadcast in Tehran, the ranking Saudi and Kuwaiti envoys had been hastily summoned to the Iranian Foreign Ministry. The two envoys had been candidly warned that "spontaneous" demonstrations would probably take place at their embassies the next day. An Iranian official, with some embarrassment according to those present, advised them to stay home. In effect, the Foreign Ministry conceded at the late-night meeting that it was impotent to contain events or to provide protection from others within the government who did indeed organize the next morning's assaults.[36] The tension throughout the Gulf had reached the point that it was, increasingly, beyond the control of any single party.

•

In August 1987, Iranian television began broadcasting a half-hour video showing Iranian naval speedboats racing through the swells of the Gulf's blue-green waters, small cannons poised for attack in front, pennants boasting of martyrdom boldly waving in the rear. Suddenly, lightning flashes of fire from larger Iranian patrol boats blazed atop the waves, erupting in thick white clouds as they hit their target, a large rusted-out freighter posing as the enemy. Eventually, the hapless freighter crippled, commandos stormed the ship and triumphantly raised the Iranian flag. Symphonic drums and cymbals echoed the sounds of war in the background.[37]

No commentary was needed to explain the message implied in the tapes of Iran's naval exercises, conducted just a few days after the Mecca massacre. In the "Martyrdom Maneuvers," as they were code-named, the Islamic Republic signaled that it would not succumb to pressure from Iraq's escalating attacks on its petroleum facilities and tankers or from the U.S. deployment in the Persian Gulf. In large red-and-white letters, a new sign in the lobby of the Revolutionary Guards headquarters in Tehran boasted more succinctly, in both Farsi and English, "The Persian Gulf will be the graveyard of the United States." Above it, in gloomy Velazquez tones, was an enormous oil painting of a ship exploding.[38]

In early August, ten days after the Mecca riots, Baghdad had upped the ante in the Gulf. First, ending a four-week lull, Iraqi warplanes flew 110 sorties against Iranian oil installations. Then, in September, the day after U.N. Secretary-General Javier Perez de Cuellar ended his first peace mission to the region to discuss Resolution 598, Iraq resumed attacks on Iranian ships. Tehran reacted by pledging to make the Gulf "a killing field for aggressors."[39] September became the deadliest month since the tanker war began; twenty-eight ships were hit. The narrow Gulf sea-lanes became a shooting gallery as Iran and Iraq repeatedly struck at large and slow-moving tankers.

The Islamic Republic's first direct confrontation with the United States took place on September 21, on the eve of the war's seventh anniversary. The timing could well have been linked to the commemoration; the theocrats may have hoped to rally new fervor behind the sagging war effort at a symbolic juncture. Shortly after midnight, American helicopter reconnaissance, equipped with infrared night scopes, spotted the *Iran Ajr* in the main Gulf channel northeast of Bahrain, an area beyond the normal route of Iranian ships where U.S. warships often anchored. The small, Japanese-built landing craft had been tracked by U.S. warships for several days after intelligence indicated it had loaded "suspect devices" at an Iranian port. Through their scopes, the pilots spotted the crew dropping mines overboard; the Iranians had been caught red-handed.

Washington had earlier informed Tehran through the Swiss government that any minelaying operation outside Iranian waters would be met with "armed resistance." So no warning was issued before U.S. helicopter gunships opened fire on the *Iran Ajr*. The choppers hit the ship's stern, knocking a large gash in the hull and setting it ablaze. Three Iranians were killed instantly and the rest were forced to flee on life rafts. After dawn broke, Navy commandos seized the ship and gathered twenty-six crew members from the Gulf waters.

In a long-scheduled speech the next day at the United Nations, President Khamenei angrily protested that the *Iran Ajr* was a food-laden cargo ship. To the cries of *"Allahu Akbar"* from supporters in the General Assembly gallery, the president charged that the Reagan administration's allegations were "a pack of lies."[40] But the evidence was damning. American troops discovered ten large, black, circular mines—all vintage models designed to float just beneath the water's surface—laid out neatly on the vessel's deck. Six others had already been dropped. The Iranian vessel was towed out of the main channel and blown up.

On October 8, less than three weeks later, a second serious shoot-out erupted. Shortly before 10:00 P.M., an American reconnaissance helicopter came under fire from Iranian gunboats. The United States again quickly responded; American attack helicopters struck three Iranian patrol boats. One sank, two were rendered useless. In light of its recent disproportionate losses, Tehran began to appear reckless. For the ruling mullahs, however, provocation was an almost necessary reaction.

In the midst of the escalating storm in the Gulf, Rafsanjani told the faithful at a Friday prayer service that the current phase of the revolution "appears very similar to the conditions of the early Islamic era, the time of the prophet." He further explained,

> The main problem of the revolution is that our enemies intend to create a barrier across the course of the revolution's movement. They intend to stop the spread of its message. We want to remove this barrier and, therefore, a clash occurs. . . . Our enemies will resort to any means. This was true in the early Islamic era too. They used to spread a rumor that the Prophet was a wizard, a magician, a liar, an ignorant person, an illiterate, etc. Now we see them making similar accusations about this revolution. We can interpret the accusations in the same way.[41]

The perception of Islam facing off the West grew in the fall as France, Britain, Italy, Holland and Belgium all reversed their earlier decisions and also deployed minesweepers or warships in the Gulf sea-lanes.

An official at Tehran's Institute for Political and International Studies also framed Iran's costly naval clash in terms of its broader mission on behalf of the Third World. "What are the consequences if Iran attacks the United States? No one expects Iran to defeat the United States militarily," he said. "But when Iran reacts militarily, it shows small countries that small powers can defend themselves."[42] The theocrats also needed to be seen, at home and in the Islamic world, to be following through on their rhetoric. Reaction was virtually required in light of the perceived confrontational stand by the United States after Irangate, the claims of an American role in the Mecca massacre and the costly American counterstrikes against Iran in the Gulf. Finally, in light of the political divisions at home, any action on the war front might serve to divert attention to issues where there was some unity.

Exactly one week after the United States shot up the three Iranian gunboats, the American-owned supertanker *Sungari* was hit by a missile inside Kuwaiti waters. The next day, October 16, the *Sea Isle City*, one of the eleven reflagged Kuwaiti tankers, was struck by an Iranian missile while anchored in Kuwaiti waters. Both shots were fired from Faw, the strategic Iraqi peninsula seized by Iran in 1986.

Again, the United States counterstruck. Three days later, Iranians on the former Rashadat oil platform seventy-five miles off the Iranian coast monitored a warning transmitted on military and international distress radio frequencies. "Rashadat, Rashadat. This is the U.S. Navy. We will commence firing on your position at fourteen hundred hours. You have twenty minutes to evacuate the platform." The Americans received no reply from Rashadat, which, rendered useless for oil drilling eleven months earlier by Iraqi air strikes, had been converted into a fortified Revolutionary Guards outpost to monitor American convoys and to provide a base for Iranian speedboats. But at least twenty men, all clad in military uniforms, were seen scrambling for boats to flee.

Four navy destroyers then pummeled the elevated rig with 1,065 rounds of artillery. The remnants were then dynamited by navy divers, leaving the platform in the central Gulf a twisted, flaming hulk. The measured and largely symbolic American action, combined with past responses, finally had an impact. Although the tanker war continued to consume growing numbers of ships,* attacks on the American operation in the Gulf ceased for the next six months. Exposed and endangered on yet another front, the Islamic Republic increasingly turned inward to sort out its own affairs.

•

On December 10, 1987, Ayatollah Khomeini summoned the government's leading figures to his austere compound in northern Tehran. In a brief ceremony, he handed over a new will, the contents of which were secret, to replace a last testament written on the same day five years earlier. The event, aired on national radio, took Iranians by surprise. Tehran's rumor mill came alive with speculation about new instructions and even a new successor, or a trium-

---

* By the end of 1987, attacks on Gulf ships were up 70 percent over 1986; Iran for the first time had hit more ships, ninety-one, than Iraq, which scored eighty-six hits.

virate of successors, upon Khomeini's passing. The imam said his
new will was necessitated by the "conditions and needs of the
times." But the ceremony instead indicated that the self-righteous
certainty with which Iran's clergy and their allies had ousted the
shah had given way to an anxious sense of transition and vulnerability.

Although Khomeini's influence on the running of government
had diminished since the Islamic Republic's early days, the revolution's dependence on the Supreme Jurisprudent was still conspicuous in 1987, even on minor issues. A dispute had recently broken
out over the content of Iranian television and radio programs, specifically over foreign music, Western and Asian films with non-
Islamic themes, and sports, such as wrestling or soccer, that exposed
the male anatomy. The topic eventually became one of the hottest
items of debate in the nation's papers, at mosques and on university
campuses. In the end, the head of the Voice and Vision of Iran,
Mohammad Hashemi, brother of the *majlis* speaker, and his advi-
sory board formally asked the imam for a ruling. Khomeini wrote
back that "Watching such films and plays is no impediment to religion, and many of them are instructive." He admonished them,
however, to be careful about nonreligious themes.[43]

The split over use of the national media underscored the diver-
gent views of how the revolution should be implemented. Tradi-
tionalist clergy favored religious and educational programming, as
much of it locally produced as possible. More pragmatic elements
recognized, however, that the revolution had conflicting constituencies with varying tastes; they sought to make the Islamic Republic
compatible with contemporary times. After the revolution's early
years, several sectors of society had turned away from the monot-
onous Islamic programming and war propaganda in favor of home
videos or, worse, Voice of America and BBC broadcasts. But the
introduction of more entertainment, including old Pink Panther car-
toons, Laurel aand Hardy classics and British docudramas about the
Victorian era (when women were appropriately attired), had created a backlash. Only Khomeini could ultimately resolve the dispute.

Reconciling the tenets of fundamentalist Islam and the require-
ments of a modern state had been one of the underlying tensions of
the revolution for nine years. The problem often led to deadlock on
basic issues, from television shows to economic reform. In 1980, for
example, the dominant Revolutionary Council had approved a law
to redistribute land among the *mostazafin*. But it gave rise to such

chaos and to so much criticism from clergy and landowners that Khomeini suspended it after seven months. Hundreds of thousands of acres were given back to their original owners.

Since then, the impasse on implementing the ideas behind the revolution had played out most visibly between the parliament and the Council of Guardians. A host of bills—on trade nationalization, price controls, expropriation of land abandoned by those who fled the country and labor laws—had been passed by the *majlis* only to be vetoed by the twelve-man Council of Guardians as incompatible with the Sharia, or Islamic law.[44]

Over the years, the 270-member *majlis*, which sought to address the raised expectations synonymous with the revolution, had become the most reform-oriented body in Iran. The Council of Guardians, the fourth branch of the Iranian government, had meanwhile evolved into one of Iran's most conservative bodies. Its strong connections with the bazaaris and the landowning clergy led it to try to protect the private sector. The clash was not simply between different centers of power, but between disparate interpretations over the role of the state.

The conflict, in practical terms, meant that key legislation—especially on land reform and trade nationalization—passed by parliament was vetoed by the Guardians on grounds that they interfered with property rights and freedom of trade or because the Sharia made no mention of the issue. The overall result, after nine years, was to leave the country in limbo on the very issues over which the revolution had been carried out.

In December 1987, with his revolution ostracized diplomatically, sapped by a costly war and surrounded by Western warships, and at an impasse on economic and other reforms, the imam initiated a series of steps designed to generate new momentum. The impetus was not his alone, but as with the decision to update his will, he clearly felt it was time to get his house in order. Khomeini was also the only one who could do it.

One of his first steps was a ruling that partly broke the impasse on labor laws. Rather brusquely, Khomeini empowered the executive branch to cut off the public utilities of businesses that did not pay minimum wages, provide social welfare contributions, or honor the laws' stipulations generally protecting workers. As he did so often, the ayatollah backed into a position, in this case endorsing laborers' rights, but the move did clarify the framework for future priorities that favored the *mostazafin* oppressed.

The next move in January 1988 was a more sweeping *fatwa*, or religious edict, in which Khomeini ruled that the authority of the state was the same today as it was in the time of the Prophet, who was the vice-regent of God. In effect, he said, the state was superior to Islam and that it was empowered to do anything necessary for the good of the faith, even suspending some of the five pillars of Islam in the state's interests. "Our government . . . has priority over all other Islamic tenets, even over prayer, fasting and the pilgrimage to Mecca," he wrote.

The *fatwa* was revolutionary because of historic Shi'ite contempt for temporal authority. Now the Iranian leader had effectively proclaimed that the power of government was most absolute—and most divine. The ruling allowed new flexibility in interpreting Islam to deal with the problems facing a modern state; it also silenced conservative clergy who advocated strict adherence to Islamic laws.[45] The ruling was such a sweeping change that some critics even called it heretical, since Khomeini was also, in effect, saying that his word took precedence over Koranic injunctions.[46]

In February, Khomeini then announced a means of settling disputes between the reform-oriented parliament and the conservative Council of Guardians. In response to a letter from several government officials, including his son Ahmad, the imam announced the formation of a new arbitration body. A thirteen-member Expediency Council—made up of six theologians from the Council of Guardians, six government officials drawn from the legislative, judicial and executive branches, and a representative of the Supreme Jurisprudent's office—would vote on any stalled legislation.

Together, the three moves outlined the powers and the future priorities of the revolution and provided a vehicle for resolving one of the deepest political divisions. Most important, they opened the way, in theory, for the next stage of the revolution to take place—even without the imam.[47]

•

Though Khomeini had been able to use his immense power to sort through some of the revolution's political problems, he was unable to break the stalemate at the military front. There had been no follow-up to the Karbala offensives a year before, and two years had elapsed since the seizure of Faw. The much-feared final, *final* offensive seemed further away than ever. Both Iran and Iraq scrambled to improve their weapons capabilities, especially missiles, to end the impasse. This time, however, Baghdad was faster.

On February 29, 1988, seventeen missiles rained down on Tehran. At first, Tehranis thought that Iraq had launched a new round of aerial bombardment in the "war of the cities." "So did the military," recalled an eyewitness. "The sky was full of antiaircraft fire. It was two or three days before we knew what had happened."[48] What had hit Tehran were Soviet Scud-B missiles modified by the Iraqis to reach twice their normal range of three hundred miles. Baghdad had actually boasted of a new capability to fire enhanced-range missiles at Iran but, like many of the claims made by both sides during the conflict, it had not been taken seriously. The modification meant that, for the first time, Iraq was able to target Tehran and other cities deep inside Iran without endangering its own air force. For the next seven weeks, the Iranian capital became an embattled city.

Tehranis either fortified or fled. At least a quarter of the capital's twelve million residents left, many for the shores of the Caspian Sea. Diplomats who tried to track down many government officials, including cabinet ministers, found they were quasi-permanently "unavailable." Streets were empty and schools closed; shops opened only sporadically. Windows of high-rise office buildings and shop fronts downtown, of clinics and mud-brick shanties in the arid south, and even of splendid villas in the wealthy northern suburbs were crisscrossed with thick strips of tape to limit the impact of implosion. Entrances and entire first floors of many government offices and all banks were protected by layers of burlap bags filled with sand. Those left in Tehran lived underground or in lower-level rooms without windows or access to an exterior wall.

Between February 29 and April 20, only 140 scuds landed in the capital, not a high total by the standards of Berlin at the end of World War II or contemporary Beirut. The death toll was also low compared with casualties at the war front. "There weren't a great many deaths," conceded a Tehran journalist who covered the bombardment. "But psychologically it was devastating. It was Russian roulette on a vast scale. Before, the capital was always separate from the war, the way America was during the second World War. This was like having raids over Washington, D.C."[49]

In the midst of the missile bombardment, Iran received another serious blow in March when Iraq unleashed another enhanced weapon in its arsenal—chemical warfare. At the Iraqi town of Halabjah, a Kurdish stronghold, Iraqi forces moved in to try to retake the town less than twenty-four hours after Iranian troops had seized it. The Kurds in this area had long sought independence from Iraq and had therefore sided openly with the Iranians. Baghdad's response was lethal. From artillery and from the air, Iraq pounded the village with poisonous mustard gas and nerve agents. Somewhere between three and five thousand people died—in their beds, at dinner tables and on the streets. While Iraq had made use of chemical warfare on numerous earlier occasions, never had civilians come under such a massive and deliberate attack.[50]

The most devastating round in the "war of the cities" and the use of chemical warfare on civilians coincided with the end of Iran's six-year domination of the war. On April 18, Iraq recaptured its Faw Peninsula. The swampy but strategic foothold, over which tens of thousands of Iranians had died in the bloody 1986 assault, was won back in a mere thirty-six hours. It was a rout, in part because of chemical warfare. The Revolutionary Guards were particularly ill equipped to defend against poison gas; many had beards that did not fit under gas masks, while the temperature of insulated suits in the smothering tropical heat made them unbearable for long periods of time.

Baghdad also, however, received massive foreign assistance in planning the attack. France, Egypt, Jordan and Iraq's other long-time arms suppliers and allies each contributed, but the United States also played a critical role. In part to restore U.S. credibility among Arab regimes after its arms sales to Tehran and in part out of fear, after the Karbala offensives, that Iran might break through, Washington advised Baghdad for more than a year on a strategy to retake Faw—despite its official policy of neutrality in the war. Besides providing intelligence on Iranian strengths and positions, U.S. military advisors mapped out how Iraqi units and weapons could most effectively strike at Iranian positions. With American and other foreign guidance, Iraq constructed a replica of Faw's junctures for practice runs.[51]

Ironically, the biggest problem was convincing Iraq to follow American advice; U.S. military and foreign policy advisors complained that Iraq's early resistance to American and other foreign counsel cost Baghdad valuable time. The scheme was straightforward. On one side, Iraqi artillery barrages hammered the underarmed Revolutionary Guards and Basij at Faw. Other Iraqi units flanked the peninsula by sea, coming up behind the Iranians. The Iraqis then announced that they would give the Iranians twelve hours to leave. Surrounded and outnumbered, with their guns pointing in the wrong direction, the Iranians fled back across the Shatt al-Arab.[52]

American involvement on Iraq's behalf in 1988 helped undo the gains achieved by Iran in the Karbala offensives courtesy of U.S.

intelligence provided during Irangate. It was the final crucial turning point in the war: Iraq made its biggest gain in more than seven years, proving that all was not lost. Iran, its vulnerability now exposed, was forced to retreat. The end game had begun.

The day of the Faw defeat, the United States Navy also intervened directly—this time in retaliation for a new Iranian minefield in the Persian Gulf that had ripped a hole in an American frigate, the *Samuel B. Roberts*, and injured ten American sailors. In one of the biggest U.S. military engagements since the Vietnam War, the Navy destroyed two Iranian oil platforms, sank a patrol boat and a frigate and badly damaged a second frigate and three smaller craft. The American warships had originally intended to hit three platforms and a frigate. But Iran upset the plan by counterstriking—at a cost of almost a quarter of its navy. The disparity of reaction— fleeing the Iraqis at Faw and making a suicidal attack on the U.S. Navy—reflected an erratic desperation. And desperate was exactly what Iran had become.

In May, the Islamic Republic's first premier, Mehdi Bazargan, issued an open letter of protest to Khomeini about Iran's war policy. In this case, "open" meant distributed in Iran and overseas but not published by the Iranian press. "Since 1986, you have not stopped proclaiming victory, and now you are calling on the population to resist until victory. Isn't that an admission of failure on your behalf?" Bazargan wrote. "You have spoken of the failure of Iraq and the crumbling of its regime, but thanks to your misguided policies, Iraq has fortified itself, its economy has not collapsed, and it is we who are on the verge of bankruptcy. You say that you have a responsibility toward the spilled blood. I answer: When will you stop the commerce with the blood of our martyrs?"[53]

It was not an isolated protest. Antiwar demonstrations were reported in several cities, including Isfahan and Tabriz. More telling were reports that mullahs were also making the pilgrimage to the Khomeini compound to tell the imam, bluntly, that the war was sapping public morale. The extent of the damage was becoming visible: The Revolutionary Guards, originally a volunteer body that had closely vetted its members' Islamic and revolutionary credentials, was, by the spring of 1988, 80 percent conscripts. The prime minister also conceded that 41 percent of Iran's 1988 budget was allocated to the war and to war-related needs. At the same time, oil revenues were a fraction of what the shah's government had regarded, two decades earlier, as basic to peacetime development.

Indeed, by the spring of 1988, the threat was not just military.

The war had also begun to threaten the revolution's economic survival. An economy that had spent $20 billion in 1982 had to make ends meet on oil revenues estimated for 1988 at less than $9 billion —at a time the war tab alone had reached $10 billion a year. Tehran had taken to barter arrangements—oil, pistachios and other goods in exchange for basic foodstuffs and necessities—with most of its major trading partners. Although it had pledged never again to be in debt to a foreign power, the theocracy was forced to negotiate one-year deferments, a form of debt, with a host of foreign suppliers. Nonvital Iranian industries were effectively seconded to help make war goods. A prominent children's clothing manufacturer in Tehran, for example, was ordered to stop its own business and to start making protective uniforms to limit the impact of chemical weapons. Imports of raw materials became increasingly restricted to war-related industries.[54]

Life was just as bad for the individual. Unemployment, officially pegged at about 25 percent, actually reached closer to 40 percent. And inflation was virtually incalculable because of the black market. The black-market rate for the dollar had doubled in just a year to twenty times the legal rate. But while Iranians earned in rials, prices for virtually all but the few subsidized goods were pegged to the dollar. A kilo of low-grade beef was more than $14.00—three times the subsidized price of $3.50. At the legal rate of exchange, a new car cost at least $140,000—more than ten times its price outside Iran. Shortages were rampant. A wood scarcity jacked up the cost of a box of matches to fifty cents, and most newspapers were down to four or eight pages. Sporadic electricity blackouts, a problem dating back to the shah's era, became daily occurrences, lasting up to eight hours.

Kayhan, a Tehran daily, reported in June that the British *Business International* had pronounced Tehran the third most expensive city in the world, after Tokyo and Osaka. Thousands of Iranian men had to take second jobs to survive, while the growing number of female workers was more often related to economic need than to manpower shortages brought on by a war. The *mostazafin* disinherited, in whose name the revolution had been carried out, were far worse off materially than they had been under the shah.[55]

A popular joke in Tehran centered on a discussion between Khomeini and a *shahid*, or martyr. "Oh, imam, tell me about paradise," the martyr asked. "Well," said the ayatollah, "There is no war, and the electricity always works." "Oh, tell me more," begged the *shahid.* "All the foods are available, the finest meat and abundant fruits," replied the imam. "More," beseeched the martyr. "There is plenty of time to play, and everyone is happy," Khomeini responded. "And more!" said the *shahid* on his knees. "Well, to summarize," the imam said, "it is like the good old days of the shah." The context was the shah's time—when oil prices were higher, relations with the world provided bustling trade and easy access to raw materials, and Iran was at peace—not the shah. Only a tiny percentage of the Iranians still in Iran proposed restoration of the Pahlavi dynasty. But, for the mullahs, the comparison was, nonetheless, couched in the worst possible terms.

As Rafsanjani admitted publicly, "Our main problem now is the war."[56] An Iranian official noted for his long years at the front, first as a soldier and later as a war correspondent for the Islamic Republic News Agency, put it another way: "From the beginning, we used the wrong motto," a reference to the implied goal of "War until victory," the standard chant of troops, at Friday prayer services and in government propaganda for almost eight years.[57] The war that had sustained the revolution had slowly begun to destroy it.

CHAPTER SEVEN

The Reckoning

~~~

"We, Iranian nation, have had no reckoning since
the revolution, but we must have one at the conclusion of these ten years."

—Ayatollah Ali Montazeri [1]

"If you people fail to be unanimous, this revolution, which is the great miracle of the century,
made under the auspices of God thanks to the
Imam's leadership and with your selflessness,
will collapse."

—Supreme Court Chief
Justice Abdul Karim
Musavi Ardabili [2]

On the elevated speaker's dais in Iran's ornate *majlis*, Ali Akbar Hashemi Rafsanjani listened in-
tently as a member of parliament whispered in his ear. The member,
hunched over at Rafsanjani's side, had been talking for ten minutes,
one of the longer discussions. For almost an hour, more than a
dozen members, including a female, had lined up at the dais steps,
waiting their turn to talk with the powerful speaker. With each,
Rafsanjani occasionally interjected a point or a question, but most
of the time he listened, until the end when he had a final word or

two. Although other members, speaking at a podium on the floor below about problems ranging from inflation to farm policies, were the first order of business on June 7, 1988, the real political action was clearly happening around Rafsanjani's chair.

Iran's parliament, a five-story, white marble building, was originally built by the shah. The changes in the nine years since his ouster, however, were telling. The main chamber, decorated with royal-blue carpeting and red furnishings and lit by an enormous crystal chandelier, was also adorned with twenty-seven large posters. Drawn against the backdrop of the green, red and white Iranian flag, each portrayed a member of parliament who had died in the 1981 bombings. On the outside, a massive replica of the shah's royal crown, complete with headfeather, which used to cover the entry had been replaced by a sentry post and a machine gun. To gain access to the *majlis* compound, all visitors had to enter a back street, pass several checkpoints and, finally, make a two-block walk by trees linked together with white banners warning, among other things, "If you hesitate today, you will be dominated tomorrow." Once inside, all bags, watches and even loose pocket change had to be checked in at a little window; all visitors had to go through at least one body search. The security and the portraits served as constant reminders of the revolution's vulnerability.

Parliament's main business on June 7 was to elect a Speaker, as happened every year. Despite heavy Iraqi missile bombardment during the spring "war of the cities," Iranians had gone to the polls in April and May 1988, for the third time since the shah's ouster, to elect a new *majlis*.* Because of the 1987 dissolution of the Islamic Republic Party, the elections had not been as predictable as earlier polls. The majority of incumbents had lost, and the number of mullahs had been almost halved.†

The outcome of the Speaker's race hardly seemed in question. Rafsanjani had run the body as its first and only Speaker during the previous two four-year terms. In the process, he had emerged as Iran's boldest and most imaginative politician. His skills were evident on the *majlis* floor. Although parliament's mandate had been established in the Islamic Republic's constitution, Rafsanjani had given it shape. The agenda he set in parliament often reflected the

---

* Iran's parliamentary elections are held in two stages. In districts where no candidate wins a majority in the first round, the two with the highest vote run in a second round.

† About 150 were new members, according to the *majlis* public relations office. And only about 27 percent of the members elected in 1988 were mullahs, compared with about 45 percent in the previous two parliaments.

framework of debate throughout the government; the laws passed usually reflected compromises that he hammered out.

Under Rafsanjani, Iran's legislature had also become the most open institution in government. Its feisty debates were similar to the heated sessions in Britain's House of Commons or Israel's Knesset. Stinging government criticism and conflicting visions of the revolution were vented on its floor; even Rafsanjani was occasionally criticized by its members. Within the inherent limitations of an authoritarian state, the speaker had built parliament into the revolution's safety valve, the voice of Iran's varied constituencies. Just as the ayatollah personified the revolution, Rafsanjani had come to personify the state.

For all the revolution's severity, its parliament had developed a rather informal air. In keeping with the taboo on neckties, the satanic symbol of Westernization, the nonclerical members wore open-necked collars with their suits. But not all members were men. Since the first election, the *majlis* had female members, and more women had run in 1988 than ever before. Although women's voting rights and the right to run for national office were among the first major issues Khomeini had protested in the 1960s, he had not sought their repeal after the shah's demise. In 1988, three women won seats in the 270-member body.

Nor were members all typecast. Jews, Armenian and Chaldean/Assyrian Christians, and Zoroastrians, members of what had been the dominant faith in Iran before the seventh-century Islamic conquest, all had seats proportionate to their population strengths. Each was sworn into parliament on his own holy book, and they were seated, like everyone else, according to numbers picked from a big box, a draw repeated every six months. The Baha'i, an offshoot of Shi'ism viewed as heretical, was the only major religious community denied representation by the constitution.*

In many ways, parliament and its speaker reflected the evolution of Iran's revolutionaries during the Islamic Republic's first decade. Like his clerical counterparts, Rafsanjani, who as a mullah took his name from his birthplace in Rafsanjan, had no experience in practical political administration when he came to power. Born in 1934, the second of a prominent pistachio farmer's nine children, he began serious religious training at the age of fourteen.[3]

---

* The Baha'i were also victims of widespread persecution. Because their ideas were viewed as heretical and because many Baha'i had served under the shah, thousands were interrogated and/or imprisoned, particularly during the revolution's first years. At least four hundred have reportedly been executed since 1979.

He first entered the political arena in 1963 as a Khomeini disciple
to oppose the shah. During the imam's exile, he had been a crucial
link in the *talabeh* network that the ayatollah had left behind. Although his activities had largely been limited to preaching, he had
been imprisoned by the shah at least four times between 1964 and
1978.[4] In 1988, a time-weathered poster of the speaker was still
visible in the window of a carpet shop on Vali-e Asr Avenue. Made
from an old mug shot, it showed Rafsanjani, his hair cropped short,
wearing a T-shirt and prison overalls. Under his round, beardless
face was number 3324–1354.

After the shah's ouster, however, Rafsanjani rose quickly in the
revolutionary hierarchy. He was a member of the secret Revolutionary Council, a cofounder of the Islamic Republic Party, and a
cabinet official. He even dabbled in the military as Khomeini's personal representative on the Supreme Defense Council that ran the
war and, briefly, as commander of the Revolutionary Guards. But
the parliament, more than any other job, exposed him to the nation's problems—and provided hands-on experience in addressing
them.

The speaker also shrewdly navigated, and survived, the labyrin-
thine Oriental intrigue of Iranian politics. To build and consolidate
his own network, he placed family and friends in key support positions. Among them was his Berkeley-educated brother, who headed
the Voice and Vision of Iran, the media network that runs national
radio and television—and controls exposure of politicians and issues. He also built up IOUs among other Iranian clans and political
cliques by mediating their disputes. During the 1985 crisis between
the president and the prime minister over control of the government, Rafsanjani scored points with both sides by finding a compromise formula that kept both in power—and, in turn, strengthened
his own position.

As a *hojatoleslam,* which translates as "authority on Islam" and
is the rank beneath an ayatollah, Rafsanjani did not have the religious credentials to inherit Khomeini's mantle—at least as the job
of Supreme Jurisprudent was originally defined. But by 1988, he
was more popular than any other contender. Although he was as
ruthless as other Iranian officials, Rafsanjani's demeanor and personal style had helped him to develop a following among ordinary
Iranians. During sermons at Tehran University's Friday prayer services, he cajoled and occasionally even joked with the crowd in his
soft, almost melodious voice. In speaking of the impact of Iraq's use
of chemical warfare, he once even wept in public. His popularity

was evident in the polls. He regularly received the highest number of votes for parliament from his district. And, in the 1983 election for the Assembly of Experts, he won the second highest tally for the body mandated to pick Khomeini's successor. By 1988, his de facto power was such that many Iranians had taken to calling him *Akbar shah*, implying that he was gaining the power of an Iranian king.

His ability to be all things to all people was reflected in a popular story in Tehran: Rafsanjani was riding in a car with President Khamenei and Prime Minister Musavi. When they came to a T-junction in the road, the driver asked which way he should turn. The president replied, "Right." The prime minister said, "Left." Rafsanjani then instructed, "Signal left, but turn right." The speaker's political positions were, indeed, often enigmatic. To the outside world, his statements on domestic practices, international diplomacy and the Gulf war had earned him a reputation as a "moderate" or a "pragmatist." And, in context of the revolution, he often was. At home, the speaker had urged a reexamination of stonings as Islamic punishment, a review of komiteh excesses, and gradual economic reforms. In foreign policy, he had urged better relations with the outside world, and he had aided in the release of the TWA 847 hostages. On the war front, he had argued against rejecting Resolution 598 outright.

But Rafsanjani had never abandoned the ideals of expanding the Islamic vision, at home or abroad. He was vehement about maintaining Iran's political and economic independence from both East and West. And he genuinely believed in sacrifice and martyrdom in defense of the faith. But having been involved in running a complex government, he also understood that the state had to survive in order for the revolution, and the ideas it represented, to succeed. That sense of realism had, specifically, led Rafsanjani to risk dealing with the Great Satan in 1986.

By the summer of 1988, having finally weathered the Irangate debacle, Rafsanjani began moving strategically to further consolidate his position. He knew that daring new steps were needed to help preserve the Islamic Republic.[5] For, Rafsanjani correctly recognized, the revolution was in serious trouble. On June 2, Khomeini appointed him commander-in-chief, a position technically reserved for the imam that the speaker managed to maneuver for himself. On June 7, the *majlis* gave him a ninth term as speaker. According to the official tally, only five of the secret ballots were blank; it was the largest vote that he had ever received. Having secured Iran's

most powerful political and military titles, Rafsanjani began seeking
a mandate for change.

•

By June 1988, the Islamic Republic almost desperately needed
change. The April defeat at Faw had been followed by a series of
further military setbacks on all three fronts. Iran countered with
several small offensives, but most were quickly beaten back. The
trickle of Iraqi victories soon became a roll. In May, Iraq took
Shalamcheh on its southern frontier. The Iranians struck back in
what appeared to be largely a face-saving or morale-boosting operation. But it, also, failed. In June, Iraq captured Mehran on its
central front and some forty strategic peaks in its mountainous
northern Kurdish province.

In late June, Baghdad regained control over the marshy Majnun
Islands, which Iran had captured four years earlier, as well as the
estimated thirty billion barrels of oil beneath it. Like the Faw offensive, the attack was a rout, lasting only eight hours.[6] Iran still occupied Iraqi territory, but Majnun had been the last strategically and
economically important property in its hands. "Because of heavy
chemical weapons attacks by the enemy, the combatants of Islam
have been deployed in new defensive positions," the Islamic Republic News Agency conceded after the loss.[7] Chemical weapons
had clearly been a major factor in Baghdad's stunning victories. A
popular, but unconfirmed, story told by foreign military attachés in
Tehran claimed that Iraq used only smoke bombs in one attack; the
psychological impact of chemical weapons was such that the Iranians had fled at the mere sight of the clouds. In the three months
since Iraq's success at Faw in April, the Islamic Republic had retreated from an estimated four thousand square miles and lost tens
of millions of dollars in war materiel.[8] Iran's military appeared to
be losing its will to fight—and, in the process, its most potent
weapon.

Meanwhile, the year-old National Liberation Army of the Mojahedin-e Khalq, the theocracy's old rival whose membership had
been forced underground or into exile in 1981, moved into Iran
alongside the Iraqis. Although the Mojahedin were widely viewed
at home as traitors because of their alignment with Iraq, domestic
discontent had reached a level in several war-torn areas that the
Mojahedin troops were welcomed. For the theocracy, the symbolism of Iranians fighting Iranians was particularly unnerving.

The theocrats had not ignored the growing antiwar sentiment,
nor were they totally opposed to a settlement. In the year since

passage of Resolution 598, Iran had probed its potential, criticizing but still never rejecting it. Tehran had hoped to alter the sequence of its provisions for ending the conflict. But the Islamic Republic had held out for an international commission to determine responsibility for launching the war before it would agree to a ceasefire; Tehran counted on a commission to apportion most or all of the blame on Baghdad. The theocrats needed a face-saving formula to sell at home and, most of all, to Khomeini. Whatever public opinion favored, any policy shift had to have his sanction. And the imam's grudge, both personal and politico-religious, against Iraqi President Saddam Hussein ran so deep that he was still calling for "war until victory."

But a year of negotiating had failed to convince the United Nations, where the Islamic Republic had few friends. And the Iraqis were clearly holding out for the original terms: a ceasefire in place before an international body investigated which party provoked the war—a formula less likely to result in Baghdad's condemnation. Meanwhile, Iran's Supreme Defense Council—made up of army, Pasdaran and other military commanders as well as government officials and the imam's representatives—had been deadlocked in divisive debates over tactics, goals and control of strategy.* The tension, often a microcosm of the broader intragovernment disputes, at least once spilled over onto the battlefront. After one loss, the long-standing rivalry between the regular army and the Revolutionary Guards broke down into open fighting.[9]

Rafsanjani's appointment as commander-in-chief had been designed, in part, to provide decisive leadership for the war effort. It had originally led to speculation that the speaker would restructure the military and launch a new mobilization. In hindsight, Rafsanjani's real intent was clearly to find a means of ending the war. He may have hoped to make gains sufficient to allow Iran to sue for a face-saving peace with Iraq that might pass as a victory at home. Other, more conspiratorial reports claimed that he was in fact prepared to tolerate further military setbacks in order to convince Iran's hawks that holding out any longer would be futile.[10]

Either way, by July 2, Iran's military predicament had deteriorated to the point that the Iranian leadership had to acknowledge

---

* One of the most hotly contested issues was whether Iran should respond to Iraq's use of chemical weapons with its own less sophisticated poison gases. Despite several strong voices against it, on grounds that Iran would lose whatever small moral edge it had gained in the eyes of the outside world, Iran did make comparatively limited use of chemical warfare, mainly mustard gas, in 1987 and 1988, according to U.S. intelligence.

the situation publicly. In an interview broadcast on nationwide television, Rafsanjani conceded, "As the present situation indicates, it appears that our enemies, the enemies of Islam, are determined to prevent Iran's vindication of our rights. . . . We are not only faced with the issue of territory or war on the battlefronts." More significantly, he noted, "Whenever there is a mention of victory on the war front, we should stress that we have also left the road to a nonmilitary end to the war open."[11] Rafsanjani's candor symbolized that the breaking point had been reached. To end the war, however, Iran still needed a pretext.

•

Just after 10:45 A.M. the day after Rafsanjani's televised interview, Iran Air Flight 655 took off from the southern port city of Bandar Abbas for the short, 140-mile hop across the Gulf to Dubai. The trip, affordable for even lower-middle-class Iranians, had long been one of Iran's most popular routes, and the United Arab Emirates was a haven for stocking up on business imports and basic necessities increasingly unavailable at home. Of all the Gulf sheikhdoms, Dubai had also maintained the warmest relations with Tehran. The flight was packed; 290, including 66 children, were aboard the giant European-built airbus. When he took off, the pilot apparently did not know that he was flying into a maelstrom.

Thirty-five minutes earlier, an American helicopter from the USS *Vincennes* had come under fire from an Iranian gunboat near the Strait of Hormuz—and not far from Bandar Abbas. As in the past, the United States had responded. One of the navy's most sophisticated cruisers, the *Vincennes*, along with the USS *Elmer Montgomery*, had fired on three Iranian gunboats positioned nearby. Two had sunk, the third had been damaged.

Tension was also high in the southern Gulf because U.S. intelligence indicated an Iranian military build up in Bandar Abbas and at the Strait over the previous two months. At Bandar Abbas airport, which served both civilian and military aircraft, Iran had deployed more of its American-made Phantom F-4s and F-14s. And, at the Strait, construction of a new launch site for Chinese-made Silkworms had been accelerated.[12] Recent history added to the pressure. The skippers of the more than two dozen American warships deployed in the Gulf all remembered what had happened to the USS *Stark* fourteen months earlier. Thirty-seven Americans had died when the captain failed to recognize the threat from an Iraqi bomber in time; the skipper had been forced to retire.

Two minutes after Iran Air Flight 655 took off, radar operators on the *Vincennes* spotted what they thought was a small, sleek F-14 fighter descending on the American warship. Mistakenly, they assumed that an Iranian aircraft was trying to avenge the American strike on the gunboats. In fact, the bulky, lumbering airbus, having received authorization to climb to flight altitude, was instead ascending into the designated commercial air corridor. The *Vincennes* radioed seven alerts warning the aircraft that it would fire if the plane did not change course. When Flight 655 did not respond, Captain Will C. Rogers III ordered the crew to commence fire. Seven minutes after Flight 655 took off, two surface-to-air missiles raced toward the civilian aircraft. At least one missile hit, breaking the plane into thousands of pieces and killing all on board. The downing of the Iran Air flight, which investigators later blamed on "human error," was the sixth-worst disaster in aviation history.

The initial reaction in Tehran was predictable. Unable to believe that the latest in radar technology could not tell the difference between "an eagle and a little sparrow," angry Iran called the accident "the greatest war crime in the contemporary era." For days, the gruesome pictures of mutilated bodies floating in the Gulf ran on Iranian television. At the official funeral in the capital, a mob of ten thousand mourners, many balancing coffins on their shoulders, surged through the streets shouting "Death to America" with chilling new energy. President Khamenei declared that the Islamic Republic would avenge the martyrs' deaths "with all our might . . . wherever and whenever we decide."[13]

Public reaction, by Iranian standards, was in fact rather muted. The crowds, including the one that assembled to hear Khamenei, were small compared with the millions who had taken to the streets in the revolution's early days. "People are angry, but they have the ability to absorb it," said a former Iranian ambassador who had five friends on the plane. "If they have the ability to absorb eight years of ferocious atrocities, including massive use of missiles and chemical weaponry, they have the ability to absorb this, too."[14] War weariness had numbed even the outrage over the shooting down of a civilian aircraft.

Within a week after the tragedy, the official posture began to take an unexpected turn. Leading officials suggested, in fact, that Iran would not retaliate. "The world knows we can respond to the crime. The United States is trying to push us to do the same thing, but we will not do anything wrong, not do as the United States did," Rafsanjani said. "If we do the same, world opinion will be against us, and the world will not listen to us." He even warned against some "amateurish action" that could, in turn, "remove the wave of propaganda that is now heaped on America's head." During the initial outburst, Tehran had been full of unconfirmed reports that the imam would issue a *fatwa*, or religious edict, declaring war against the United States.[15] But that, too, never came to pass.

Behind the scenes, Rafsanjani moved quickly. He first called together Iran's military commanders in mid-July for an assessment. It appears to have been a calculated move; he surely had little doubt about what they would say. For most of the session, the commanders reportedly did the talking: listing what war materiel had been lost, outlining the reasons for recent losses, projecting what was needed to counterstrike. The overall assessment was that the Islamic Republic had neither the time nor the resources, human or financial, to hold out indefinitely. Any further losses, they conceded, might even increase the danger of an outright defeat and a public backlash against the revolution. In the end, Rafsanjani won an endorsement, although not with total consensus, to pursue a means to end the war.

Again with calculated effect, Rafsanjani, with the support of President Khamenei, then called together ranking officials from all four branches of government—the cabinet, the *majlis*, the Supreme Court and the Council of Guardians—on July 16. The debate was again heated and lasted well into the night; several of the theocrats reportedly argued that ending the war short of victory was a betrayal of the war's martyrs, of the country and, most of all, of Islam. But when presented with the hard facts, military and economic, the majority finally conceded that, to preserve the revolution, something had to be done. They agreed to let Rafsanjani and Khamenei take the issue to Khomeini. The third and final step was to consult Ayatollah Montazeri in Qom. The heir apparent reportedly told emissaries that he not only endorsed an effort to end the war but had been urging it for more than a year.[16] The ground was well laid for what would be Rafsanjani's most daring political venture.

•

Shortly after his return to Iran in 1979, Ayatollah Khomeini and his entourage had moved to an austerely simple compound in the northern Tehran suburb of Jamaran, which the regime's opponents relished pointing out translates as the "haven of snakes." The imam had originally located in Qom, but his presence in Tehran was vital to the revolution's direction and cohesion. So the ayatollah, his wife, Batoul, his only surviving son and chief of staff Ahmad, and assorted aides and grandchildren had settled in a complex centered around a mosque in the foothills of the Elburz Mountains less than a mile from where the shah used to live.

By July 1988, a huge white banner was stretched across Jamaran's high entrance gates manned by a police unit of the Revolutionary Guards. "God, God," it beseeched rather plaintively, "Keep Khomeini alive until the Mahdi's revolution." The Mahdi is the "rightly guided one" awaited by Muslims to restore the original order and purity of the Islamic faith. Tehran's walls were full of such signs, and speeches in the *majlis* and official letters to Khomeini's office often ended with felicitations on the imam's health. The depth of feeling that the revolution's fate depended on the ayatollah was reflected, perhaps inadvertently, in another sign at the airport, "Islam will be in our blood as long as Khomeini is our leader."

While the cohesion of the revolution did clearly still depend on the imam, its future was, in fact, increasingly being decided by the younger theocrats who, over the previous decade, had been implementing his vision. The ayatollah kept in touch through his son, Ahmad, through the stream of visitors and theologians who provided reports and intelligence about developments throughout Iran, and through nearly obsessive monitoring of local and foreign radio programs. His days were full. Yet his isolation in the Jamaran compound cut him off from the mood on the streets. His frame of reference was the memory of adoring millions who stampeded to catch a glimpse of him when he first returned to Iran. He knew little firsthand about the depths of disillusionment or the growing hardships.

Even if he had, his unyielding commitment had always been to Islam first, then to the faithful. His version of Islam meant submission and sacrifice, which he still practiced in starkly simple surroundings. Others, he believed, should too. The revolution was thus sacrosanct, and compromise was, literally, anathema—first with the Pahlavi dynasty, then with the United States and now with Iraqi President Saddam Hussein. For all his wily genius, the imam had become the lonely, valiant crusader, the ideologue so committed to the war that he was endangering his own dream.

Khomeini's intransigence on the war was symptomatic of a broader problem for the Islamic Republic: The revolution had been virtually locked in place for the better part of eight years because of the war. Breaking the logjam had become a necessity. Conventional wisdom, both inside and outside Iran, had always been that the war would not end before Khomeini's death. But Rafsanjani and others knew that, without the imam's imprimatur on a ceasefire falling short of Saddam's ouster, Iran's war policy would almost certainly become a centerpiece of the power struggle after his passing—potentially at even greater cost to Iran. Ending the war was thus also vital in getting the revolution back on track and in establishing its direction before the imam died. In effect, the potentially violatile post-Khomeini era was also at stake.

Against this background, Rafsanjani and Khamenei made their pilgrimage to Jamaran on July 17 to present the issue of the war for Khomeini's ruling. Rafsanjani clearly hoped to swing the imam around—as many Iranians believed that he had done in presenting Khomeini with a virtual fait accompli to win his endorsement of the arms-for-hostages swap with the Great Satan. But the evidence had to be overwhelming.

No one but the few present knew the content of the delicate discussions. The tragedy of Flight 655 and the potential of future mass civilian deaths as well as the possibility of a military defeat were undoubtedly the basis of the talks. Historic and religious parallels, including the early setbacks of the Prophet Mohammad and of the first Shi'ite communities, were almost certainly a topic; they were later used in public to justify the decision. Diplomats from countries with close ties to Iran later claimed that Rafsanjani also made it clear that he, and the government, could no longer function under the pressures of the war. Some even said that he subtly implied that, under those circumstances, he might feel forced to resign if the war were not brought to an end.[17] Whatever the approach, Khomeini, in the end, succumbed.

The next day, fifteen days after the downing of Iran Air Flight 655, Khamenei officially notified the United Nations secretary-general. The war, he said in an accompanying letter, had grown to "unprecedented dimensions . . . engulfing innocent civilians. Under these circumstances, we have decided to officially declare that the Islamic Republic of Iran—because of the importance it attaches to saving the lives of human beings and the establishment of justice and regional and international peace and security—accepts the Security Council resolution."

The imam, with obvious reluctance, publicly decreed his support for the decision two days later. "I had promised to fight to the last drop of my blood and to my last breath. Taking this decision was more deadly than drinking hemlock," said a statement released in his name. "I submitted myself to God's will and drank this drink for His satisfaction. To me, it would have been more bearable to accept death and martyrdom. Today's decision is based only on the interest of the Islamic Republic." By August 20, the day the United Nations officially declared a truce, most guns had fallen silent.

For Rafsanjani and others who had put their necks on the line, a turning point had been reached. The conflict's conclusion represented an opportunity to breathe new life into the revolution and to address issues stalemated or deferred by the war. The imam's decision had set a precedent, compromising the revolution's ideals for the sake of the state's survival. They intended to use it as a mandate for further changes. The day after the cease-fire was in place, Rafsanjani declared, "Thanks to God, a new era is starting." [18]

•

The war's end did, indeed, appear to herald a new era. Once the shock and confusion about the abrupt decision, which stunned Iranians as much as it did the outside world, wore off, the changes began. Almost overnight, the Islamic Republic's rigid lifestyle showed signs of relaxation. Tapes crisscrossed on windows to limit the impact of implosion from missiles finally came off. The black-market value of the dollar more than halved. Refugees spoke of returning to rebuild their lives in the war-ravaged western provinces, while families who had sent their draft-age sons abroad made plans for their homecomings. Many exiles also inquired about returning home. While bitterness ran deep among the Hizbollah faithful who served as the revolution's backbone and among many families who had lost martyrs, the overwhelming mood in Iran was relief.

The shifting winds were evident in even small changes. Khomeini rulings opened the way for the return of chess and disputed forms of music. Chess had been banned since the shah's ouster, in part because of the pieces' association with the monarchy; the imam ruled that it was again permitted—as long as gambling was not involved. He also ruled that the sale and use of certain musical instruments was not forbidden by Islam. In the fall of 1988, the music of Beethoven and Mozart returned to the concert halls of Tehran. On September 1, Shakespeare's *The Merchant of Venice* translated into Farsi, opened at a theater complex built during the shah's reign. [19]

The changes did not occur without controversy. One of Iran's most conservative papers published an eloquent poem entitled "For Whom Do the Violin Bows Move?" It suggested that the Beethoven and Mozart concerts catered more to "the worm of monarchic culture"—specifically women with "pushed back scarves" who did not observe modest Islamic dress and men with "protruding bellies" who had grown fat off the black market—than to the *mostazafin* poor who were martyred in the war. The regime, however, stood firm. Khomeini told his followers not to "pay too much attention to what the stupid, backward or illiterate clergy might think."[20] Iran's Supervisor of Revolutionary Songs and Tunes told a press conference that the decision to have Tehran's symphony orchestra play the European classics was "a serene policy in the direction of recruiting music fans."[21] The revolution was, in effect, also trying to recruit support from outside the circles of religious zealotry. The day after the cease-fire, Rafsanjani conceded candidly, "A revolution in which people are not involved will not survive."[22]

The "new era" affected more than domestic policies. Iran's tentative opening to the outside world, launched shortly before the war ended, rapidly gained momentum. On the same day that the Islamic Republic accepted the cease-fire, it also announced resumption of relations with Canada. Again, Iran had made a concession. After eight years of demanding that Ottawa formally apologize for sneaking out six American embassy employees hidden for three months during the 1979–81 hostage affair, the precondition was dropped.

Rafsanjani had hinted earlier at a new accommodation in Iran's foreign policy. "One of the incorrect measures was that, in the revolutionary atmosphere, we made enemies of [some Western countries]. We pushed those who could have been neutral into hostility," he said. "Now the Foreign Ministry has been instructed to tread the correct path at this stage. It is one that we should always have followed."[23] The day after the cease-fire, he went further, "Our postwar foreign policy will be more open than that during the war."[24]

The extent to which Tehran was prepared to go to rebuild diplomatic bridges had been evident during its first gesture of rapprochement with France. After almost a year of tension over the nastiest chapter in Iran's "war of the embassies," Paris and Tehran had come to terms in June. In a "no-deal deal" reminiscent of the United States' resolution of the TWA hostage episode, France returned one-third of a billion-dollar loan from Iran dating back to the shah's era. In exchange, the final three French hostages—two diplomats and a French cameraman held by the pro-Iranian Revolutionary Justice Organization—in Lebanon had been released in May. Formal relations were restored a month before the cease-fire.

Overtures were also made to Britain. One public offer included intervention to help win release of one Irish and two British hostages in exchange for London's aid in winning freedom for the four Iranians abducted in 1982. Relations were on the verge of being restored during the summer; negotiations soured temporarily when Prime Minister Margaret Thatcher backed Washington's claim that the United States was acting defensively when it shot down the Iran airbus. But, by the end of September, Tehran and London announced their intent to restore relations.

Kuwait also reopened its embassy, which had been closed since the attack following the 1987 Mecca massacre. Iran even sent a twenty-nine-man team to the Seoul Olympics, where it picked up a silver medal.[25] "In an interdependent world, Islam will be the loser if one does not participate in the Olympics because of its adverse psychological impact; if you are not part of the United Nations; and if we are not present in every international arena today," Rafsanjani told a Friday prayer service in September.[26] Commenting on the burst of activity, an Iranian official conceded that the *majlis* speaker and his allies were "picking up where they left off at Irangate."[27]

The diplomatic thaw was not one-way. Foreign trade delegations from such diverse countries as Italy and China, Turkey and Nigeria, the Soviet Union and Australia flooded Tehran to discuss their share in Iran's potentially profitable reconstruction. For the first time since the revolution, Iran's annual International Trade Fair opened in Tehran to an overwhelming response. Thirty-six countries, including some of the United States' closest allies, responded to the Islamic Republic's invitation to display their wares. Britain, which had sent no representation the previous year, sponsored more than 60 companies in 1988; another 120 were turned away for lack of space.

At the opening ceremonies, President Khamenei said, "We have bitter experiences with foreign investments in our country. But these experiences will not be an obstacle for those countries wishing to establish healthy ties and trade. We accept the world's knowledge and technology as a standard and an inseparable part of foreign trade. . . . We must make use of the knowledge, expertise and resources of the foreigner" in reconstructing the war-ravaged country.[28]

To counter potential disillusionment over Iran's failure at the war front, the theocrats had begun to shift the focus of the revolution away from the war and export of the revolution to reconstruction and long-delayed development at home. Two weeks after the United Nations cease-fire took effect, Khomeini ruled that the government should "allow people to import consumer goods from abroad and sell them. If the people do everything by themselves, without any control, there will be corruption. But neither can the government do everything by itself because it has neither the means nor the power. . . . People should be free to run businesses."[29] After almost a decade of failing to decide whether or not to nationalize foreign trade, the theocracy finally had guidelines guaranteeing at least some rights of free enterprise.

Reconstruction and normalizing foreign relations, however, also led to further divisions. In September, Prime Minister Musavi resigned. The official reason was his fear that as many as eight of his cabinet ministers would not be confirmed by parliament, which would cripple his government. But, in the kind of subterfuge that so often undermined the regime, Musavi's office then leaked a letter to President Khamenei outlining the real reasons. Power, he implied, was centered in the hands of a few, an inner clique, especially on budget and foreign policy issues; powers rightfully belonging to his office had been usurped.[30] Musavi, the regime's ranking noncleric, was among those most committed to strong government control over the economy and other aspects of national life. The president rejected the resignation, while Khomeini admonished him, "In moments of anger, we should not do things that will be taken advantage of by the enemies of Islam."[31]

Throughout the fall of 1988, an undercurrent of tension ran through Tehran as the so-called pragmatists consolidated their hold on government. When the *majlis* did finally hold its vote of confidence on the cabinet, key hard-line ministers were either ousted or narrowly approved. Revolutionary Guards Minister Rafiqdoost was rejected, while Interior Minister Mohtashami, who as ambassador to Syria had earlier been linked to several terrorist attacks against Western targets in Lebanon, was roundly condemned before mustering just enough votes for reconfirmation. Of Mohtashami, one member of parliament said, "He is well-known for his hiring and firing; he regards himself as the only power. He neither consults the clergy, nor does he pay attention to the deputies. With regard to the law, he acts wherever he sees fit and in accordance with his own will."[32] The reconfirmation hearings put hard-line elements in check —and in an angry, defensive posture.

The divisions were particularly evident on two issues: relations with the United States and a new wave of political executions. The apparent contradictions in the debate on both underscored the delicacy, even volatility, of shifting the revolution's course.

In early November, Iran, as usual, marked the anniversary of the 1979 seizure of the United States embassy with protests in front of the former "den of spies" in downtown Tehran. But this time the crowd was small and the demonstrations without much fervor. More telling was an anniversary editorial in the country's most conservative paper, which boldly commented,

> It is extreme pessimism, shortsightedness and lack of confidence to take any kind of relation with the West as compromise, surrender and a beginning of dependency. . . . We must begin to believe that, if necessary, we can have relations with the United States with complete self-reliance and confidence from a position of strength. . . . We have nothing to lose by establishing proper relations with the superpowers of the West based on justified rights of the Islamic Republic. Not only will we have nothing to lose, but also by using proper means we will . . . regain our lost rights in the world.[33]

The issues of relations with the Great Satan had become a topic of open conversation and speculation. Within three weeks after the war's end, a deputy foreign minister had said, "Our reluctance to talk with Washington does not imply fear. We do not regard any talks to be disagreeable per se. If they change their policies and treat us with mutual respect and nonintervention in our affairs, the relations with the United States will be like that with other countries."[34] And in early October, an Indian lecturer with U.S. residency, who along with three American professors had been abducted in Beirut by Islamic Jihad for the Liberation of Palestine twenty-one months earlier, was freed. The release was widely viewed by Washington and by foreign envoys in Tehran as a harbinger of a tentative thaw.

Musavi was again among the most vehement opposition, charging that "the resumption of relations with Washington is a betrayal of the ideals of the revolution and of those who have made sacrifices and have been guarding it."[35] More important was the imam's last word. In a nine-point edict outlining the priorities of reconstruction, Khomeini effectively reprimanded the theocrats for even conceiving of the idea. He said,

> Recently, overt and covert Eastern and Western hands have resorted to a new trick to cause rifts and differences among the supporters of

the Islamic revolution. They have tried to make dear senior officials
of our country, certain *majlis*, government and spiritual figures, think
and act in ways that lean toward dependence, to deviate from previous positions, and ultimately to lean toward the East or the
West. . . . It is religiously incumbent on all of you to try to wipe
away the last traces of this country's dependence on foreigners. . . .
And I am confident that the Iranian people, particularly our youth,
will keep alive in their hearts anger and hatred for the criminal
Soviet Union and the warmongering United States. This must be until the banner of Islam flies over every house in the world.[36]

Less public was the debate over the wave of arrests and executions.
As Tehran began peace talks with Baghdad, the ruling mullahs went
to war at home again with domestic rivals. The majority of those
detained and almost summarily executed were members or sympathizers of the Mojahedin, which had demonstrated an ability to
challenge Iran militarily, as well as other leftist groups.[37] Amnesty
International described the three hundred known executions as
"the tip of the iceberg." The human rights group reported that the
sweep, which began in July and continued through the fall, was
"the biggest wave of secret political executions since the early
1980s."[38] Among the victims were teenagers, women and some
who had been rearrested after serving earlier prison terms.

   The security sweep also did not have unanimous backing. Ayatollah Montazeri, the heir apparent, wrote the warden of Tehran's
Evin Prison, "One does not fight a doctrine by killing because no
problem can be settled this way. One fights back with a fair doctrine."[39] He warned theology students that, if the government continued to ignore the voices of dissent, then "the dissenting words
will turn into bullets."[40] And, finally, in an open letter to the imam
in January 1989, he wrote, "For what valid reasons . . . has our
judiciary approved these executions, which can result in nothing
but damaging the face of our revolution and the system?"[41] But the
decisive voice had again been Khomeini's. Angered by the Mojahedin's betrayal in fighting alongside Iraq, he reportedly personally
ordered the hangings of Mojahedin members, either those captured
or those already imprisoned who had not "repented" their opposition. The order was interpreted with wide latitude. By early 1989,
an estimated twenty-four hundred had been sent to the gallows and
before firing squads.[42]

   At a time when the revolution badly needed direction and resolution of its long-standing disputes, Khomeini held it back. For each

bold new move undertaken by Rafsanjani, Khamenei and others, the imam issued a check. Despite the new latitude the imam allowed in rulings on chess, music and free enterprise, he had not deviated from his fundamental premise. "As long as I live, I will not allow the revolution or the regime to deviate from the path set for it," Khomeini had warned in the autumn.[43] It was a chilling omen of things to come.

•

In February 1989, the Islamic Republic held nationwide celebrations to mark the tenth anniversary of the revolution. Despite the parades, fireworks displays and self-congratulatory speeches, there was, in fact, little to celebrate. For all the apparent movement in the heady days after the war's end, Iran had made virtually no progress in securing a permanent peace or in launching reconstruction. United Nations mediation between Iran and Iraq remained deadlocked over every major issue, from the return of prisoners of war to control of the Shatt al-Arab. At home, the imam blocked reconstruction that might, even peripherally, involve the outside world. With no new capital and limited foreign help, Iran was again drifting, particularly economically.

In early 1989, the dollar's black-market value approached the high rates of the war years. Costs of basic necessities surpassed the wartime peak, and the wartime rationing system for meat, sugar, rice, butter, eggs, cheese, kerosene, gasoline and soap powder was still in force. Few men returning from the front found employment, one of the reasons for the growing drug epidemic; because of military and economic pressures and the banishment of alcohol, the use particularly of opium, a popular narcotic in Iran both before and during the revolution, had soared. The electricity crisis was so serious that the government asked Iranians to be sparing in using the strings of bright-colored lights normally put up for celebrations. The lack of repairs and reconstruction continued to mean blackouts for up to six hours a day.

During the tenth anniversary commemorations, three of the nation's leading theocrats were surprisingly candid about the revolution's mistakes. In interviews with Iranian journalists, Rafsanjani called Tehran's demand for a military victory over Baghdad "too big a bite." He added that the constitution had been written too quickly and that it was "incomplete." President Khamenei conceded that the revolutionaries who took over the state had initially been "inexperienced." On the war's end, he said that Iran had not "calculated" on the possibility that the United States would send its navy to the Gulf and "pull the world along with her." And Supreme Court Justice Musavi Ardabili said that he believed the 1979–81 American hostage ordeal had lasted too long. On the war, he claimed that it "should have been stopped after the liberation of Khorramshahr" in 1982. And of the revolution's status ten years after the takeover, he admitted, "We are still at a stage that we are trying to blame others for our sins." [44]

In contrast, the imam appeared intractable about the revolution's purity and almost oblivious to the postwar deterioration. "The people should make their choice: Either welfare and consumerism, or hardship and independence," he warned in early 1989. "This could take several years, but the people will definitely choose the latter." [45] And he showed no sign of tolerating less than total devotion to the faith or even human error. The week before the tenth anniversary, four men from the Voice and Vision of Iran were sentenced to jail terms of four and five years, plus fifty lashes. Their crime was airing an interview with an Iranian woman who, the imam believed, had insulted the Prophet's daughter by suggesting that she might not be the ideal role model for the Islamic woman. If there was intent, Khomeini added, then the men should receive the death sentence.* [46] Nor, finally, had he been humbled after a decade. Shortly before the anniversary, he had brazenly written Soviet President Mikhail Gorbachev to suggest that Moscow make a study of Islam because the faith "can undo the knots of fundamental problems of humanity" and "easily fill the ideological vacuum of your system." [47]

Indeed, Khomeini appeared to be prepared to allow his nation to face even further convulsions.

•

The trouble actually began outside Iran. Demonstrations in Muslim communities from India and South Africa to Britain first drew international attention to Salman Rushdie's *The Satanic Verses.* The novel's satirical and profane treatment of the Prophet Mohammad, whose human weaknesses undermine his credibility as God's messenger, and of Islam's origins had ignited Muslim rage. In mid-February 1989, the anger turned into a rampage when riots outside the American Cultural Center in the Pakistani capital led to six deaths and more than a hundred injuries; violence spread to India, where another died during a mass protest. Under growing pressure,

---

* His daughter eventually talked him into pardoning the four.

nations with large Islamic communities in Asia, the Middle East and Africa condemned or banned a book critically acclaimed in the West.

Despite the brewing storm, the Islamic Republic virtually ignored *The Satanic Verses* since its initial publication in Britain five months earlier. So, no one was prepared for the bombshell dropped on Tehran Radio's 2:00 P.M. news bulletin on February 14, three days after the revolution's tenth anniversary. Khomeini had just issued a *fatwa*, the radio announced. "The author of *The Satanic Verses* book, which is against Islam, the Prophet and the Koran, and all those involved in its publication who were aware of its content, are sentenced to death," declared the imam's religious edict. "I call on zealous Muslims to promptly execute them on the spot they find them so that no one else will dare to blasphemize Muslim sanctities."

At first, the edict seemed little more than a tantrum. But Khomeini clearly intended to follow through. The next day was declared "a day of public mourning to protest the Great Satan's new plot." In cities throughout Iran, thousands once again took to the streets amidst shouts of "Death to America," "Death to Britain" and "Death to Salman Rushdie," the book's Muslim author who, although Indian-born, lived in Britain. Crowds who surrounded and stoned the newly reopened British embassy were reminiscent of the early American hostage crisis. Tehran also offered a $2.6 million reward to Rushdie's executioner—with a provision for another million if the avenger were an Iranian. The imam's outburst had quickly become a tangible threat, made all the more frightening by the Islamic Republic's record on aiding and abetting terrorism. The momentum sparked the most rupturous literary clash in Islam's thirteen-hundred-year history.

The impact was felt throughout the world. Rushdie and his American wife went into hiding, under the protection of Scotland Yard. American and British book dealers initially pulled the volume off their shelves, abandoning the principle of free speech for fear of violence. Anonymous callers threatened to blow up British airliners flying to India. A Canadian official who ruled against banning the book was put under guard after reported death threats. Four bookstores, two in London, one in Italy, and one in Berkeley, California, were firebombed, as was a New York City newspaper that ran an editorial supporting the right to read *The Satanic Verses*. In Belgium, a local Muslim leader who had opposed the death sentence was assassinated, while Nigerian Muslim militants called for the death sentence on local Nobel laureate Wole Soyinka for defending Rushdie.

Even ordinary people and remote corners of the globe were caught up in the furor. The government of the Comoro Islands, a former French colony in the Indian Ocean, seized all foreign newspapers carrying excerpts of the book and notified foreigners that they would be expelled if found in possession of the book. Overnight, any issue seen as offensive to Islam was hands-off. French singer Véronique Sanson pulled the song "Allah" from her repertoire, while *Veiled Threat,* a film critical of Khomeini, was withdrawn from the Los Angeles Film Festival. Pakistan banned copies of *Newsweek* that carried a forbidden picture of the Prophet Mohammad.

European Community members responded to the death threat by jointly condemning Khomeini's edict and then, individually, by recalling their ambassadors. But the theocracy appeared unfazed, pushing even further. Unless Britain formally condemned *The Satanic Verses* within a week, Iran announced, it would break off relations. The British foreign minister's subsequent concession that the novel was, regrettably, offensive to Muslims and Rushdie's qualified apology from hiding were not enough. On March 7, Tehran terminated its new diplomatic ties with London.

For Khomeini, blasphemy was a genuine issue. Two weeks after his death sentence, Tehran pulled its films out of the Istanbul Film Festival and publicly condemned the event because of plans to show *The Last Temptation of Christ,* a controversial film about Jesus' life. He also saw the book in conspiratorial terms, as the outside world's latest plot to defame and suppress his religion. But the imam's edict also served to address his personal, domestic and regional agendas, each of which had little to do with the book.

For the previous decade, the aging imam had sought to be the spokesman of the Islamic world—for his ideas as well as for himself. But the initial recognition had quickly dissipated because of the revolution's excesses at home and its support for extremist groups abroad. While fundamentalism had increased in the region, few except a handful in Lebanon joined *his* cause. And many in the Sunni world openly reviled his revolution as a strictly Shi'ite phenomenon. *The Satanic Verses* thus represented an opportunity. Picking up on the growing fury among both Shi'a and Sunni over the novel, Khomeini deliberately moved to the forefront of opposition, in part to demonstrate that he and his revolution did represent all Muslims. Indeed, having claimed the leadership role, he almost had little choice. But the edict was mainly an attempt to reclaim lost legitimacy.

The novel was also published at a crucial juncture in the revolution. The theocracy needed a rallying point to divert attention from domestic problems, which had grown worse rather than better since the end of the Gulf war. In the past, the ruling mullahs had used, and in some cases created, crises to mobilize public support for the troubled regime. The furor over Salman Rushdie conveniently countered the growing frustration, discontent and sense of malaise at home.[48]

Finally, the imam used the book as a pretext to correct, even reverse, the course increasingly being charted by Rafsanjani, Khamenei and others to ensure the state's survival. As the international furor grew, Khomeini declared that the book had been a "godsend" that had helped Iran out of a "naive foreign policy."[49] He all but listed names in a direct warning, "As long as I am around I shall not allow the government to fall into the hands of the liberals." Even renewed economic sanctions would not "force us to retreat and forgo God's decree," he declared.[50]

But the imam, once again, acted at an enormous cost to the Islamic Republic. In the name of his reputation, Khomeini was prepared to undo all the diplomatic gains achieved by his government over the previous year. Indeed, he was willing to allow Iran to be even more vilified than during the hostage ordeal. And in the name of his faith, the ayatollah was, in effect, also prepared to undercut his own government's attempts to interest the outside world in improving trade and eventually assisting with reconstruction of his war-ravaged country. His naïveté and his growing distance after a decade sequestered at Jamaran were reflected in his boast "I am fully confident that in principle all the people, as before, support the regime and their Islamic revolution."[51]

The imam did not stop with the Rushdie affair. In a move that had even deeper ramifications at home, Khomeini fired Ayatollah Montazeri, his own successor, six weeks later. The official exchange of letters on March 28 cited Montazeri's unwillingness and lack of preparedness to take on the sweeping powers of the Supreme Jurisprudent. The real reason, however, was clearly Montazeri's public criticism of the revolution. On the tenth anniversary, he had conceded that the revolution had failed to fulfill several of its promises. He had also called on the government to "correct past mistakes." And in the midst of the Rushdie furor, he complained, "People in the world got the idea that our business in Iran is just murdering people." [52]

For Khomeini, the heir apparent had finally gone too far. The curt dismissal amounted to a complete reversal; the imam had for years called Montazeri, a Khomeini student and disciple since the 1950s, "the fruit of my life." Pictures of the two men had hung side by side in government offices, banks, hotels, hospitals, airport lobbies and businesses throughout Iran since the 1985 selection.

The ouster had dangerous long-term implications. Although the heir apparent had neither the imam's charisma nor his religious authority, Montazeri had come to symbolize continuity. Three years had been invested in his selection, and there was no obvious or qualified single successor. Of the less than half dozen grand ayatollahs who were eligible to inherit Khomeini's title, not one agreed with Khomeini's dream. The constitution stipulated that a council of three to five senior mullahs could assume the position of guiding the country. In the meantime, however, the insecurity and anxiety of the nation further undermined its stability. The imam had undercut the very system he had worked for decades to create in the name of keeping the revolution pure—and supreme.

Epilogue

"Our path is the same as Imam Khomeini's and we will continue the path vigorously and decisively."

— Khomeini's successor,
Ali Khamenei, at
Khomeini's funeral [1]

"We cannot apply European standards of conduct to Persia with any expectation that they will furnish a reliable gauge of action."

— Lord Balfour, 1921 [2]

Tehran Radio's late news bulletin on June 3, 1989, was brief but, for many Iranians, chilling. Eleven days after he had undergone surgery to stop intestinal bleeding and just after doctors had predicted a full recovery, Ayatollah Khomeini's condition suddenly turned critical. Throughout the Islamic Republic, tens of thousands, heeding the government's appeal to pray for his welfare, flocked to mosques in near panic; somehow, after having defied death for so long, his passing at age eighty-six was still unthinkable. But the crisis was, in fact, already over. His system weakened by disease and age, Khomeini had suffered a heart attack, and hours of attempts to restore his breathing had failed.[3] On the first news broadcast the next morning, Tehran Radio made the announcement, "The lofty spirit of the leader of the Muslims and the leader of the noble ones, His Eminence Imam Khomeini, has reached the highest status, and a heart replete with love of God and his true people, who have endured numerous hardships, has stopped beating."

The paroxysms of grief overwhelmed the streets of Tehran. Iranians poured into the capital from all corners of the country to view Khomeini's body, encased in a refrigerated glass box atop a thirty-foot funeral bier. Despite the hundred-degree heat, crushing mobs created an impassable sea of black for miles as they wailed, chanted and rhythmically beat themselves in anguish. "We have been orphaned. Our father is dead," one group of women cried over and over again. Children and even babies were passed hand to hand above the crowd to the ring of Revolutionary Guards at the bier so they could be held aloft for a final look at the imam. As the hours passed, fire trucks had to be brought in to spray water on the crowd to provide relief from the heat, while helicopters were flown in to ferry the eight killed and more than four hundred injured, including Khomeini's son Ahmad, to hospitals. Thousands refused to leave, holding all-night vigils beside the body.

The mourning and burial were full of historic ironies. The imam died just two days short of the twenty-sixth anniversary of his first arrest by the shah, a day normally marked by nationwide commemorations. A year earlier, attendance had been noticeably, even pitifully, small. The millions who turned out to mourn Khomeini, however, indicated that public loyalty to the man, if not his vision, was still strong. As an Iranian political scientist had commented a year before his death, "Khomeini may have created a hell, but most Iranians believe that he created it with good intentions."[4] Shortly before his burial, many were reluctant to let him go—literally. In attempts to touch Khomeini or grab bits of the traditional white burial shroud, distraught Iranians surged toward the open wooden coffin, overturning the litter and exposing the gaunt, half-naked body and the deep scars of his recent surgery as the corpse fell to the ground. Again, a helicopter was flown in to pick up the body; the final rite had to be delayed for six hours. As Khomeini's body was finally emptied into the simple grave, this time from a closed aluminum casket, an Iranian television correspondent broadcasting live succumbed to emotion: "Oh stars stop shining. Oh rivers stop flowing," he lamented in tears.[5] Only once before had Iran witnessed such wild displays of passion and adulation—on the day the imam returned to Iran.

Khomeini was buried in Behesht-e Zahra, or Paradise of Zahra, a cemetery on the outskirts of Tehran named after the Prophet Mohammad's daughter. It was here that the imam had chosen to give his first major address upon his return to Iran a decade earlier. He had wanted to pay homage to the thousands who had died in confrontations with the shah's security forces and who had helped make possible his rise to power. The burial site selected for his final trip to Behesht-e Zahra was near the section, now stretching for miles and miles, allocated for martyrs killed in the war with Iraq that Khomeini had prolonged for almost six years.

On the day he returned to Iran, the imam's first speech was an appeal for unity behind the Islamic Revolution and for strong action to "cut off the hands" of Iran's enemies, notably the United States. His appeal from the grave was almost identical. In a wordy and occasionally obtuse last will and testament addressed to "all Muslim nations and to the oppressed of the world, of whatever country or religion," Khomeini appealed once again for unwavering loyalty to his dream. Foreign propaganda, he charged, "claim[s] clumsily and explicitly that the laws of Islam, which were recorded 1,400 years ago, cannot be used to administer countries of the contemporary world, or that Islam is a reactionary religion, or that it is against any innovation or symbols of civilization." But Islam and its laws "are not things that grow old with the passage of time" and instead provide the power "to lead mankind to the desired status of evolution." He called on his followers, in Iran and elsewhere, not to "deviate in the slightest" and to "sacrifice their own lives and the lives of their dear ones" to perpetuate the "divine revolution"— especially against "enemy conspiracies and world-devouring America."[6]

The imam's death, the political threshold that the ouside world had long awaited, led to bold predictions by Iranian opposition groups ranging from Marxist to monarchist. "We are going to witness the downfall of the regime in the near future," claimed the Mojahedin-e Khalq, the Islamic socialist group that had been the theocracy's nemesis. Its leadership pledged an imminent military assault from bases in Baghdad supported by clandestine cells within Iran to bring down the regime.[7] Reza Pahlavi, who crowned himself shah after his father's death in 1980, forecast from his base in the United States, "The Islamic Republic is dead with the passing away of Khomeini. The people who are the remnants of Khomeini's government are not people with the authority to issue decrees from the Islamic vantage point. Technically, today, the regime is no longer an Islamic Republic."[8] And the Islamic Republic's first president, Abolhassan Bani-Sadr, predicted from exile in Paris that a power struggle between pragmatic and hard-line mullahs could turn bloody, resulting in civil strife comparable to Lebanon's breakdown.

But for all the public chaos generated by his death, the men Khomeini left behind to run his revolution moved surprisingly quickly to fill the vacuum. Within twenty-four hours, the Assembly of Experts selected a successor. Since none of the half-dozen grand ayatollahs qualified to inherit Khomeini's mantle actually agreed with his interpretation of Islam, a council of three to five junior mullahs was widely seen as a more viable option to replace the imam, an alternative provided for in the Islamic Republic's constitution. Instead, after eight hours of debate, the Assembly selected President Ali Khamenei. Only a *hojatolislam,* or "authority on Islam," Khamenei was scheduled within the next five months to finish his second and final presidential term. As a former Khomeini student and disciple twice jailed by the shah and as one of Iran's most experienced politicians, he was, however, a logical choice to provide transition leadership. "The most important thing is that we made very swift movement," *majlis* Speaker Rafsanjani said later. "We astonished the world, and right now all of those wrong interpretations of power struggles and radicals versus moderates are dismissed."[9] Khomeini's political heirs managed, at least initially, an orderly succession.

•

Because of his impact on Iran, on the Middle East and on the world, *Time* magazine selected Khomeini as its 1979 "Man of the Year." "Rarely has so improbable a leader shaken the world. Khomeini's importance far transcends . . . the overthrow of the shah of Iran," it wrote. "The revolution that he led to triumph threatens to upset the world balance of power more than any political event since Hitler's conquest of Europe."[10]

On some counts, the Islamic Republic fulfilled those expectations. It survived a decade, a war lasting almost as long as World War I and World War II combined, economic devastation and sanctions, diplomatic isolation and its own internal divisions. Indeed, after ousting the shah and establishing an Islamic state, Khomeini's main contribution may simply have been surviving a full decade and thus allowing the revolution to become entrenched and the clergy to gain experience in running a state. No single group from either the right or the left and no alliance could muster sufficient support either inside or outside the country to threaten the theocracy seriously during the vulnerable first days after the imam's passing, and no Napoleon had yet appeared on the sidelines ready to step in.

Khomeini also succeeded in restructuring the domestic political apparatus, spreading power for the first time beyond the wealthy, Westernized elite. He also succeeded in upsetting the regional and international balance of power, forcing the superpowers to take both Iran and Islam more seriously. Along with the Vietnam War and the Soviet occupation of Afghanistan, the Iranian revolution may prove to be a historic turning point, teaching the superpowers that military intervention and strong-arm political pressure cannot sway determined Third World societies. And for his faith, Islam was taught at home to a whole new generation as a way of life and a means of governance, and the outside world was given notice that religion could be a potent political force in the world's most secular age.

On other counts, however, the messianic hopes of an Islamic utopia were dashed. Khomeini's early promise—that submission to God would create a just society at home, empower Iran to defeat external oppressors and reunite the Islamic world in a new power bloc—was largely unfulfilled. Iran's revolution did not carry universal relevance for either the Islamic world or the Third World.

Indeed, at crucial junctures, the imam failed his own revolution. Politically, despite his absolute authority, Khomeini's vacillation and delicate balancing of Iran's political factions often resulted in policy paralysis on key issues rather than reform.[11] His self-righteous inflexibility also cost Iran international acceptability and his revolution credibility in the Islamic world. Tehran's brand of Shi'ite extremism never took hold except in neighborhoods of chaotic Lebanon and among handfuls of Gulf Arabs. And in the West, "Shi'ite" had virtually become a dirty word, usually synonymous with terrorism. Iran's isolation was visible at Khomeini's funeral. Only one foreign leader, the president of Pakistan, came to pay his respects.

Militarily, Khomeini's personal and political grudge against Saddam Hussein prevented mediation after it became clear in 1986 that the war was unwinnable; tens of thousands died as he held out. Economically, he failed his own constituency, the *mostazafin* disinherited, who were even more impoverished during the revolution's first decade than under the shah with little to show for the "dignity" that Khomeini had promised. Finally, despite his own advanced age and failing health, he left the state and his own disciples vulnerable without a successor—all in the name of revolutionary purity. In many ways, the imam's followers managed the initial stage of the transition despite Khomeini.

When he died, the Islamic Republic's agenda for its second decade was burdened with more problems than when the theocrats seized power. Costs of reconstruction for the western provinces and the oil industry have been estimated as high as $350 billion. Billions more will be needed to restock Iran's depleted arsenal, which the theocrats have indicated will be a top priority because of fears of future outside intervention. Hundreds of thousands of war refugees, who turned the fringe areas of Iran's major cities into massive slums, will also have to be relocated. And those costs do not include long-delayed but basic development projects.

Meanwhile, the birth rate—estimated, at 4 percent, to be among the highest in the world—means that Iran's population will almost double to a hundred million soon after the turn of the century.[12] In a country with subsidized food and education, the future demographic burden could drain the oil-rich nation. The bill to import food, in a country that until the shah's final years had been an exporter, consumed $3 billion in 1988—at a time oil revenues brought in only about $9 billion.[13] Shortages, inflation, unemployment and price gouging were all many times worse than during the final year of the shah's rule. Food prices were particularly troublesome; in a single week in the spring of 1989, the already exorbitant cost of rice, milk, tomatoes, chick-peas and beans again increased between 7 and 30 percent—for no specific reason.[14] The average Iranian was finding it difficult to afford the revolution.

Most daunting of all were the political challenges. Society was deeply polarized and politically exhausted: For all the fervor displayed at Khomeini's funeral, there were limited reserves for the imam's successors to tap beyond the *hizbollahi* faithful. Even shortly before his death, a new wave of mass executions had still been deemed necessary to keep potential opposition in check. A decade of power struggles within the leadership had also left deep bruises and some scars that portended further trouble, leaving the revolution infused with a crisis mentality.

The revolution still has to prove that it can endure beyond Khomeini, which will be its single biggest challenge. Despite the limitations of his leadership, the imam's charisma and authority held the

revolution together for ten years and, short-term, neither Rafsanjani nor Khamenei has sufficient popular appeal or religious standing to replace him. They will not be able to rule in the name of God.
And, although the mullahs coalesced after his passing, they will, at
some stage, surely have to sort out their long-standing differences.
Rafsanjani appeared to be the favorite to lead the post-Khomeini
era, but his longevity is not immune from the political or physical
challenges of an unstable environment.

To survive a second decade, Iran's revolution will almost certainly have to redirect its energies, focusing less on exporting the
revolution and more on domestic problems. Two particular issues
will have to be addressed: First, to broaden its base of support,
particularly crucial after Khomeini's death, the theocracy will have
to show greater tolerance of diverse tastes and beliefs at home. That
may not mean an end to the chador or hejab for women or changing
the Islamic curricula in schools, but it must mean less cruelty and
greater discipline of revolutionary institutions such as the komitehs.
The continued use of force and repression may be effective short-
term, but it is a tactic that, according to the pattern of past revolutions, will only alienate its constituency. Second, the Islamic Republic will have to end its parish status in the eyes of the West, a process
launched but then aborted during Irangate and after the war's end.
Even with its oil wealth, Iran cannot reconstruct and develop alone;
Western technology and expertise are vital in keeping the Islamic
Republic in the twentieth century. In other words, the revolution
will have to come to grips with its limitations.

•

In the ten years since Ayatollah Khomeini's return to Iran, the
revolution has appeared, on the surface, to have become entrenched, right down to the smallest detail. During rush hour on a
dusky evening, an old blind violin player, led by a young boy,
worked his way down the middle of Tehran's busy intersection at
Dr. Hosain Fatami Street and Vali-e Asr Avenue—two of the many
streets renamed after the shah's exile. Dr. Fatami, a fiery critic of
the shah executed in the 1950s, was revered by the revolutionaries;
Vali-e Asr translates as "the expected one," a reference to the
Mahdi. Elizabeth Avenue, running in front of the British embassy,
was pointedly renamed for Bobby Sands, the Irish Republican
Army prisoner who fasted to death. Roosevelt Avenue had been
renamed for a noted mullah.

As the blind beggar played, the boy temporarily abandoned him
in traffic to dart to car windows for coins. "He has been here for-

ever, since I was fifteen," said a middle-aged cabbie. "The boys change, but he is always here. He used to play jazz and popular Iranian music," including the lilting love sonnets of great Persian lyricists. "But that is all forbidden. Now he plays only Islamic music and the anthem. Mostly the anthem."

Lest Tehranis forget what the revolution was about, the streets were covered with graffiti to remind them. On the brick wall surrounding the British embassy compound, the setting for the 1943 Tehran Conference Summit of Roosevelt, Churchill and Stalin, neat calligraphy pronounced, "Our duty is to protect Islam." At Niavaran Palace, the shah's favorite residence, the exterior wall was adorned with instructions from Khomeini: "Talk about God and don't think about anything else." At Tehran's Great Bazaar, the carpets of the shah and John F. Kennedy had been replaced by a carpet woven in Khomeini's image.

Yet the revolution had not completely abrogated the past. The women who strolled down Vali-e Asr Avenue hand in hand with their children or with each other, gossiping or gazing through modern steel-and-glass shop windows, were hidden behind all-enveloping black chadors or the cover of hejab headscarves. But the high heels or jeans peeking from underneath their covers told another story. In the lobby of the former Intercontinental, renamed the Laleh, or "tulip," after the symbol of martyrdom, an Iranian Jewish family went through the courtship rites for one of its daughters. The potential bride, her mother and three sisters dipped into ice cream sodas and chatted with a young man the parents had selected as an appropriate husband. If this interview and, usually, a second went well, the couple would probably be married—a tradition dating back centuries.

Traces of foreign influence had also not been totally eliminated. American flags had been painted on hotel walkways for guests to tread on, but pirated copies of *Top Gun* and *Rambo* were the most popular movies on the video circuit. At the half-dozen former Kentucky Fried Chicken outlets, Col. Sanders's picture had been replaced by a drawing of a mustachioed gentleman who looked a bit like the Islamic Republic's first president, and the red-and-white marquee had been changed to read "Try Our Fried Chicken, the Ultimate Taste," but the aroma and taste were unmistakably familiar. Most bookstores had English-language sections, which carried everything from William F. Buckley's novels and the Woodward and Bernstein account of Watergate to a rather dated copy of traveling in New York on twenty-five dollars a day. A local restaurant

still served Waikiki shrimp, while a Tex-Mex diner that opened
eight years after the revolution attracted a booming business. Despite the revolution's Islamization of society, Tehran had not lost
its diversity or its interest in the outside world.

Encounters with Iranians in visits during the first decade of the
revolution were usually complex, often confounding, and occasionally amusing. At the war front in 1982, Iranian troops performed
the ritual "Death to America" chant for Western television cam-
eras. But once the TV crews moved away, army and Revolutionary
Guard soldiers surrounded an American reporter and asked
whether Nebraska had beaten Oklahoma the previous fall and if
Pink Floyd had released any new albums. In Tehran's tatty southern
suburbs in 1987, a young bearded *hizbollahi,* one of the young
faithful, angrily derided the United States, yet he had no aversion
to talking to an American. Like many in the Third World, he differ-
entiated between a government and its people. His complaints were
standard fare: The United States' all-consuming bias, as he saw it,
in favor of Israel at the expense of the world's Muslims; its schemes
to exploit the have-nots of the Third World economically; and its
attempts to dominate any weaker ally politically. But his fashionable fatigue trousers reflected the revolution's incongruities: A conspicuous label on the back pocket read, "Made in the USA."

On another visit in 1988, a group of women employed as researchers and scholars at the Foreign Ministry's think tank eagerly
offered lunch to an American woman. For all the animosity between the two societies, they were intrigued with the United States.
They were, with some degree of unanimity, rather disparaging
about Ronald Reagan. One of the women who had been educated
at a major American university commented: "I think Art Buchwald
knows more about Iran than Ronald Reagan. I love his columns. I
loved the one best about an Iranian moderate that ran after Irangate." She had read it in the *International Herald Tribune.* The
think tank's library was filled with copies of the latest *New York
Times, Washington Post* and *Christian Science Monitor* as well as
scholarly American journals and their counterparts from all corners
of the globe. They were quite proud of their ability to keep up with
the outside world. Any lingering doubt that the Buchwald fan had
about Reagan, she said, had been lost when she read about former
White House chief of staff Donald Regan's claims that the president's schedule was determined by an astrologer. "Could this really
be true," she asked, "of an American president?"

Despite outside perceptions, Iranians do not speak with a single voice, even about their own revolution, which played out one after-noon in 1988 at Luna Park. The amusement center, decorated throughout with storybook characters, funny ducks and cheerful mice clearly based on Disney personalities, was always crowded. But a female American reporter, dressed in a locally bought rou-poosh, was stopped at the gate by a rather thuggish member of the local komiteh. Her loose overcoat, he said, was not sufficiently Islamic to allow entry. It turned out that the roupoosh, which fell to her ankles, had a tiny slit up the back to allow movement. This, he apparently thought, was suggestive, and no press card or expla-nation would help. An official from the Ministry of Islamic Guid-ance, which accredits the foreign press, was outraged when he learned of the exchange. "Acchhh," he said, "these people are so stupid. They are there mostly to stop the young boys and girls from becoming too familiar. I will take you back and you will get in wearing the same thing."

Ten years after the mullahs seized power, the revolution still conveyed conflicting signals. In April 1989, thousands turned out at a sports stadium in the southern port city of Bushehr to watch eleven prostitutes and pimps being stoned to death. The prisoners were hooded and buried—men to the waist, women to the chest—in a hole in the ground. Following custom, the sentencing judge threw the first stone. Amid shouts of *"Allahu Akbar,"* other police and judicial officials pelted the convicts until they were pronounced dead. The eleven were among fifty-two found guilty of "spreading corruption on earth" for running a prostitution ring. The others were flogged or jailed. Although dozens had been stoned to death since 1979, it was the largest group executed by ritual Islamic pun-ishment at a single time.[15] At the time this book went to press, U.S. intelligence also believed that hard-line Iranian elements played a role in the December 1988 bombing of Pan Am 103, in which all 259 on board were killed. The revolution's cruelty had not abated in either intensity or scope.[16]

The revolution, however, was not uniformly severe, for freedom of expression, in body and soul, had long been a Persian passion. And, like women covered by chadors, there is another layer under-neath that runs deep in Iran, sometimes in surprising ways. The window of Tehran's La Boutique, which was what its name implied, carried several rather daring frocks. One was a loosely knit and therefore potentially revealing black evening dress. It had precar-iously thin spaghetti straps and featured sequins shaped into vines suggestively curling down the front into clusters of green leaves.

The young salesgirl said it cost the equivalent of $2,239 at the legal rate of exchange, or $113 at the black-market rate. Between the price and the design, it seemed unlikely that anyone would buy it. But the next day, it was gone from the window. Asked if someone had ordered it taken from public view, the salesgirl laughed aloud, "Oh no. It's gone. These are my best sales. A lot of women wear them under their roupooshes and chadors. You'd be surprised." Equally surprising was her disclosure that this dress and several similarly skimpy designs were not imports, but made on hand looms in Iran.

More worrisome were the apparent policy contradictions. At annual religious services commemorating Jerusalem day in May 1989, Rafsanjani urged Palestinians to kill Westerners, hijack aircraft and threaten U.S. interests worldwide to stop Israeli repression. "If in retaliation for every Palestinian martyred in Palestine they kill and execute . . . five Americans or Britons or Frenchmen," the Israelis "would not continue to do these wrongs," he told a cheering crowd in reference to the more than 450 deaths in the Palestinian uprising. "God knows there is a solution if you announce today that from now on you will threaten American interests throughout the world." [17] As the architect of at least two earlier attempts to better relations with the Great Satan and other Western nations, Rafsanjani's call to terrorism was incongruous and alarming.

Although he backtracked a few days later, Rafsanjani's speech indicated the ongoing pressures to prove one's revolutionary loyalty and to accommodate the fluctuating political climate. In this case, he appeared to be playing to the atmosphere created three months earlier by Khomeini's death threat on Salman Rushdie. In the run-up to presidential elections, in which he was the leading candidate to succeed President Khamenei, he may have been, in effect, campaigning in the currently popular idiom. Ayatollah Montazeri's ouster as heir apparent had also been a warning to all mullahs about the price of talking out of school. But Rafsanjani's speech indicated that the revolutionary environment was still volatile— and unpredictable. Khomeini's death did little to alleviate the pressures.

•

Forecasting the future of the Islamic Republic would be foolish, for the course of revolutions is so often surprising and their impact at home and on other societies usually cannot be fully assessed in contemporary times. British scholar Fred Halliday rightly pointed out, "It took the Bolshevik revolution nearly three decades, until the end of World War II, to spread eastwards and westwards. It took Castro until 1979, two decades after he entered Havana, to establish a beachhead in Central America. It was Mao who told Nixon, in 1972, that it was still too early to assess the international consequences of the French revolution." [18]

The shifting course of revolutions was evident on the chaotic day that Khomeini returned to Iran in 1979—the same day that the United States was formalizing the final stages of détente with China. Sharing the headlines with the Iranian revolution was President Jimmy Carter's welcome for Deng Xiaoping, the highest-level Chinese official to visit Washington since China's 1949 revolution. Deng, whose visit symbolized his interest in cementing relations with the West, was at the time considered a moderate—and a relief from the eccentric extremism of Mao Zedong's final years. But on the day Khomeini died in 1989, China was in chaos. The very hour that Tehran Radio announced the imam's passing, the Chinese People's Liberation Army began slaughtering an estimated three thousand students camped out in Beijing's Tiananmen Square to demand democratic reforms from those now perceived as hard-liners in Deng's government. After a decade of increasingly close trade and diplomatic ties, the United States condemned China's extremism and offered refuge to Deng's political opponents. The sequence of events over a decade underscored, once again, that revolutions are not single events that end with the overthrow of the ancien régime; they are ongoing processes that take decades to unfold fully.·

There are no guarantees that Iran's revolution will survive. While two revolutions in less than twenty years seem unlikely, the Islamic Republic's authoritarian populism may go too far and, in the process, devour itself. Disillusionment among the faithful may also eventually grow to intolerance because of the failed promise of God's intervention. Rarely, if ever, has a revolution claimed such absolute justification. Like secular ideologies, however, religion is unlikely to be able to provide perfect temporal solutions, and the revolution has already proven to be neither pure nor infallible.

For all the anecdotes and indicators accumulated over a decade, it is nearly impossible for any outsider to judge just how far beneath the surface the revolution penetrated during the Khomeini era— and thus to evaluate its fate. The bottom line is that, ten years after Khomeini's return, the Islamic Republic is still struggling to come to terms with itself. As a result, the revolution could still turn in any of several directions. Like the Jacobins, Iran's theocrats could ulti- mately fail and be replaced in a counterrevolution, assuredly, however, leaving behind precedents and a powerful ideology. Or, like the Bolsheviks, they may become sufficiently entrenched that the various opposition forces will find it difficult to overthrow them. Khomeini launched the revolution and left his mark; it will be up to his successors to determine whether the Islamic Republic survives. The next ten years could well be as interesting, even as tumultuous, for Iran as the past decade.

Chronology

❧

For the convenience of the reader, the following outline of major events during the first decade of Iran's revolution links together series of events over a period of days according to the subject, such as domestic politics, international affairs or the war. The chronology is drawn from three primary sources: the excellent quarterly review of major events in the *Middle East Journal*, published by the Middle East Institute; the daily translation of Middle East news in *Foreign Broadcast Information Service*; and the annual *Middle East Contemporary Survey* yearbook. Assorted other books, periodicals and newspapers cited in the Source Notes and the Bibliography supplement the chronology.

1979

February 1: Ending fourteen years in exile, Ayatollah Ruhollah Khomeini returned to Iran. Before a crowd of three million, he demanded the resignation of Premier Shapour Bakhtiar's government and criticized the presence of foreigners in Iran. The next day, he called on the public to "destroy" the Bakhtiar government. On February 5, the imam appointed Mehdi Bazargan prime minister of a provisional government, while the United States reiterated its support for the Bakhtiar government the next day.

February 7: U.S. Ambassador to the United Nations Andrew Young praised Islam as "a vibrant cultural force in today's world" and predicted Ayatollah Khomeini would someday be hailed as "somewhat of a saint."

February 11: Following two days of clashes between pro-Khomeini supporters and government troops, the army's Supreme Council declared neutrality in the political crisis to prevent further bloodshed and ordered troops to return to their barracks. The Bakhtiar government resigned following withdrawal of army support, ending a week of dual governments. Many members of the military high command were subsequently arrested.

February 12: The Carter administration said that the United States would "honor the will of the Iranian people" and "attempt to work closely" with the existing government of Iran. On February 14, the U.S. embassy in Tehran was stormed, trapping the ambassador and his staff until the deputy prime minister led forces to end the assault. One U.S. marine was wounded and held by government forces until February 21. On February 16, the United States announced its intention to maintain diplomatic relations with Iran.

February 13: Ayatollah Khomeini appealed to Iranians to turn in their weapons and to end attacks on public property. Not all groups, including some aligned with Khomeini, complied. On February 15, four army generals were executed, followed by four more on February 20, which marked the beginning of a major purge of the military.

February 17: Prime Minister Bazargan pledged to resume oil exports to "all parts of the world," including the United States. Tankers began loading oil on March 5.

February 18: Iran terminated diplomatic relations with Israel the day before Palestine Liberation Organization chairman Yasir Arafat arrived in Tehran for talks and to open PLO offices in the former Israeli mission. Relations with South Africa were severed on March 4. On March 12, Iran withdrew from the Central Treaty Organization on grounds that "the treaty only incorporated the interests of the superpowers."

March 7: From his exile in Morocco, Mohammad Reza Shah Pahlavi said that he did not intend to abdicate. Ayatollah Khomeini ordered women employed in government to dress according to the Islamic code.

March 14: Prime Minister Bazargan condemned summary trials. In a meeting the next day with Ayatollah Khomeini, he offered his resignation, which was rejected. On March 16, Ayatollah Khomeini ordered an end to trials until new regulations were drafted.

March 18: Fighting erupted in Kurdistan between Kurdish dissidents and Iranian troops. Similar clashes over minority rights erupted on March 27 in Turkoman areas and on March 29 among Baluchi tribesmen.

March 30–31: A national referendum was held on the formation of an Islamic republic, which reportedly received more than 90 percent support. Ayatollah Khomeini declared April 1 "the first day of a government of God."

April 5: New trial procedures were announced. They were followed by the executions on April 7 of former Prime Minister Hoveyda and, between April 9 and May 18, of at least forty ranking military and cabinet officials from the shah's government. At least two hundred thirteen had been executed since the shah's overthrow.

May 1: Ayatollah Murtiza Mutahhari, Revolutionary Council chairman and Khomeini aide, was assassinated in Tehran. On May 25, Revolutionary Council member Ali Akbar Hashemi Rafsanjani was shot and wounded by gunmen in Tehran.

May 5: Formation of the Revolutionary Guards Corps to "protect the Islamic revolution" was reported.

May 13: Ayatollah Khomeini declared that death sentences should be limited to those proven to have killed people or to have issued such orders. On May 17, the U.S. Senate passed a resolution deploring summary executions without due process in Iran, leading Tehran to protest American intervention in Iranian affairs. Iran recalled its Washington envoy and, on June 4, rescinded its approval of the new U.S. ambassador.

June 8: Iran announced the takeover of private banks, followed by nationalization of private insurance companies on June 25 and further takeovers of private industry on July 5.

June 12: In a meeting with the Soviet ambassador, Ayatollah Khomeini accused Moscow of supplying arms to his opponents and of aiding Iran's minorities, especially the Kurds. Criticism of the Soviet Union increased throughout the summer.

June 18: The draft constitution was put forward.

July 1: Prime Minister Bazargan again offered his resignation, which Ayatollah Khomeini refused to accept.

July 9: Ayatollah Khomeini declared a general amnesty for anyone who had committed offenses during the shah's rule, except those charged with murder or torture.

July 11: A provisional press bill was published prohibiting newspaper publications by anyone who had prominently served the shah and providing for up to two years' imprisonment for slandering Islam. On August 20, twenty-two opposition newspapers, including the Tudeh Party's *Mardom*, were ordered to close. By the end of September, forty papers were closed, although a few later were allowed to reopen.

July 18: Construction of a pipeline to supply gas to the Soviet Union was reportedly canceled.

July 19: Four leading clerics—Rafsanjani, Khamenei, Bahonar and Mahdavi-Kani—became the first mullahs to join the Bazargan cabinet, beginning the process of a clerical takeover of the state.

August 3: Elections were held for the seventy-three seats on the new Assembly of Experts mandated to finalize a new constitution. The polling was boycotted by twenty political groups that Ayatollah Khomeini described as "enemies of the revolution." Clergymen won fifty-five seats. Dissident groups' offices were raided on August 13, sparking several street clashes.

August 10: Iran canceled a $9 billion U.S. arms deal made during the shah's reign.

August 18: Khomeini appointed himself commander-in-chief and ordered a general mobilization against the Kurds. Fighting in northern Kurdistan continued until the fall of Kurdish strongholds on September 3.

August 31: Prime Minister Bazargan again offered his resignation, which Khomeini rejected. The Soviet Union was accused of aiding Iran's opponents, which was followed by a Soviet press commentary calling Khomeini's regime "a disaster." Tension remained high until a September 27 meeting at the United Nations between Foreign Minister Ibrahim Yazdi and Soviet Foreign Minister Andrei Gromyko.

September 1: An Iran oil company official said that Iran might be forced to change its agreement to sell oil to the United States because of a controversy in the United States over selling heating oil and kerosene to Iran.

September 7–8: An Alitalia plane was hijacked by three Lebanese Shi'a to protest the 1978 disappearance of Lebanese religious leader Imam Musa Sadr in Libya. The plane was flown to Tehran, where the hijackers surrendered to Iranian officials.

October 2: Washington announced a U.S.-Iran agreement on a new American ambassador. On October 5, delivery of military spare parts for aircraft were resumed to Iran, according to the Pentagon. Iran and the Soviet Union signed an agreement for construction of a power station in Isfahan.

October 14: The Assembly of Experts approved a constitutional clause providing for Khomeini to become Iran's Supreme Jurisprudent and head of the armed forces. The draft stipulated that he would also have ultimate veto power over selection of candidates, including those for the presidency.

October 22: After brief residences in Egypt, Morocco, the Bahamas and Mexico, Mohammad Reza Shah Pahlavi flew to the United States for cancer treatment.

November 1: Ayatollah Khomeini broadcast a statement urging students to expand attacks against the United States and Israel to force the return of the shah. The U.S. embassy was the site of protests. The same day, U.S. National Security Advisor Zbigniew Brzezinski met with an Iranian delegation led by Prime Minister Mehdi Bazargan in Algiers.

November 4: Students seized the U.S. embassy in Tehran, taking diplomats and staff hostage. The United States said that Iran had assured Washington that it would try to resolve the crisis. The next day, Iran canceled the 1957 Treaty of Military Cooperation with the United States as well as a 1921 pact with the Soviet Union allowing military intervention in Iran when Moscow's interests were threatened. The U.S. consulates in Tabriz and Shiraz were seized by students, while students in Tehran briefly occupied the British embassy. The United States said that the shah would not be returned to Iran.

November 6: Because of the hostage affair, Prime Minister Bazargan again offered his resignation, which was accepted, and the Provisional Revolutionary Government was dissolved. The previously secret Revolutionary Council took over the government.

November 10: In his first act as new foreign minister, Abolhassan Bani-Sadr praised the U.S. embassy seizure and called for return of the shah, whom he labeled "the greatest criminal history has seen." On November 12, President Carter announced suspension of Iranian oil imports, which was followed by Iran's announcement of a cutoff of oil exports to the United States.

November 14: Iran revealed plans to withdraw all funds from American banks due to banking interests' role in the shah's admission to the United States. The Carter administration ordered a freeze on the estimated $6 billion worth of official Iranian bank deposits and other assets in the United States.

November 15: The Assembly of Experts approved a new constitution for the Islamic Republic of Iran. On November 17, Ayatollah Khomeini ordered that the female and black American hostages not guilty of espionage be freed. But on November 20 he pledged that if the shah was not returned to Iran, the remaining hostages would be tried. The United States sent a naval task force into the Indian Ocean on November 20 after warning that, while it preferred a peaceful solution, other options were available. Students holding the hostages threatened to "destroy" the American captives if the United States resorted to military options.

November 21: The United Nations proposed a resolution to the hostage crisis, which was followed the next day by an appeal from twenty-one European nations to free the Americans. On November 29, the United

States appealed to the World Court to order Iran to free the hostages. Iran filed a $56.5 billion suit in the United States against the shah.

November 23: Foreign Minister Bani-Sadr announced that all foreign commercial bank loans had been repudiated. On November 25, the petroleum minister threatened an oil boycott against any nation hostile to Iran.

December 1: After initially pledging to attend a U.N. Security Council session on the hostage crisis, Iran announced it would boycott the meeting. On December 4, the Security Council unanimously passed a resolution urgently calling on Iran to free the hostages, offering the secretary-general's office to help. Students began releasing documents seized at the U.S. embassy.

December 2–3: In a national referendum, more than 99 percent of Iranian voters accepted a new constitution based on Islamic law.

December 15: The World Court ordered Iran to free the hostages as the shah flew to Panama. On December 17, the U.N. General Assembly passed a resolution outlawing the taking of hostages. On December 22, the Carter administration announced plans to propose international economic sanctions on Iran at the United Nations.

1980

January 1: U.N. Secretary-General Waldheim arrived in Tehran to discuss the hostage issue. On January 7, he disclosed that Iran would not respond to the U.N. appeal for the hostages' freedom. The Soviet Union on January 13 vetoed a U.N. resolution to impose sanctions on Iran, which the United States charged was due to Moscow's designs on Iran.

January 23–March 2: Ayatollah Khomeini was hospitalized for a heart ailment.

January 25: The first presidential elections were held nationwide, in which Bani-Sadr received more than 75 percent of the vote. He was sworn in by Ayatollah Khomeini during a hospital ceremony on February 4.

January 29: Canada disclosed that six Americans who had escaped from the U.S. embassy the day it was seized had been hidden by Canadian diplomats and subsequently flown out of Iran. On February 6, President Bani-Sadr criticized the captors of the U.S. hostages as "children" who behaved like a government within a government.

February 11: Ayatollah Khomeini declared that Iran would resist the United States until "all economic, military, political and cultural dependence" was broken, after which "ordinary relations" could be established. President Bani-Sadr said the hostages might be released if the United States conceded its past "crimes" in Iran, promised not to interfere in Iranian affairs and recognized the right of Iran to demand the shah's extradition. On February 16, President Carter said he hoped eventually to establish normal relations with Iran and that he regretted misunderstandings between the two nations.

February 19: Ayatollah Khomeini appointed President Bani-Sadr commander-in-chief of the military.

February 23: A U.N. Commission of Inquiry arrived in Tehran to begin hearings on Iranian grievances and to expedite release of the hostages. After talks with Iranian officials, hearing testimony of 140 Iranian victims of torture during the shah's reign, and a meeting with the three U.S. hostages held outside the embassy, the commission left on March 11.

March 14: Iran held the first parliamentary elections since the revolution, after which a commission was appointed to investigate charges of electoral misconduct. Voter turnout was low, estimated at about 50 percent. A second round of elections in districts where no candidates had won an absolute majority in the first round was held on May 9. The Islamic Republic's first parliament, which was heavily weighted by clerics, convened on May 28.

March 24: The shah arrived in Cairo, where he underwent surgery on his spleen. The move triggered a new round of demonstrations in Iran.

March 29: Iran publicized a letter from the Carter administration that allegedly admitted U.S. policy "mistakes" in Iran; Washington initially denied sending such a message, then admitted that two letters had been relayed via the Swiss. On April 2, the White House said the United States would show restraint on the hostage issue as long as it felt progress was being made.

April 7: Ayatollah Khomeini said the captors would retain custody of the hostages until the new parliament determined their fate. President Carter broke off diplomatic relations with Iran, froze Iranian assets in the United States and imposed sanctions. The United States asked allies to follow suit. Ayatollah Khomeini welcomed the breaking of relations as a "good omen." Further U.S. political and economic sanctions were imposed on April 17.

April 8: Ayatollah Khomeini called on the Iraqi army to overthrow the Iraqi leadership. On April 20, Iraq's deputy foreign minister, Tariq Aziz, escaped an assassination attempt, reportedly by Iraqi Shi'a. Baghdad subsequently deported thousands of Iraqi Shi'a.

April 23: Iran announced an agreement with Moscow on importing goods through the Soviet Union in the event of an American naval blockade.

April 24–27: The U.S. hostage rescue attempt began, but mechanical malfunctions at an Iranian desert staging post led Washington to abort the mission. During withdrawal, a helicopter crashed into a transport plane, killing eight American troops. President Carter said the attempt was "not directed against the people of Iran" and that he would continue to seek a peaceful resolution of the crisis. The hostages were then dispersed throughout Iran. After public displays in Tehran of the eight servicemen's bodies, Iran returned them to the United States on May 6.

April 30–May 5: Five Iranian-Arab gunmen took over the Iranian embassy in London and held the staff hostage, demanding release of nine Arab political prisoners in Iran. President Bani-Sadr said Iran was prepared to accept the "martyrdom of our children in England" rather than succumb to the demands. Three hostages were released and two killed before British commandos stormed the embassy and freed the hostages. Three of the captors were killed.

May 22: The Islamic Conference Organization passed a resolution opposing sanctions against Iran and any threat to the nation's territorial integrity. The European Economic Community trade embargo on Iran went into effect, while Japan froze all contracts with Iran signed since the hostage seizure.

May 23: The World Court ruled unanimously that Iran should end the unlawful detention of U.S. hostages and said that Iran could not subject the hostages to judicial proceedings. A court majority also said Iran should pay reparations to the United States.

May 23: Iran revealed a coup plot by army officers. A second plot was reported on June 12, a third on June 22, and a fourth, involving a plan by military officers to bomb Khomeini's home and strategic installations, was disclosed on July 10. The plotters reportedly confessed on July 13 that they hoped to bring former Prime Minister Bakhtiar, then in exile in France, back to power. All borders were closed for forty-eight hours to help track other plotters. More than two dozen were eventually executed. On July 18, gunmen failed in an assassination attempt on Bakhtiar in Paris.

June 2–6: Ten Americans, including former Attorney General Ramsey Clark, arrived in Tehran for an international conference on U.S. intervention in Iran. After offering to take the place of any of the hostages, Clark agreed to an Iranian request to form a commission in the United States to investigate American involvement in Iran during the shah's rule. The final conference document labeled Clark a "latter-day Rudolf Hess." Six American delegates met with the student captors on June 6. On June 18, the U.S. Senate passed a resolution deploring intervention by private citizens in hostage mediation.

June 10: Ayatollah Khomeini warned that Iran was in "chaos" and that "the Islamic Republic could be defeated by those who are on our side."

July 11: American hostage Richard Queen was released due to an undiagnosed illness that turned out to be multiple sclerosis.

July 20: Revolutionary Council member Ali Akbar Hashemi Rafsanjani was elected speaker of parliament, followed on July 22 by the formal swearing in by the *majlis* of President Bani-Sadr.

July 27: The shah died in Cairo at age sixty of cancer. The United States said the death marked "the end of an era in Iran, which all hope will be followed by peace and stability." Demonstrations by both shah loyalists and Khomeini supporters were held in Washington, during which more than 190 were arrested. Iran charged that the United States had savagely attacked Khomeini supporters, who were "chained in prison and under torture" after being transferred to prisons in New York. On August 4, the U.S. State Department offered to allow a U.N. investigation of the detainees' prison conditions. Speaker of Parliament Rafsanjani announced that *majlis* debate on the American hostages would be delayed due to the treatment of Iranian prisoners in the United States. On August 5, 250,000 demonstrated in Tehran against alleged maltreatment of Iranian detainees in the United States. American officials disclosed on August 7 that they had evidence of Iranian government funding and aid to supporters in the United States to foment civil disturbances. Another round of demonstrations by rival groups was held on August 8 in Washington.

August 8: Iran threatened to recall its ambassador to Moscow after complaining about Soviet-supplied arms facilitating Iraqi attacks on Iran. In Paris, former Premier Bakhtiar announced formation of a national resistance front to overthrow the new Iranian government.

August 28: Amnesty International, citing at least one thousand executions since the revolution, appealed to Iran to end executions and imprisonment based on beliefs or ethnic origins.

September 11: After the Revolutionary Council was formally dissolved because of the establishment of a new government, Ayatollah Khomeini appealed to all government officials to end their differences.

September 16: Parliament established a commission to study the hostage issue, followed the next day by a U.S. State Department announcement that Washington was willing to have a commission investigate past U.S. involvement in Iran. But President Carter said on September 18 that "to preserve the honor and integrity" of the United States he would not apologize to Iran to free the hostages. Secretary of State Muskie said on September 22 that the United States accepted the right of Iranians to select their own form of government without foreign intervention.

September 22: Following weeks of clashes between Iranian and Iraqi forces along the border and the September 17 abrogation by Iraqi President Hussein of a 1975 treaty on the border, Iraqi troops invaded Iran. Baghdad's conditions for peace included Iranian recognition of Iraqi claims to the entire Shatt al-Arab waterway and disputed territory, and the return of three Gulf islands occupied by Iran in 1971. Iraq quickly penetrated deep into Iranian territory. Oil installations were targeted by both nations, leading to a suspension in oil shipments. PLO chairman Yasir Arafat began the first mediation effort on September 25, which was followed by a similar attempt by an Islamic Conference Organization delegation on September 27. The U.N. Security Council passed a resolution on September 28 calling on both nations to cease hostilities.

October 1: Iran said it would do its part to keep the Strait of Hormuz open to oil-tanker traffic in spite of regional hostility. Heavy bombardment was reported on cities in both nations, while fighting on the ground centered around the southern cities of Khorramshahr and Abadan. On October 7, the United States said it would respond to requests for assistance from nonbelligerent Gulf allies.

October 17: At the United Nations, Iranian Prime Minister Raja'i charged that the United States was aiding Iraq with military intelligence from AWAC surveillance planes and pledged that a settlement would be reached only if the "aggressor is conquered and punished." On October 20, Secretary of State Muskie warned that the Iraqi invasion had threatened Gulf stability and offered a framework for peace, which included: no territory should be seized by arms and no intervention by either state in the other's domestic affairs. Iraq claimed to have cut off southern Iran's oil-rich Khuzistan Province on October 22, while Iran captured Iraq's oil terminals in the Gulf and cut off much of Baghdad's export capability.

October 20: In a campaign speech, President Carter said he would unfreeze Iranian assets and end trade sanctions against Iran if the hostages were freed. On October 28, he added that the United States would be neutral in the Iran-Iraq war, but that, if the hostages were freed, he would honor delivery of war materiel purchased and paid for during the shah's reign.

October 27: A day after Iran conceded the loss of Khorramshahr, Iraq offered a cease-fire on condition that it was granted sovereignty over the Shatt al-Arab and disputed territories. By October 31, Iraq claimed to have encircled Abadan.

October 31: Crown Prince Reza Pahlavi, son of the late shah, proclaimed himself shah at a Cairo ceremony under the name of Shah Reza II. After the war erupted in September, he had sent a message offering his "life's blood" in the war with Iraq.

November 2: Parliament approved a special commission's report that outlined four conditions for release of the hostages, which President Carter called a positive basis for ending the crisis. The next day Prime Minister Raja'i announced that Algeria would conduct the mediation. U.S. Deputy Secretary of State Warren Christopher began negotiations with Algerian

officials. On November 20, Secretary of State Muskie said the United
States had accepted the Iranian terms in principle.

November 5: After several days of heavy fighting around Abadan, Dezful,
Ahvaz, Mehran and Hermanshah, Ayatollah Khomeini said there would
be "no compromise with the invaders" and ordered that the Iraqi siege of
Abadan be broken. The cost of the war was reflected on November 9,
when Iran announced that the price of gasoline and kerosene would be
trebled and that sugar would be rationed.

November 12: Kuwait charged Iran with an attack on its border post with
Iraq; a second attack was reported November 16. The Cuban foreign
minister visited Iran and Iraq to attempt peace mediation, the terms of
which Iran rejected in December. On November 18, new U.N. special
envoy Olof Palme began peace mediation, but after talks in both capitals
he reported on November 24 that rapid results should not be expected.
Fighting remained intense near Abadan and Susangerd. An Arab summit
in Jordan urged a cease-fire on November 27, while expressing support
for Iraq's legitimate rights in territory and waters. Warships from both
nations clashed in the Persian Gulf on November 28.

December 5: As heavy fighting continued in Khuzistan, Iran hit the Iraq
oil terminal at Faw and Iraq struck an Iranian oil pipeline at Bandar Abbas.
On December 16, OPEC appealed to the two nations to end the war.

December 15: President Bani-Sadr said that the main obstacle in the
hostage settlement was return of Iran's financial assets. Iranian press disclosure on December 21 of the terms, which involved $24 billion in frozen
assets and additional, unspecified sums from the shah's wealth, were
termed unreasonable by the United States. The next day Parliamentary
Speaker Rafsanjani warned that the hostages would go on trial if Iranian
terms were not met. On December 24, President-elect Reagan called the
hostage captors "nothing better than criminals and kidnappers." The Algerian ambassador to Iran visited the hostages on December 25 and reported they were all in good health. Intense negotiations continued
throughout December.

December 22: Iran announced a counteroffensive in Khuzistan and positions farther north. On December 26, Iraq said it had invaded the northern
Iranian province of Kurdistan. Heavy fighting ensued in both provinces.

1981

January 4: The Iraqi defense minister claimed Iraqi triumphs over Iran,
adding that the "myth of Iranian hegemony" was over. The next day,
President Bani-Sadr said Iran had launched its long-awaited counteroffensive in the Gilan area, which was largely unsuccessful. Heavy fighting was

reported in Gilan as well as in Ahvaz, Susangerd, Dezful, Abadan and Ilam.

January 6: After a meeting with Khomeini, Prime Minister Raja'i said that the imam had consented to acceptance of U.S. proposals on the hostages. The next day U.S. Deputy Secretary of State Christopher flew to Algeria to mediate final terms of a deal.

January 14: U.N. envoy Palme began another round of peace talks to end the war, but he reported on January 18 that neither side would back down from their hard-line positions.

January 19: After a series of last-minute hitches were resolved, Iran and the United States announced agreement on terms to end the hostage crisis. The fifty-two Americans flew from Tehran late the next day, arriving in Algeria just hours after President Carter left office. After the hostages were flown to a U.S. military hospital in West Germany, President Carter flew in to meet with them. He said they were the victims of "acts of barbarism" that could "never be condoned."

January 27: President Bani-Sadr said that two plots to assassinate him had been uncovered earlier in the month and in November 1980.

January 28: President Hussein told an Islamic Conference Organization summit in Saudi Arabia that he was prepared to return captured Iranian territory in exchange for recovery of territorial and offshore rights usurped by Iran by force. Ayatollah Khomeini said troops would fight until final victory.

February 4: Ayatollah Khomeini told squabbling politicians to stop "biting one another like scorpions," which was followed on February 11 by another warning to clergymen in government that they "should by no means interfere in areas outside their competence." President Bani-Sadr noted on the same day that the economy was in "terrible" shape; unemployment was growing and foreign currency reserves were dwindling.

February 16: In a public letter, thirty-eight intellectuals complained that prisons were being filled with "militants and libertarians" who were also being tortured. On February 18, former Prime Minister Bazargan and thirty-nine members of the parliament warned in another letter that ending the street violence was vital to avoid charges that extremists had "infiltrated the organs of the republic." On February 26, more than one hundred intellectuals charged the government with torture of political prisoners and attacks on democratic rights and liberties. On April 1, Ayatollah Khomeini urged the judiciary to establish delegations to examine the nation's court system and to dismiss unsuitable judges. He also urged prosecution of Revolutionary Guards who were interfering in judicial matters.

February 16–23: U.N. special envoy Olof Palme began mediation efforts on the war in Baghdad and Tehran, but concluded that the time was not right for negotiations. Tehran refused a cease-fire until there was an Iraqi withdrawal from Iranian territory.

February 28–March 12: With heavy fighting reported in southern Khuzistan, an Islamic Conference Organization peace delegation put forward a cease-fire proposal to both the Iranian and the Iraqi governments, which Iran rejected. Baghdad said it would not pull out of Iran until Tehran recognized Iraqi rights. After two weeks, the delegation admitted failure. Parliamentary Speaker Rafsanjani said on March 23 that the ouster of Iraqi President Saddam Hessein's regime was the "strategic goal on which we will not compromise."

March 6: More than forty people were injured in clashes between supporters and opponents of President Bani-Sadr. On March 8, Revolutionary Courts Justice Sadeq Khalkhali said that the president should be tried for committing treason. Ayatollah Khomeini established a three-man reconciliation committee on March 16 to study complaints related to the war and domestic politics.

March 30–April 8: The Islamic Conference Organization attempted another peace mission in Tehran and Baghdad. On May 8, the Nonaligned Conference initiated peace efforts, which were followed by the return of U.N. special envoy Olof Palme on June 19, as heavy fighting was reported in the Susangerd area.

June 1: The commission investigating President Bani-Sadr said he had violated the constitution and contravened Ayatollah Khomeini's instructions. The next day he was accused of violating the constitution for failing to allow the prime minister to make government appointments. Chief Justice Beheshti suggested that Bani-Sadr be tried. On June 7, a newspaper licensed to Bani-Sadr was banned along with five other papers. Riots erupted on June 9 when Bani-Sadr supporters were blocked from demonstrating. Ayatollah Khomeini removed Bani-Sadr as commander-in-chief on June 10. Demonstrators the next day called for the president's trial and execution. On June 12, Bani-Sadr claimed a government plot was trying to unseat him and went into hiding.

June 16: Parliament began impeachment proceedings against Bani-Sadr. On June 20, twenty-four were killed and more than two hundred injured in Tehran demonstrations between Bani-Sadr opponents and supporters. Riots in six other cities were also reported. The president was formally declared incompetent by parliament on June 21, and his arrest was ordered. Ayatollah Khomeini officially removed him from office on June 22. The former president arrived in France with Mojahedin-e Khalq leader Masoud Rajavi on July 28 on an Iran Air plane hijacked by sympathizers.

June 26: Amnesty International reported that at least sixteen hundred had been executed since the revolution.

June 27: Supreme Defense Council member (and later President) Ali Khamenei was wounded by a bomb during a mosque sermon in Tehran. The next day a massive bomb destroyed the Islamic Republic Party headquarters. More than seventy were killed, including IRP chairman and Chief Justice Beheshti, ten cabinet ministers and deputies and twenty-seven members of parliament. On July 1, the government reported that more than fifty members of the Mojahedin had been arrested as they tried to blow up parliament. More than two hundred Mojahedin members or supporters were reportedly executed over the next few months.

July 24: Elections were held for the presidency and forty-six parliamentary seats, many left vacant after the June 28 bombing. Prime Minister Raja'i overwhelmingly won the presidency. Ayatollah Khomeini confirmed Raja'i as president on August 2, a day when bombs, blamed on the Mojahedin, exploded near the presidential office. Education Minister Bahonar was named prime minister on August 3.

July 28: Meat rationing began.

August 5: Shah Reza II announced new plans to overthrow the Khomeini regime and called for "a national uprising to destroy the forces of evil."

August 6: A new round of mediation on the war was initiated by the Nonaligned Conference, but after talks in Tehran on August 8 Iran said that the war would continue until "final victory."

August 7: Khomeini opponents took over the Iranian Interests Section in Washington; one demonstrator was shot before order was restored. On August 11, the Iranian embassy and its staff in Norway were seized by Iranian dissidents, and on August 25 Iranian students opposed to Khomeini occupied Iranian embassies in Belgium and Holland.

August 17: Iran's press reported twenty-three executions related to sedition charges. On August 24, the Iranian justice minister said that revolutionary courts had ordered seven hundred executions since Bani-Sadr's ouster.

August 30: President Raja'i, Prime Minister Bahonar and three others were killed by a bomb blast in government offices. Supreme Defense Council member Khamenei was elected to replace Bahonar as Islamic Republic Party leader on September 1, and Interior Minister Madavi Kani was nominated as prime minister on September 2. On September 5 and 11, two prominent ayatollahs were assassinated. On September 5, Ayatollah Khomeini said Iran was the most stable country in the world because it could survive assassinations and quickly replace slain officials.

September 3: In the heaviest fighting reported since the war began, Iraq claimed it had repulsed an Iranian offensive near Susangerd and caused thousands of Iranian casualties.

September 18: The day after the Western press reported an average of one hundred executions daily since Bani-Sadr's ouster, Chief Justice Musavi Ardabili announced that protestors and dissidents would be tried immediately upon arrest and executed if two people testified against them. A wave of executions followed. Dissidents briefly seized the Iranian embassy in Turkey to protest political executions. On October 7, former prime minister Bazargan condemned the mass executions.

September 27: Iran claimed to have driven Iraq back across the Karun River from Abadan to Ahvaz on the southern front, capturing three thousand Iraqi troops.

October 1: Kuwait charged Iran with attacks on its oil installations and recalled its ambassador from Tehran, which denied the charges. Iran reported new offensives near four cities on the southern front.

October 2: New presidential elections—the third round in twenty-one months and the second in ten weeks—were held. Voter turnout was comparatively low. In a four-way contest, Islamic Republic Party leader Khamenei won 95 percent of the vote. Khamenei was sworn in on October 13. On October 31, former engineer and newspaper editor Mir Hosain Musavi was appointed prime minister.

October 13: The Supreme Defense Council was formed to coordinate the war effort and to supervise a military reorganization and an intense period of training.

October 26: Iran's press reported that more than one thousand government officials had been killed over the past four months, including the prosecutor general, judges, police officials, Islamic Republic Party officials and Khomeini's aides and personal representatives to the provinces.

November 5: Iraq offered a one-month cease-fire during the holy month of Muharram, which Iran rejected on November 10.

November 15: Iran said that more than six thousand political prisoners had been detained since the shah's ouster.

November 22: Ayatollah Khomeini approved a plan to partially nationalize foreign trade.

November 24: In a wave of attacks, bombs exploded at Tehran's central train station and, on November 27, at Tehran's largest department store. In separate December and January incidents, members of parliament, a Friday prayer leader and a personal representative of Ayatollah Khomeini and several others were killed, followed by a wave of arrests. By December 29, Iranian press reported detention of more than 170 members of the Mojahedin and other leftist dissident parties in Tehran.

November 29: Heavy fighting was reported in southern Khuzistan Province. Iraq rejected Iranian claims of recapturing several villages. On December 3, Iran announced a major offensive in the area. Iran's Khuzistan gains led Iraqi President Hussein on December 9 to tell his troops, "It is very important that you not lose any more positions." Iran claimed further victories on December 11. On December 15, Hussein said he was prepared to end the war if Iran recognized Iraqi borders.

December 2: Iran denied purchasing arms from Israel.

December 29: Syria and Kuwait announced a new mediation effort in the war. On December 31, an Iranian delegation met with Syrian President Assad in Damascus.

1982

January 4: Six Baha'i leaders were executed, according to the Baha'i National Assembly office in London. On January 24, the *Tehran Times* reported that executions of the Baha'i were justified because of Baha'i collaboration with the shah.

January 22: Parliamentary Speaker Rafsanjani announced, "Iran does not want to attack the small countries of the Persian Gulf and does not want to interfere in their internal affairs." The next day, Bahrain's prime minister accused Iran of instigating Shi'ite communities throughout the Gulf to overthrow their governments in favor of revolutionary Islamic regimes. Bahrain's statement followed the uncovering of a coup attempt linked to Iran in December 1981. On January 28, Jordan announced that troops would be sent to aid Iraq.

February 3: Foreign Minister Ali Akbar Velayati announced at the United Nations that Iran's two preconditions for peace were "withdrawal of Iraqi troops from all Iranian territory and compensation for damage inflicted." He also said that Tehran was not ready for diplomatic relations with the United States.

February 8: Iran announced a raid on a Tehran home during which the ranking Mojahedin leader in Iran, his wife and the wife of the exiled Mojahedin leader were killed and twenty people involved in the escape of former President Bani-Sadr were arrested. On February 10, Iran's press reported that the underground opposition group Paykar had been "totally dismantled" after raids on twenty-two safe houses. On February 22, a bomb in Tehran, which was blamed on a monarchist group, killed fifteen and wounded sixty.

February 15: Iranian officials signed a protocol for economic and scientific cooperation with the Soviet Union after talks in Moscow.

March 1: Following weeks of heavy fighting around Susangerd, Shush and Bostan, Special U.N. Envoy Olof Palme announced failure to mediate a truce between Iran and Iraq. Jordanian volunteers left to join Iraqi troops.

March 4: The pardon of more than ten thousand prisoners was announced to mark the third anniversary of the founding of the Islamic Republic, but seventeen leftists were executed on March 6 for rebellious activities.

March 6: The Islamic Conference Organization initiated a new peace effort to end the Gulf war. On March 7, the U.S. press reported that Tehran was buying millions of dollars of war materiel from Israel, North Korea, the Soviet Union and Europe. On March 9, Ayatollah Khomeini announced that President Hussein was "past salvation and we will not retreat even one step."

March 10: Iran signed a food-for-oil barter agreement with Turkey. On March 17, Iran and Syria signed a ten-year trade agreement providing Damascus with sixty-three million barrels of oil annually. The Nuclear Technology Center director said that Iran would resume imports of nuclear materials and technology.

March 20: Iran's press reported that the Revolutionary Guards had raided the underground Fidayan-i Khalq movement and killed forty of its leaders.

March 22–29: Iran claimed major territorial gains in the Susangerd and Dezful areas during Operation *Fath*. On March 27, President Hussein called for a cease-fire and, on March 30, told troops "not to feel bitter over the rearrangement of the Iraqi defense lines." An Iranian military commander claimed on April 2 that "the end of the war with Iraq is near." On April 12, Hussein said Baghdad would withdraw its troops from Iran if Tehran agreed to end the war.

April 10: The arrest of former foreign minister Sadeq Qotbzadeh and others for plotting to assassinate Ayatollah Khomeini was confirmed by Iran's press. On April 16, more than one thousand were arrested in connection with a plot to assassinate the imam. On April 19, former Foreign Minister Qotbzadeh confessed on television to plotting to overthrow Khomeini. On April 20, Ayatollah Shariatmadari was stripped of his religious rank by Qom theology faculty for complicity in the plot against Khomeini; he was also placed under house arrest.

April 19: The Iranian chargé d'affaires in Rome resigned to protest political executions and repression in Iran. On April 23, the Iranian chargé d'affaires in Yemen resigned on similar grounds.

April 30–May 24: Iran announced that a new offensive had crossed the Karun River, forcing Iraqi troops from a three-hundred-square-mile area in southern Khuzistan; Iraq conceded a loss of territory. Heavy fighting ensued. On May 4, a plane carrying an Algerian mediation team crashed en route from Baghdad, killing all on board; Iran blamed Iraq. By May 7, Iran claimed that Operation Jerusalem had carried troops to the prewar borders. Iraq on May 8 admitted withdrawing troops from west of Ahvaz and Susangerd in preparation for the defense of Khorramshahr. On May 23, President Hussein called for Arab assistance to help defeat Iran. On May 24, Iran recaptured most of Khorramshahr, marking the largest offensive of the war.

May 2: Ten Mojahedin safe houses in Tehran were raided, during which at least fifty leaders were killed and which marked a new phase of repression against opposition groups. On May 12, Revolutionary Guards disclosed raids on ten Paykar hideouts and the arrest of seventy members. Arrests, particularly of Mojahedin supporters, and executions continued into August.

May 27: Israeli Defense Minister Sharon said the United States was aware in advance of Israel's sale of American war materiel to Iran, which was refuted by the U.S. State Department on May 28. Sharon claimed again the next day that the sale of $27 million of weaponry was made with the full knowledge of Washington officials.

May 28: Parliamentary Speaker Rafsanjani said Iran would not interfere in the Persian Gulf, and he repeated Iran's terms—reparations, Iraqi withdrawal and the trial of Iraqi President Hussein as conditions—to end the war. Iran said the fighting had shifted to the central front near Sumar, eighty miles from the Iraqi capital.

June 12: Iran dispatched a contingent of a thousand Revolutionary Guards to Lebanon a week after Israel's invasion.

June 20: President Hussein announced that Iraq had begun to pull out of Iran, which would be complete within ten days. Ayatollah Khomeini said on June 21 that the pullback would not end the war. Iraq announced completion of its withdrawal on June 29, which Iran said was "a lie." On June 30, Baghdad proposed a multinational force to patrol the border. On July 9, Parliamentary Speaker Rafsanjani announced that Iran would not honor a cease-fire until Iraq met Iranian demands. On July 12, a U.N. cease-fire resolution was rejected by Iran. The same day, Iraq reported a new Iranian attack near the southern Iraqi oil port of Basra. On July 13, U.S. intelligence reported that Iran had pushed ten miles into Iraq.

July 16: Iran held high-level economic talks with China in Beijing.

July 16–23: Heavy fighting was reported on a new northern front and on the southern front. Parliamentary Speaker Rafsanjani said that Iran's crossing into Iraqi territory was defensive and that Iran made no claims against other Gulf states, although it would take action against nations aiding Baghdad. Foreign Minister Velayati said the ouster of President Hussein was not a precondition for ending the war. Ayatollah Khomeini called for an Iraqi admission that it was the aggressor as a precondition to stop the fighting. The U.S. State Department said that, if requested, the United States was willing to conduct joint military exercises with Persian Gulf states.

July 24: Iran said that it was prepared to allow Algeria to mediate in the war. Ayatollah Khomeini warned Gulf nations against aiding Iraq "for the sake of their own futures." On July 28, President Hussein said he wanted a cease-fire to take effect in September. Parliamentary Speaker Rafsanjani declared that Iran would stay in Iraq until Tehran's conditions were met. U.S. Secretary of Defense Weinberger said Iran was "run by a bunch of madmen" who could endanger the Gulf if Tehran won the war.

August 1: Sixty-five members of the Mojahedin were reportedly killed or captured in Tehran raids, while twenty-four Jews in Mashad were arrested on smuggling charges. On August 8, three hundred members of the Mojahedin were reportedly killed, wounded or captured in Khuzistan over the previous four months.

August 14: Former Foreign Minister Qotbzadeh's trial began in Tehran on charges of plotting to overthrow the state. On August 16, he denied plans to kill Ayatollah Khomeini while admitting plotting to remove several clerics from the regime. Seventy officers were reportedly executed in connection with the plot. On September 16, Qotbzadeh was found guilty and executed by firing squad at Evin Prison.

August 15: President Hussein threatened to bomb vital oil targets unless Iran agreed to a cease-fire, which was followed by several weeks of sporadic Iraqi shelling of Iran's oil terminals at Kharg Island and tankers ferrying Iranian oil. On September 24, Parliamentary Speaker Rafsanjani said Iran would withdraw its pledge not to bomb Iraqi cities if Baghdad refused to meet Iran's terms to end the war.

August 24: Iran called for the Islamic Conference nations to boycott the United States due to its support for Israel.

September 6: Twenty were killed and more than one hundred wounded by a bomb in Tehran. On September 12, two bombs exploded in Tehran near Tehran University and at Enqilab Square. Another bomb went off on September 20 at Tehran's central bus station. On October 1, sixty were killed and seven hundred wounded by a bomb blast in central Tehran.

September 21: Parliament passed legislation outlining penalties for moral offenses.

October 1: Iran launched an offensive on the central front one hundred miles northeast of Baghdad, involving the heaviest fighting since July. Iraq asked for a U.N. Security Council meeting to debate the Iranian attack. On October 4, the U.N. Security Council unanimously voted for an end to the Gulf war and a withdrawal of all forces from occupied territory. Tehran rejected the move, while Baghdad said it would accept a cease-fire.

October 4–5: Dissidents hijacked a military plane to the United Arab Emirates, where they released passengers and asked for political asylum, which was denied. The plane returned to Iran, where the hijackers were arrested.

October 6–15: Heavy fighting was reported near the Shatt el-Arab waterway and on the central front as Iran amassed thousands of troops for what Western analysts predicted might be a final offensive. On October 23, the Islamic Conference Organization attempted a new round of mediation on the war, but reported a deadlock the next day.

November 1: Iran launched a new offensive near Dezful, with heavy fighting and high casualties. Iran reported gains inside Iraq on November 7. On November 8, President Khamenei said that Iranian troops would proceed toward Baghdad.

December 10: Iranians went to the polls to elect eighty-three members to an Assembly of Experts to determine the succession procedure after Ayatollah Khomeini's death.

December 15: Ayatollah Khomeini issued a warning to the judiciary and the Revolutionary Guards against abusing individual rights in arrests, searches and seizures. He outlined eight points as the basis of human rights regulations to prevent excesses. On December 22, he said that "to spy and search is contrary to Islam. . . . We should not engage in oppression. We should not investigate what is going on in people's homes." On December 28, the Tehran and Qom prosecutors were dismissed. On December 30, Khomeini approved appointment of a court president to try revolutionary prosecutors and judges charged with rights offenses. On January 1, further purges of the revolutionary tribunals were undertaken.

December 18: Ceremonies at Tehran University marked the reopening of several institutions of higher education throughout the country.

1983

January 4: Iran announced an end to three years of gasoline rationing. On January 11, parliament passed legislation allowing confiscation of property of Iranian exiles who did not return within two months.

January 18: Foreign Minister Velayati told an Austrian magazine that the ouster of President Hussein "never was a main condition for peace negotiations." On January 19, Iran announced its war budget for fiscal 1983 was $4 billion.

January 19: Iran-Soviet relations deteriorated after the expulsion of the Tass news agency and the January 25 execution of twenty-two members of the Union of Iranian Communists. On February 5, the communist Tudeh Party leader and other officials were arrested on charges of spying for Moscow. On February 14, Tass reported that "reactionary elements" were working to hurt Soviet relations with Iran.

February 6: Iran launched a ground offensive on the southern front, crossing into Iraq. On February 10, Iraq launched a counteroffensive backed up by heavy aerial bombardment. On February 14, Parliamentary Speaker Rafsanjani admitted Iran's offensive was making slow progress, while Western analysts said the offensive had failed. On February 17, Iran said that Iraq still occupied 350 square miles of Iranian territory.

February 28: Iran's press reported that a general amnesty freed more than eight thousand prisoners.

March 29: Parliament passed a law permitting women to initiate divorce proceedings, followed on April 16 by legislation imposing prison terms of up to one year on women violating Islamic dress codes. On May 17, parliament passed a law establishing a new Ministry of Intelligence. And legislation to Islamicize banking, including scrapping interest in favor of fluctuating dividends, was passed on May 31.

April 10: Iran launched another offensive in the south. Fighting ensued, with heavy casualties reported on both sides. On April 16, Iraq approved a cease-fire proposal from the Islamic Conference Organization meeting in Baghdad. On April 27, Saudi Arabia asked for Soviet assistance in ending the Gulf war.

April 30: Iran's press said that the communist Tudeh Party leader had confessed to spying for Moscow. On May 4, Iran dissolved the Tudeh Party and expelled eighteen Soviet diplomats for interfering in Iran's domestic affairs. On May 10, a Revolutionary Guards commander announced that more than one thousand Tudeh members had been detained. On May 25, Moscow expelled three Iranian diplomats.

May 11: Ayatollah Khomeini appealed for an end to disagreements among government officials. The International Red Cross accused both Iran and Iraq of "grave and repeated violations" of international law in treatment of enemy troops, while the United Nations approved an Iranian proposal to send delegations to inspect civilian areas damaged in the war.

May 20: An Arab peace mission reported encouraging signs from Tehran and Baghdad. On May 25, Iraq said it was prepared to sign a U.N. agreement to end attacks on border cities and civilian sites, which Iran rejected. On June 7, President Hussein said he would sign a limited cease-fire agreement allowing free passage of oil and ending border shelling during the holy month of Ramadan, which Iran rejected the next day.

May 21: President Reagan called for an end to persecution of the Baha'is, a statement that was criticized by Ayatollah Khomeini. On June 19, Baha'i officials charged that sixteen Baha'is had been executed during the previous two days.

May 29: A summit of industrialized nations, including the United States, said that the West should promote better relations with Iran.

July 1: Iraq's naval commander claimed that more than one hundred Iranian ships had been sunk in naval battles since 1980.

July 10: Prime Minister Musavi condemned illegal activities in Iran's bazaars. On July 13, thirteen bazaar merchants were arrested for hoarding. On July 18, new regulations were issued to prevent hoarding and profiteering.

July 14: The Assembly of Experts, elected to select Ayatollah Khomeini's successor, held its first meeting. In a July 19 address, Ayatollah Khomeini told the council that disagreements among the clergy were hurting the revolution and he called for unity and cohesion.

July 17: President Hussein appealed to the superpowers and the Gulf states to help end the war, followed on July 20 by Iraqi claims that Iran was being supplied with U.S. weapons.

July 23: Iraq conceded that Iran had penetrated territory during heavy fighting in the northern Kurdish areas after a new Iranian offensive launched the previous day. Clashes continued for several days. On July 29, Iran announced a new offensive along the central sector near Mehran. On August 5, Iran claimed that it had taken strategic northern mountain positions. On August 9, Iraq admitted a partial withdrawal on the central front.

August 23: Reflecting concern about internal squabbling, Ayatollah Khomeini urged unity between the military and the Revolutionary Guards. On September 4, he claimed the clergy would retreat from political life when the public "gets on the right track . . . as long as they have not found pious and competent people to replace them." In a October 5 talk to Tehran clerics, he warned against "satans" fomenting discord.

September 16: All Baha'i groups were banned.

September 17: President Hussein said Baghdad wanted peace with Tehran based on mutual noninterference. The next day Iran repeated threats to block oil exports if its shipments were disrupted.

October 17: The U.S. State Department said the United States would not allow Iran or anyone else to threaten access to the Gulf through the Strait of Hormuz, which was followed on October 19 by a statement from President Reagan that the Free World would not permit Iran to close the Gulf.

The issue was brought up by France's delivery of Super Etendard fighters equipped with Exocet missiles to Iraq and by Iran's subsequent warning that it would close the Gulf if its shipping was closed down by Iraqi attacks.

October 19: Iran launched a limited offensive in northeast Iraq. On October 22, Iraq claimed to have mined approaches to Iran's Bander Khomeini port. Iran claimed that ninety-five civilians had been killed and four hundred wounded in Iraqi missile attacks. Heavy fighting was reported on October 24 on the northern front, with high Iranian casualties.

October 23: A suicide car bomber drove into the U.S. Marine battalion headquarters in Beirut, killing 241 American military personnel. The United States later implicated Iran for aiding the plan and suggested a similar link to the April 1983 bombing of the U.S. embassy in Beirut.

October 26: Iran said that it would not accept U.N. Security Council resolutions on the war until the United Nations ended its favoritism of Baghdad. On October 31, the United Nations passed Resolution 540, calling on Iran and Iraq to safeguard shipping through the Gulf, which Tehran rejected. Iraq agreed to a cease-fire.

November 7: Opponents of the Khomeini regime attacked Iran Air offices in London, Vienna, Paris, Brussels and New Delhi.

November 10: Iran moved to sever economic relations with France after the sale of French warplanes to Iraq. On November 13, Parliamentary Speaker Rafsanjani repeated the threat to close the Gulf if Iraq cut off Iran's oil shipments. The United States expressed grave concern on November 25 about any attempt by Iran or Iraq to disrupt shipping.

December 6: Members and sympathizers of the communist Tudeh Party, including military officers, went on trial in Tehran. Trials of more than one hundred members, divided into small groups, lasted through January. On December 24, one hundred members of the Mojahedin were arrested.

December 8: Ayatollah Montazeri, later to become Khomeini's heir apparent, urged government reforms, noting that the revolution lacked "a certain moral courage and administrative audacity."

December 13: Iraq fired missiles at five Iranian towns as reprisals for six car bombings in Kuwait the previous day that hit the U.S. and French embassies and strategic Kuwaiti installations.

December 25: Three French diplomats were expelled from Tehran for unspecified undiplomatic activities. France responded on December 30 by expelling five Iranian students allegedly trained as terrorists.

December 31: The U.S. press reported a U.S. policy shift toward Iraq because Washington believed an Iraqi defeat would hurt U.S. interests.

The Soviet press criticized Iran and the Tudeh Party trial as a "judicial farce."

1984

January 7: Iran claimed territorial gains in northern Kurdistan during a week-long drive. Iraq launched air strikes of Iranian positions along the central front on January 17.

January 21: Eighty-seven Tudeh Party members were imprisoned for one year to life; a second trial of thirty Tudeh members began on January 29.

January 23: Following U.S. threats of preemptive strikes to prevent Iranian attacks on American targets, Iran warned the United States against any adventures directed against Iran. The U.S. State Department added Iran to the list of nations supporting international terrorism. On February 10, President Khamenei warned that Iran would close off the Gulf oil flow if the United States intervened directly in the Gulf War.

January 31: To mark the fifth anniversary of his return to Iran, Ayatollah Khomeini warned of internal disputes, especially within the military, that might lead to destabilization.

February 11: Iraq attacked civilian targets in Dezful, triggering a new phase of the "war of the cities." Iran responded on February 12 by shelling seven Iraqi cities. After repeated incidents, Iran accepted an Iraqi cease-fire offer on February 18. Both agreed to allow a U.N. mission to assess damage in civilian areas.

February 13: Iran announced a new offensive on the northern front, followed by a new offensive along the central front on February 16 and a major new push on the southern front on February 21. On February 27, Iraq announced a siege of Kharg Island and warned oil tankers not to approach the area. Iran captured part of the Majnun Islands on February 29. On March 3, Iran charged Iraq with using chemical weapons, a practice which the U.S. State Department condemned on March 5.

March 7: The Soviet Union charged that the U.S. presence in the Gulf was endangering peace. Iran claimed that it had repulsed an Iraqi effort to recapture Majnun Islands. From March 12 to 20, heavy fighting was reported on the southern front near Basra and in the marshlands around Majnun Islands. On March 14, the Arab League appealed for a worldwide ban on aid to Iran and condemned Tehran for blocking mediation efforts.

March 27: Iraq claimed use of French-made Super Etendard aircraft for the first time in the tanker war, hitting a Greek oil tanker. The tanker war escalated through April.

April 1–10: Heavy fighting was reported along the northern and southern fronts. Intense clashes were reported east of the Tigris River.

April 25: The United States urged a worldwide ban on the sale of nuclear materials to Iran, which led Iranian officials to ridicule Western speculation that Iran was building a nuclear bomb.

April 26: Opponents of the Khomeini regime attacked the Iranian consulate in London, the Iranian embassy in the Hague, Iran Air offices in Frankfurt and an Iranian U.N. delegation office in Paris.

May 1: Egypt disclosed that the Nonaligned Conference was preparing a mediation effort on the Gulf war, which Iran rejected the next day.

May 13: After a run of at least six Iraqi strikes on tankers doing business with Iran since April 18, Iran for the first time attacked a Gulf ship, the Kuwaiti *Umm Casbah*, marking the outbreak of the "tanker war." Lloyd's of London doubled the insurance rate for Gulf tankers. Parliamentary Speaker Rafsanjani declared on May 15, "Either the Persian Gulf will be safe for all or for no one." The next day Iran hit the Saudi tanker *Yanbu Pride*. U.S. officials claimed that Washington had offered air cover to Gulf states in April, but had been turned down. The six Gulf Cooperation Council states condemned Iranian aggression on May 17. On May 20, the twenty-two-nation Arab League called on the United Nations to take action to end the crisis. A Syrian mediation effort began on May 24. U.N. debates on May 25 led to condemnation of attacks on shipping out of neutral Gulf ports and a call for all states to respect international rights of free navigation. Lloyd's raised insurance for ships going to Iran's Kharg Island oil terminal from 3 percent to 7.5 percent. On May 29, the United States disclosed that it had shipped four hundred antiaircraft missiles to Saudi Arabia because of the tanker-war escalation. Between May 14 and May 30, Iraq claimed strikes on fifteen Iran-bound ships, and Iran was held responsible for three hits. On May 31, President Reagan said that Iran had prolonged the Gulf war by demanding unconditional victory while also going "beyond bounds" with strikes on neutral shipping.

May 17: Voters went to the polls in the second round of parliamentary elections since the revolution.

June 4: Algeria launched a Gulf-war mediation effort. On June 5, Saudi Arabia, aided by U.S. AWACS radar aircraft, shot down an Iranian plane in Saudi airspace. Iran pledged to strike Iraqi residential areas in retaliation for an Iraqi air raid killing six hundred Iranian civilians. The "war of the cities" raged until a U.N. appeal to end strikes on civilian cities, which both Iran and Iraq began observing on June 12.

June 21: Fighting escalated along the war front, with new charges of strikes on civilian targets in both nations the next day. On July 6, Parliamentary Speaker Rafsanjani pledged that Iran's "final offensive" was inevitable and could occur any time within the next year. Strikes on Gulf shipping continued.

July 22: At the end of an official visit, the first by a high-ranking Western official, the West German foreign minister said that Iran wanted to reestablish contacts with the West. On August 14, Foreign Minister Velayati said Iran should abandon its present foreign policy and take a more positive approach to diplomacy.

July 31–August 2: An Air France plane was hijacked to Tehran. The hijackers threatened to kill passengers unless five prisoners in France convicted of trying to murder former Iranian Premier Bakhtiar were freed. They surrendered after blowing up the cockpit. On August 8, two Iranian dissidents hijacked an Iran Air plane to Rome and surrendered.

August 9: Ayatollah Khomeini denounced Islamic Jihad's claims of mining the Red Sea and criticized Tehran Radio for implying support.

August 17: After weeks of fighting in northern Kurdistan, the Iranian press issued a final warning to Kurdish rebels to surrender and be pardoned or face death.

August 23: Seventeen were killed and three hundred wounded in a Tehran car bomb. On September 6, two car bombs exploded in Tehran, killing three.

August 28: An Iran Air plane was hijacked to Iraq by an Iranian couple, who asked for political asylum. On August 30, two Iranians flew an F-4 to Iraq and asked for political asylum. On September 8, an Iran Air plane was hijacked to Bahrain, Egypt and Iraq.

October 18: Iran launched an offensive on the central front, with Iraq counterstriking on the southern front the next day. Heavy fighting ensued in both regions. On October 27, both nations accused the other of breaking a U.N. cease-fire on striking civilian areas.

November 6: A Saudi jet hijacked to Tehran by two Yemenis was stormed by Iranian troops, who freed the hostages. On December 4, a Kuwait Airways plane was hijacked to Iran by Lebanese Shi'ites, who killed two American hostages before Iranian troops stormed the plane on December 9 and freed the remaining passengers. On December 11, the United States charged that Iran had initially encouraged the four hijackers. On December 18, Tehran refused to turn over the hijackers, saying they would be tried in Iran.

November 8: New courts were established to deal with bribery, embezzlement and fraud in Iran's new campaign against corruption. The next day, five Ministry of Heavy Industry officials were sentenced for bribery.

November 23: The International Red Cross accused Iran of grave and repeated violations in the treatment of fifty thousand Iraqi POWs.

December 22: Iran rejected an Islamic Conference Organization resolution on Islamic mediation to end the war.

December 25: Four were killed and fifty wounded in a Tehran car-bomb explosion, followed the next day by another bombing in which no casualties were reported.

1985

January 27: Iraq announced that it had launched the first ground attack in almost three years to recapture the Majnun oil fields. On January 27, the Greek ship *Serifos* became the first tanker to be struck by Iraq's newly acquired French-made Exocet missiles. On January 31, Baghdad also announced a new offensive on the central front. Heavy fighting ensued in both areas.

February 8: The "war of the cities" escalated as both countries charged the other with strikes on civilian areas in defiance of the 1984 U.N. agreement. On February 13, Iran charged that Iraq had struck its incomplete nuclear power plant. On February 21, a U.N. group reported that both Iran and Iraq regularly violated the Geneva Convention on POW treatment.

February 14: One hundred and fifty shops were shut down in Tehran for spreading "decadent Western culture."

March 6: Iran and Iraq escalated the "war of the cities" with air and missile attacks on civilian areas. A U.N. appeal on March 10 to both nations to abide by a 1984 agreement on residential areas contributed to a twenty-four-hour lull on March 23–24, which was quickly broken.

March 7: Baha'i sect officials told the U.N. Human Rights Commission that 140 Baha'is had been executed in Iran and that many others had been imprisoned and tortured.

March 11: Iran launched a new offensive aimed at cutting off the southern Iraqi city of Basra and at taking part of the river Tigris. Iran reached the east bank of the Tigris, but by March 20 Iraq had pushed the attackers back. Casualties were heavy on both sides, particularly for Iran due to Iraqi use of chemical weaponry. Iraq launched a new round in the "war of the cities" on civilian areas.

March 15: Five worshippers were killed by a suicide bomber at Friday prayer services being conducted by President Ali Khamenei in Tehran. On April 6, two explosions killed fourteen and wounded more than thirty. On April 7, Iran announced discovery of a sabotage network in possession of explosives.

March 20: The United States urged Iran to accept a negotiated settlement of the war and abandon hopes of a military victory. On March 25, an Arab League resolution announced "total solidarity" with Iraq and urged an end to the war. On March 26, the U.N. secretary-general presented a plan to reduce hostilities and to promote an end to the conflict, including a moratorium on strikes on civilian targets and an end to the tanker war. Parliamentary Speaker Rafsanjani said it would accept those terms, but to end the war Iran demanded $350 billion in war reparations, the ouster of the Iraqi regime and the return of Iraqi refugees to Iraq.

March 30–April 9: The U.N. secretary-general toured the Gulf states, Iran and Iraq to pursue peace efforts, but left after concluding that the gap in positions was "as wide as ever." Iraq pledged to raid Iranian cities until Iran agreed to a comprehensive peace.

April 1: The United States warned that Iran would be held responsible if American hostages in Lebanon were harmed, to which Iran responded on April 3 that it was not involved in kidnappings. By midsummer, Washington had begun dealing with Iran for an arms-for-hostages swap.

April 24: Ayatollah Khomeini called for unity between the army and the Revolutionary Guards to prevent divisions from hurting the war effort. On May 2, President Khamenei's sister fled to Iraq to join her dissident husband.

May 12: Fifteen people were killed and fifty wounded in a car-bomb blast in Tehran.

May 17: Iraq offered a thirty-one-day cease-fire during the holy month of Ramadan, which Iran rejected. A Tehran rally reportedly protested continuation of the Gulf war.

May 18: The Saudi foreign minister began an official visit to Tehran, the first by a high-level Saudi official since the revolution. The U.S. press reported that the Iranian government was split over conditions to end the war, primarily whether the overthrow of President Hussein's regime should be a precondition.

May 19: Mehdi Bazargan's Freedom Movement, the only legal opposition party, was allowed to reopen its Tehran office, which had been ransacked three months earlier, and was officially invited to participate in 1985 presidential elections.

May 27: The "war of the cities" escalated as both sides struck at civilian targets and residential areas, including both capitals, until Iraq called for a cease-fire on June 16 and Iran complied. Baghdad also increased military pressure on Iran's Kharg Island and on tankers doing business with Iran.

June 2: During a visit to Japan, Parliamentary Speaker Rafsanjani called on the United States to initiate restoration of relations with Iran. Later that month, he played a role in ending the hijacking of TWA 847 and the seventeen-day hostage ordeal of thirty-nine Americans in Beirut in talks with Lebanese Shi'ite extremists in Syria, which was acknowledged by the

U.S. State Department. On July 25, Ayatollah Montazeri urged Iranian diplomats to improve relations with Western nations.

June 8: Iran announced a new offensive in Marivan sector, and a second offensive on June 17. On June 22, Iraq claimed to have repulsed Iranian attacks on the southern front. On July 12, Iran launched another attack on the southern front, which Baghdad claimed to have repelled. Between July 15 and 29, fighting was reported on the northern front.

August 14: The second of two shipments of 508 TOW antitank missiles was shipped to Tehran from Israel. The same day, the Rev. Benjamin Weir became the first American hostage to be freed in an arms-for-hostages swap.

August 15: Iraq claimed to have destroyed Kharg Island, which initially triggered a major increase in oil prices in Europe. Baghdad continued sporadic air strikes on Kharg throughout the fall, crippling the Iranian oil refinery's loading capacity and leading Iran to develop alternative export routes farther south.

August 16: Presidential elections were held. From a field of three candidates, President Khamenei won reelection by a decisive majority. Supporters of Mehdi Bazargan boycotted the poll once the Freedom Movement leader was among the twenty-seven candidates not approved by the Council of Guardians.

August 18: Thirty were wounded by a Tehran car bomb. On September 11, another Tehran car bomb wounded three, and a third bomb on September 19 killed one and wounded eighteen.

September 8–30: In heavy fighting, Iran reportedly recaptured key northern Kurdish territory.

October 22: Iran announced an offensive in the Sumar area, which Iraq claimed to have repulsed, although fighting continued for several days.

November 3: A car bomb in Tehran wounded two. On November 7, another bombing injured three. On December 7, two were killed and eighteen wounded by a car-bomb blast.

November 22: Eighteen HAWK antiaircraft missiles were shipped to Tehran from Israel as the second phase of an arms-for-hostages swap. But the deal fell far short of what was promised, and Tehran ordered a refund of payment and a resupply.

November 23: The Assembly of Experts elected Ayatollah Montazeri as Ayatollah Khomeini's successor.

1986

January 9: The U.S. press reported that Paris was attempting to better relations with Tehran to help win freedom for French hostages in Lebanon.

But on Februrary 24, five French citizens, including a diplomat, were arrested in Tehran, a week after four Iranians were ordered to leave France in connection with a wave of bombings in Paris, and then expelled.

January 17: President Reagan signed a special finding to permit negotiations with Iran on hostages and to help promote "moderate" elements in Tehran. This was followed by shipments totaling a thousand TOW antiaircraft missiles from Washington via Israel at the end of February.

February 9: Iran launched a two-pronged offensive on the northern and southern fronts. Little progress was made in the north, but in the south Iran captured strategic Faw Peninsula, which it held despite heavy casualties and repeated Iraqi counterattacks. Fighting was reportedly heavy throughout the spring. A year later, Iraq claimed that the loss of Faw was due to misleading intelligence from the United States.

February 24–26: Iran announced a new offensive on the northern front in the Kurdish mountains.

March 2: To mark Women's Day, Ayatollah Khomeini opened the way for greater participation of women in public life, including military service.

March 11: Tehran demonstrators protested against Kuwait and Saudi Arabia for their war policies. On March 13, Iran said that the Gulf states faced possible military action if they did not end their support for Iraq. On March 14, the U.N. secretary-general announced that a team of experts had confirmed Iraqi use of chemical weaponry against Iran, which was formally condemned at the Security Council a week later.

April 3: Ayatollah Shariatmadari died of cancer at age eight-seven after being under house arrest for five years.

April 19: A Friday prayer leader in Azerbaijan was killed in a bomb explosion. On May 9, two Iranians were killed in a Tehran bus-bomb explosion.

April 22: Three Israelis were among seventeen indicted in New York on conspiring to sell Iran American war materiel. Israel denied any links with the ring. Israel, however, was at this stage deeply involved in the U.S. arms-for-hostages swap with Iran. Two more Israelis were arrested in New York on May 15. An Israeli official accompanied the National Security Council team, led by former chief NSC advisor Robert McFarlane, to Tehran the following month.

May 15: Iran barred a British diplomat from taking a post in Tehran after London's rejection of an Iranian diplomat connected with the 1979 U.S. embassy seizure.

May 13: Jordan and Syria attempted a joint peace effort in the Gulf war, while heavy fighting intensified on the central and southern fronts. On

May 17, Tehran conceded that Iraq had captured the Iranian city of Mehran. Iran retook Mehran in early July and claimed to have crossed into eastern Iraq.

May 20: A high-level Iranian mission arrived in Paris for talks on normalizing relations, which reportedly centered on repayment of a $1 billion loan by the shah to a European uranium-enrichment consortium and on the French hostages in Lebanon. On June 7, Mojahedin leader Masoud Rajavi was expelled by France, reportedly as part of a French deal to free its hostages.

May 25–28: Former National Security Advisor Robert McFarlane, Lieutenant Colonel Oliver North and others made a secret trip to Iran to deliver a secret arms shipment.

June 18: American telecommunications engineer John Pattis was arrested in Iran for espionage.

July 8: Thirty-seven were wounded by a bomb in a Tehran café. An August 5 bomb in Tehran killed one. Eleven were killed in a Qom car bomb and twenty died in a Tehran car bomb on August 19.

July 26: After more than a year in captivity, Father Lawrence Martin Jenco was freed in Lebanon as part of the arms-for-hostages swap. On August 3, the United States delivered new HAWK missiles to Iran.

July 27: An Iraqi air raid on Arak that killed more than seventy marked a new round in the "war of the cities." President Khamenei vowed on August 2 that Iran would retaliate against Iraqi industrial centers. Sporadic air and missile strikes on several cities in both nations continued through mid-September.

August 25: Iran announced plans to resume natural-gas exports to the Soviet Union after high-level talks in Moscow.

September 5: In a clandestine broadcast on Iranian television, Shah Reza II, son of the former shah, declared himself ruler of Iran and called for the overthrow of the Khomeini government.

September 9: American educator Frank Herbert Reed was abducted in Beirut, followed on September 12 by the kidnapping of Joseph Cicippio, an American University of Beirut administrator. Between September 19 and 20, a new Iranian channel related to Rafsanjani visited Washington for talks on arms, hostages and improved relations.

October 2: The Foreign Ministry announced another round of talks with France to improve relations. On October 29, Iran and France announced agreement on partial repayment of a 1975 Iranian loan to a French energy agency, reportedly as part of a deal to free hostages in Lebanon.

October 8: Demonstrators attacked the West German embassy in Tehran in retaliation for violence by anti-Khomeini elements at a recent Frankfurt Book Fair in which pro-Khomeini Iranians had been injured.

October 12: Mehdi Hashemi, head of the World Islamic Movement and protégé of Ayatollah Khomeini's designated successor Ayatollah Montazeri, was arrested in Tehran and charged with treason, murder, sabotage and other crimes. On October 21, American writer Edward Austin Tracy was abducted in Beirut. Between October 26 and 29, the United States provided one thousand new TOW antitank missiles to Iran. On November 2, hostage David Jacobsen was freed in Beirut. On November 3, the Lebanese magazine *As Shiraa* revealed the secret trip of former National Security advisor Robert McFarlane to Iran, which was denied by the State Department. The leak was reportedly from allies of Hashemi, who were trying to sabotage the U.S.-Iran deal.

November 4: On the seventh anniversary of the U.S. embassy seizure, Parliamentary Speaker Rafsanjani confirmed the McFarlane trip, but claimed that he had been "uninvited." The White House claimed the arms embargo against Iran was still in effect. The next day, Ayatollah Montazeri said that if the United States "comes to its senses" then it would be correct to reestablish humanitarian relations.

November 6: President Reagan said reports that the United States and Iran had reached a secret agreement on hostages had no foundation and were endangering efforts to win their release. On November 7, Parliamentary Speaker Rafsanjani said that Iran would try to help free American hostages in Lebanon if Washington released weapons sold to Iran during the shah's reign. On November 11, Israel denied supplying arms to Iran.

November 11: Iraq renewed air raids on Iran and a new round in the "war of the cities" began as Iran retaliated for each strike. Attacks on civilian areas and strategic oil installations continued through December.

November 13: In a television address, President Reagan said reports that the United States sold arms to Iran in exchange for hostages were "utterly false." He said small shipments of arms were to start "a new relationship" with Iran. The next day, President Khamenei said Iran could not help the United States with hostages "under the present circumstances."

November 20: Ayatollah Khomeini said U.S. officials "have come back meekly and humbly at the door of this nation wishing to establish relations. . . . Our nation rejects them." On November 23, questions raised earlier in Iran's parliament about U.S.-Iran contacts were withdrawn.

November 25: Foreign Minister Velayati defended Iran's foreign policy of "neither East nor West" by explaining "having relations with countries is different from accepting their hegemony."

November 25–26: The United States disclosed that profits from arms sales to Iran had been diverted to the Contras and confirmed that the undisclosed third country involved in the Iran arms sales was Israel. On November 27, the Jewish member of Iran's parliament was arrested on morals charges.

December 1: The Soviet press charged that Iran aided U.S. interests in Afghanistan. After a six-year gap, Iran and the Soviet Union began talks on December 9 on economic cooperation, which culminated on December 12 with a new protocol on trade, banking, transport, steel mills, fisheries and power generation.

December 10: Mehdi Hashemi confessed to murder, weapons violations and collaboration with the shah's secret police on national television.

December 23: A high-level French delegation began talks in Tehran about settling Iran-French financial disputes.

December 25: Iran launched its offensive, code-named Karbala, on the southern front around Basra.

1987

January 6: The southern Iraqi oil port city of Basra came under intense shell fire as Iran launched Karbala-5 around Iraq's Fish Lake. Karbala-5, one of the war's longest offensives, lasted through February 25 and made major inroads in southern Iraq.

January 17: A new phase in the "war of the cities" erupted when Iraq bombed Tehran as well as other Iranian cities for the first time in two years. Iran responded on January 22 with a surface-to-surface missile attack on Baghdad. With the exception of a brief, Iraq-initiated cease-fire on January 27, civilian residential areas in both countries were the site of frequent bombardment until February 18, when Iraq announced a two-week cessation of attacks on cities. The tanker war also escalated during this period.

January 20: Hostage mediator Terry Waite disappeared in Beirut. On January 24, three Americans and an Indian with U.S. residency, all professors at Beirut University College, were abducted in Beirut. On January 31, *Wall Street Journal* reporter Gerald Seib was detained in Iran. After four days of interrogation about his Israeli connections, he was released on February 3.

January 21: Secretary of State Shultz reported that he had approved a meeting between his officials, the CIA and unnamed Iranians the previous month. He ordered an end to negotiations when Iran offered another arms-for-hostages swap, although the CIA reportedly continued the talks. On January 23, President Khamenei said Iran had rebuffed a U.S. effort to maintain contacts. On January 28, Parliamentary Speaker Rafsanjani showed journalists the Bible autographed by President Reagan, whom he said was "serious and honest" in his decision to resume ties with Iran but demonstrated "weakness" in his actions.

February 10: Ayatollah Khomeini, appearing in public for the first time in almost three months, called for "war until victory" against Iraq.

February 11: President Khamenei discounted speedy reconciliation with the United States. On February 13, Foreign Minister Velayati held talks with Soviet Foreign Minister Eduard Shevardnadze in Moscow.

February 17: Iran expelled two German diplomats and closed consulates in Hamburg and Frankfurt to protest a German television documentary on Iran.

March 14: U.S. sources reported Iranian deployment of Chinese Silkworm missiles along the Strait of Hormuz, which led to a U.S. warning on March 20 against Iranian interference with Gulf shipping. Tehran replied on March 22 that it had no intention of affecting freedom of navigation.

April 7: Parliamentary Speaker Rafsanjani said normal relations with the United States would be possible once Tehran was sure the United States did not pose a threat to Iran.

April 21: Parliamentary Speaker Rafsanjani said that if the United States showed "goodwill" by releasing frozen Iranian assets in the United States, Tehran would try to mediate the release of American hostages in Lebanon, adding that U.S.-Iranian relations need not remain poor until "doomsday." The United States confirmed that it had been negotiating with Kuwait about flying the American flag on Kuwaiti tankers. The Soviet Union said it would respond "firmly" to any attack on ships flying the Soviet flag in the Gulf.

April 22: Iraq charged that the United States and Israel still supplied Iran with arms and "military expertise." American John Pattis, a telecommunications engineer arrested in mid-1986, was sentenced to ten years for spying for the CIA. On April 24, President Ali Khamenei warned Kuwait against seeking American and Soviet protection for its tankers. Iran launched Karbala-10, the final phase in the Karbala series, against Iraq. It ended three days later.

April 23: The U.S. State Department admitted that it had occasional contacts with the Mojahedin.

May 7: Secretary of State Shultz said the United States would continue to press for an arms embargo against Iran until Tehran agreed to negotiate an end to the war.

May 13: A U.N. team announced that Iraq had begun using chemical weapons on Iranian civilian targets. The United States returned $451 million in frozen assets, which had been left over from the 1981 Algiers accord on American hostages, after a May 5 decision by the World Court in the Hague.

May 16: A Soviet tanker leased to Kuwait hit a mine. The next day, the USS *Stark* was attacked by an Iraqi missile in the Gulf, killing thirty-seven crewmen. Parliamentary Speaker Rafsanjani said the Iraqi attacks demonstrated that the United States was a "paper tiger" and presented no danger to Iran. The *Marshal Zhukov*, one of three Russian tankers leased to Kuwait, hit a mine in the Gulf. On May 19, the United States expanded its role in the Gulf to protect reflagged Kuwaiti tankers.

May 28: British diplomat Edward Chaplin was abducted and beaten in Tehran in apparent retaliation for the May 9 arrest of an Iranian diplomat in Manchester for shoplifting. Chaplin was released the next day. Between June 4 and 6, five Iranian diplomats were ordered to leave Britain, and Iran's Manchester consulate was closed due to impasse on the Chaplin incident. Iran retaliated by expelling Chaplin and four other British envoys. Between June 10 and 12, Iran was ordered to reduce its London embassy staff by two; Iran expelled four more British diplomats. Between June 15 and 18, Britain recalled six more diplomats from its embassy in Tehran and ordered fifteen Iranian diplomats to leave Britain.

June 2: The Islamic Republic Party was dissolved. Parliamentary Speaker Rafsanjani said it was no longer needed and that polarization would hurt national unity. Khomeini responded by warning against "sowing discord."

June 3: Ayatollah Khomeini announced formation of a five-member committee to study the hostage situation in Lebanon.

June 4: Iranian Foreign Ministry officials toured European capitals urging U.S. allies to reject Washington's plans to patrol the Gulf because an increased presence would prove dangerous. On June 5, Parliamentary Speaker Rafsanjani warned Gulf states against providing facilities to the United States, or Iran would "occupy that base and port and drive the Americans from there."

June 9: The summit of industrialized nations endorsed the principle of freedom of navigation in the Gulf but did not go along with U.S. urging to warn Iran. On June 15, Bahrain said the Gulf states would not grant facilities to the United States or the Soviet Union, and that neither nation had requested access. President Reagan said that if the United States did not protect Gulf shipping, the Soviet Union would.

June 19: In Baghdad, Mojahedin leader Masoud Rajavi announced the formation of the Iranian National Liberation Army to overthrow the Tehran government.

June 30–July 2: France set up barricades around the Iranian embassy in Paris because of Iran's refusal to hand over an Iranian interpreter who was suspected of having links to a group responsible for a wave of 1986 bombings in France. Iran claimed that he had diplomatic immunity; France said he was only a staff employee. Iran retaliated by preventing French diplomats in Tehran from leaving the French embassy. On July 14, a French diplomat was summoned before an Iranian court on charges of spying. On July 17, France and Iran severed relations over a diplomatic standoff at respective embassies in Paris and Tehran.

July 5: Iran reportedly began deployment of Chinese-made Silkworm missiles.

July 7: The Soviet Union offered to withdraw its warships from the Gulf if the United States did. On July 20, the U.N. Security Council unanimously passed Resolution 598 calling for a Gulf war cease-fire, which Iraq welcomed and which Iran criticized but did not reject outright.

July 22: The USS *Bridgeton*, the first reflagged Kuwaiti tanker escorted by the U.S. Navy, entered the Persian Gulf; the *Bridgeton* hit a mine on July 24. Lloyd's of London announced that 333 ships had been hit in the Gulf since the war began, including 65 in 1987.

July 30: Ayatollah Khomeini called for Haj pilgrims in Mecca to hold demonstrations of "disavowal." Iranian demonstrations on July 31 led to clashes with Saudi security forces, during which more than four hundred were killed. Crowds in Tehran stormed the Saudi and Kuwaiti embassies the next day, ransacking and burning the embassies.

August 3–7: Iran conducted "Martyrdom" maneuvers in the Gulf to train suicide squads to ram warships with explosive-laden speedboats.

August 4: A Soviet delegation visited Tehran to discuss building oil pipelines and a railway linking the Soviet Union to the Gulf, which led to a preliminary joint agreement on August 12 to convert a gas pipeline to transport Iranian oil to the Black Sea.

August 6: Shah Reza II, son of the former shah, announced that he was ready to emerge from eight years of low-key opposition to unite exiled groups under his leadership.

August 8: A U.S. F-14 fired two missiles at an Iranian warplane.

August 10: Iraq began the first in a series of sporadic bombing raids against industrial and other nonmilitary targets in several Iranian cities that lasted through August. On August 29, an informal cease-fire in the tanker war expired, and Baghdad ordered a series of raids on ships doing business with Iran and offshore installations.

August 11: Britain and France announced dispatch of minesweepers to the Gulf. On August 13, the United States blamed Iran for planting mines in the Gulf, but called on Iraq to show more restraint in attacks on Iranian shipping traffic after Baghdad resumed strikes. Iran began its own minesweeping operations in the Gulf of Oman on August 14.

August 15: The trial of Mehdi Hashemi began in Tehran. On August 28 he was convicted of treason and sentenced to death, a sentence carried out on September 28.

August 31: The Reagan administration protested renewed Iraqi attacks on Iranian ships and oil facilities, which Iraq said on September 2 were justified to force Iran to accept a cease-fire.

September 3: The United States postponed a call for an international arms embargo at the United Nations while the secretary-general conducted a peace mission to the region beginning September 11. Parliamentary Speaker Rafsanjani said Iran would accept a cease-fire if Iraq was identified as the aggressor by the United Nations. Iraq called for United Nations punishment of Iran for not accepting a cease-fire. On September 4, Italy agreed to send warships to the Gulf. The secretary-general left for the region on September 15.

September 21: U.S. helicopters hit and set ablaze the *Iran Ajr* on a minelaying mission. Three Iranians were killed, twenty-six captured. At the United Nations, President Khamenei said that the *Iran Ajr* was a merchant ship and that the American version was "a pack of lies." Captured sailors were returned to Iran on September 26, and the United States blew up the *Iran Ajr*.

September 29: After the U.S. press reported that Iran had become the second largest supplier of crude oil to the United States, the Senate voted to ban the import of Iranian oil and other products.

October 3: Iran and Iraq officially severed diplomatic relations and closed their respective embassies in Tehran and Baghdad.

October 8: U.S. helicopters struck and sank three Iranian gunboats after they shot at a U.S. helicopter. Four captured Iranians were returned nine days later. On October 15, an American-owned tanker was set on fire inside Kuwaiti waters by an Iranian missile. The next day, the U.S.-reflagged Kuwaiti tanker the *Sea Isle City* was also hit inside Kuwaiti waters by an Iranian missile.

October 19: In retaliation for the *Sea Isle City* attack, the United States struck Iran's Rashadat offshore oil-drilling platform. The next day Kuwait's northern desert was hit by artillery shells, reportedly Iranian. On October 22, an offshore Kuwaiti terminal was hit by an Iranian missile. The United States announced a ban on Iranian imports and on military-related American exports to Tehran. On October 29, Israeli Defense Minister Yitzhak Rabin alleged that Baghdad had manipulated the United States into a confrontation with Tehran.

October 21: Tehran reportedly began a diplomatic initiative to better relations with Britain, France and the Soviet Union. Aeroflot flights to Iran had resumed on October 15, and the new Soviet ambassador presented his credentials in Iran on November 3. Rafsanjani revealed that Tehran and Moscow were negotiating a new agreement.

November 2: The United Nations received written responses from Tehran and Baghdad on Resolution 598. Iran demanded that a commission first determine guilt for starting the war before a formal cease-fire; it also linked withdrawal of troops to reparations for war losses. Iraq agreed to a truce before guilt was established. On November 4, Iranian Premier Musavi said the United Nations was unlikely to be able to organize a truce.

November 8: The Arab League began a three-day summit in Jordan. The final resolution unanimously backed Iraq in the Gulf war.

November 13: Iran announced a ten-point plan for mobilizing new troops and new financial support for the war effort. Three days later, President Khamenei was quoted on Iranian radio as having ordered 20 percent of government employees to enlist. New Iranian offensives were launched in Sulaymaniya on November 22 and in Irbil on November 23.

November 27: Two French hostages were freed in Lebanon, marking a new effort at rapprochement between France and Iran. Return of more than $300 million loaned to France by the shah was at the center of a multifaceted deal. On November 30, the two nations also exchanged embassy employees who had been at the center of a diplomatic dispute since July. France later expelled Iranian opposition figures.

December 3: Iranian Deputy Foreign Minister Larijani concluded talks on the U.N. peace proposals in New York. On December 9, the Iraqi foreign minister repeated Baghdad's acceptance of Resolution 598. No progress was reported. On December 16, U.S. officials claimed that Moscow was prepared to consider an Iranian arms embargo on condition that a U.N. naval force be involved.

December 10: A secret new Khomeini will, replacing an earlier document, was presented to government officials for safekeeping.

1988

January 1: Lloyd's of London disclosed that 178 ships were attacked in the Persian Gulf in 1987, compared with 107 in 1986, making it the worst year of the tanker war. December's hits included 34 confirmed attacks. Attacks on Gulf shipping remained high throughout January.

January 5: Two-year mandatory military service in Iran was extended by four months.

January 7: In response to growing disputes within the hierarchy, Khomeini issued a ruling strengthening the powers of the Islamic government. On February 6, the imam announced the formation of a new council to adjudicate disputes between Iran's *majlis* and the Council of Guardians in the event of a deadlock on new legislation.

February 12: U.S. reconnaissance helicopters near a Kuwaiti convoy came under fire from Iran, which claimed that the aircraft had flown near two Iranian islands.

February 27—April 20: The new and most deadly stage of the "war of the cities" erupted when Iraq struck Tehran. Iran responded with missile strikes on Baghdad and Basra. On February 29, Iraq for the first time used enhanced Soviet-made Scud-B missiles to hit Tehran seventeen times in twenty-four hours. Iraq's new capability to strike deep into Iran without using its air force led to devastating hits on a dozen major cities over the next seven weeks. Two cease-fires quickly collapsed. Iran responded with use of its missiles and extensive shelling along the border and at Baghdad.

February 28: Montazeri said Iran had no desire to keep even "one foot" of Iraqi territory. On March 4, Iran's U.N. ambassador claimed Tehran had written the secretary-general expressing willingness to accept Resolution 598, but the United Nations did not accept the statement as a full endorsement.

March 6: Just over a day after an American ship fired on small gunboats moving near U.S. barges, U.S. reconnaissance helicopters came under fire in the central Gulf. The Soviet embassy was attacked by mobs in Tehran following reports that Moscow provided Baghdad with the missiles used in the "war of the cities."

March 17: Tehran charged that Iraq had made massive use of chemical weapons, killing between three and five thousand Kurds, after Iranian troops seized the Iraqi border town of Halabjah. On March 22, Iran again claimed Iraqi use of chemical warfare in the Marivan area. Baghdad's use of chemical weapons was reported again in early April. The United States later confirmed and condemned Iraqi use of chemical warfare in Kurdish areas but claimed that Iran had also made more limited use of chemical weapons.

April 12: The first round of parliamentary elections were held; the second round took place on May 13. The vote was the third *majlis* poll since the revolution. Only one-quarter of the seats went to clerics, compared with almost one-half in the two previous contests.

April 14: The USS *Samuel B. Roberts* struck a mine in the Gulf; ten American sailors were injured. On April 18, in its first major offensive in almost two years, Iraq retrieved its Faw Peninsula in a thirty-six-hour rout. In retaliation for Iran's new mining in the Gulf, the United States struck two Iranian oil platforms, sank a patrol boat and a frigate and badly damaged a second small frigate and three small craft. The United States lost one helicopter and two men. On April 20, an Iranian missile landed near a Kuwaiti oil field. On April 22, the United States announced it intended to authorize the navy to protect non-American ships in the Gulf upon request. From early May through early June, the tanker war heated up again with assaults by both Iraq and Iran on Gulf ships.

May 18: Following the release of the final three French hostages on May 4, France announced an intention to restore diplomatic ties to Tehran. Relations were formally restored in mid-June.

June 2: In response to recent military losses, Parliamentary Speaker Rafsanjani was appointed commander-in-chief of the military by Khomeini. The appointment also followed circulation of a letter by former Premier Bazargan in late May openly criticizing Khomeini for a failed war policy. On June 7, Rafsanjani was also reelected parliamentary speaker of the new *majlis*.

June 19: The Mojahedin's National Liberation Army claimed thrusts inside Iran. On June 25, Baghdad reported the recapture of Majnun Islands. Baghdad claimed a series of significant gains on its southern and northeastern fronts.

July 2: President Khamenei admitted that Iran had made military mistakes and had "missed opportunities" on the war front. The same day, Rafsanjani conceded that Tehran had "incorrectly created enemies." On July 3, the United States damaged three Iranian gunboats after they fired on American helicopters. Less than an hour later, the USS *Vincennes* fired at an Iran Air airbus, downing the plane and killing 290. On July 12, American helicopters and Iranian gunboats exchanged fire near Farsi Island.

July 18: President Khamenei notified the United Nations that Iran accepted Resolution 598 to end the war. The same day, Lloyd's of London reported that during the eight-year Gulf war at least 546 ships had been hit. On July 20, Khomeini formally endorsed an end to the war, calling it worse than "drinking hemlock." On July 22, both Tehran and Baghdad said they would send their foreign ministers to New York for formal peace talks.

July 18: On the same day that Iran agreed to a United Nations cease-fire, Tehran and Canada announced agreement to restore diplomatic relations. On July 26, Rafsanjani disclosed that Iran was prepared to help win the release of American hostages in Lebanon in exchange for Iran's military and financial assets frozen in the United States since the revolution. Washington rejected the terms.

July 25: In an apparent attempt to make last-minute gains, the Mojahedin National Liberation Army (NLA) made a push into Iran, claiming gains the next day in Bakhtaran Province. Within four days, the NLA claimed it had withdrawn, while Iran claimed it had surrounded and destroyed the Mojahedin force.

August 1: A U.N. report announced that chemical weapons had been used by Iraq on "an intense and frequent" scale in the war. Tehran claimed that Baghdad continued to use chemical warfare in Kurdish areas even after Iran's agreement to end the war. Despite initial obstacles, the United Nations announced on August 8 that a formal cease-fire would begin on August 20, with formal talks to begin five days later in Geneva. Throughout the fall and winter of 1988, the two sides did not agree to a permanent truce because of differences over rights to the Shatt al-Arab as well as the sequence of a prisoner exchange and the pullout of troops from each other's territory. Iran demanded a return to the terms of the 1975 Algiers accord.

September 3: Khomeini ordered the government to allow people to import and sell foreign consumer goods, thus guaranteeing the right of free enterprise. The ruling coincided with other edicts allowing Iranians to use certain musical instruments and to play chess again.

September 5: A government crisis over confirmation of the cabinet was diverted when President Khamenei refused to accept the resignation of Prime Minister Musavi. The premier reportedly sent a letter to the president complaining of his lack of control over government policies. The next day, Khomeini scolded Musavi and other officials for bickering and diverting attention from reconstruction. Three cabinet members subsequently received votes of no confidence.

September 29: Two Kuwaiti envoys reopened the embassy in Tehran. Cyprus and Iran also reportedly reestablished formal relations. On September 30, Britain announced the intention of restoring relations with the Islamic Republic; its Tehran embassy formally reopened on December 4. Throughout the fall, nations from Europe, Asia and Africa sought visits to Tehran to discuss closer relations and joint economic projects.

October 3: Khomeini announced a nine-point plan on reconstruction priorities, giving emphasis to adherents of "barefoot Islam" and war "martyrs." He also declared, "As long as I live, I will not allow the true direction of our policies to change."

October 3: Mithileshwar Singh, an Indian-born lecturer with American residency who was abducted in January 1987 along with three American professors, was freed in Beirut. In two letters dated October 30, former

President Jimmy Carter wrote Khomeini and Rafsanjani that release of the remaining hostages in Lebanon would "remove a fundamental barrier to the resumption of friendly relations." Iran responded that the letters were a "new trick." On October 31, the United States announced that, in light of the end of the tanker war, it would soon pull out the first American warship from the Persian Gulf. Iran held its annual celebrations to mark the November 4 seizure of the U.S. embassy in Tehran. The same day, a conservative Iranian daily said that, in light of Iran's greater self-confidence and security after a decade, relations with the West, including the United States, no longer had to mean domination.

November 3: A U.N. report charged that a "large number" of Iranians, mainly from opposition groups, were executed in the three months after Iran accepted the cease-fire. On December 13, an Amnesty International report claimed that at least three hundred had been executed in a wave of political executions since the August cease-fire. It called the confirmed executions "the tip of the iceberg."

December 4: The government announced that it would approve political parties, under certain conditions, but it warned groups applying for permits to "learn from past experiences." On December 31, Khomeini told the Expediency Council to give up some of its decree-making powers wielded during the final months of the war.

1989

January 4: Khomeini's emissaries carried a letter to Soviet leader Mikhail Gorbachev from the imam suggesting that Moscow study Islam as a means of filling the "ideological vacuum" in the Soviet system. On February 26, Khomeini received Soviet Foreign Minister Eduard Shevardnadze in Tehran. The imam said he wanted strong ties with the Soviet Union to fight the "devilish" West.

January 21: Iran introduced a stiff new antidrug law that stipulated the death sentence for anyone caught with thirty grams of heroin or eleven kilos of opium or hashish.

February 1–11: Iran celebrated the "ten days of dawn," which marked the tenth anniversary of Khomeini's return to Iran through the fall of the shah's caretaker government. At least three thousand prisoners were eligible for a pardon by the ayatollah during the anniversary.

February 14: Following riots in Pakistan that killed five people, Khomeini issued a religious edict calling on Muslims worldwide to track down and execute Salman Rushdie, author of *The Satanic Verses*. The next day an Iranian cleric offered a $2.6 million dollar reward for Rushdie's execution. The European Community jointly criticized the death sentence on Rushdie and individually withdrew their ambassadors. On February 28,

Iran's parliament voted to give Britain one week to condemn the book and its author, or Tehran would sever relations. Iran broke off relations on March 7.

March 28: Khomeini's office announced the resignation of Ayatollah Ali Montazeri, his heir apparent, on grounds that Montazeri was both reluctant and not prepared to assume the sweeping powers of the Supreme Jurisprudent. The resignations of Iran's U.N. ambassador Mohammad Mahallati and the deputy foreign minister in charge of American and European affairs, Mohammad Javad Larijani, were also confirmed.

June 3: After eleven days in a hospital for an operation to stop internal bleeding, Ayatollah Khomeini suddenly lapsed into critical condition and died. Within twenty-four hours, the Assembly of Experts selected President Ali Khamenei as the temporary new "Revolutionary leader." A final decision on succession would await the conclusion of a referendum on constitutional reforms and a presidential election scheduled, before the imam's passing, for August.

Source Notes

Prologue

1. Interview in Tehran, June 1988.

2. James A. Bill, *The Eagle and the Lion: The Tragedy of American-Iranian Relations*, pages 27–30.

3. General Robert E. Huyser, *Mission to Tehran*, page 88.

4. "Chronology," *The Middle East Journal*, volume 36, number 1, Winter 1982, page 75, citing *The New York Times*.

5. Nisha Desai, "The Cost of the War in Lives and Money," *Dialogue: A Magazine of International Affairs*, volume 1, number 1, page 3.

6. Brian Jenkins and Robin Wright, "The Fearsome New Forms of Hostage-Taking," *Newsday*, July 23, 1988.

7. Robin Wright and Geoff Kemp, "Shifting Sands," *New Perspectives Quarterly*, volume 5, number 2, Summer 1988.

8. Hamid Algar, translator and annotator, *Islam and Revolution: Writ-*ings and Declarations of Imam Khomeini*, page 48.

9. James A. Bill, "Why Tehran Finally Wants a Gulf Peace," *The Washington Post*, "Outlook" section, August 28, 1988.

10. Robin Wright, "A Reporter at Large: Teheran Summer," *The New Yorker*, September 5, 1988.

11. During two summer visits to Tehran in 1988, the legal exchange rate was sixty-seven rials to the dollar. But on the black market, the dollar could fetch up to fourteen hundred rials.

12. Based on interviews conducted during two visits to Tehran in summer 1988, after the April and May 1988 elections for parliament.

13. "Islamic Revolutionary Komiteh, Gendarmerie to Have Unified Command," from *Kayhan*, in *Akhbaar News and Translation Service*, September 15, 1988.

Chapter One

1. Michael M. J. Fischer, *Iran: From Religious Dispute to Revolution*, page 1.

2. Sign painted on the fence around the former shah's Niavaran Palace in Tehran.

3. Ronald Koven, "Travelers Share Sense of Danger on Exile's Plane," *The Washington Post*, February 2, 1979.

4. John Simpson, *Inside Iran: Life Under Khomeini's Regime*, page 27.

5. Paul Lewis, "On Khomeini's Flight: The Morning Prayers on Newspaper Mats," *The New York Times*, February 2, 1979.

6. Shaul Bakhash, *The Reign of the Ayatollahs: Iran and the Islamic Revolution*, page 16.

7. R. W. Apple, "Bakhtiar Warns Foe; Says He Will Take Strong Steps If Ayatollah Tries to Name a Regime," *The New York Times*, February 1, 1979.

8. R. W. Apple, "Khomeini Threatens to Arrest Bakhtiar If He Stays in Post," *The New York Times*, February 2, 1979.

9. Ibid.

10. Jonathan C. Randal, "Graveside Homage Paid to Martyrs," *The Washington Post*, February 2, 1979.

11. Fred Halliday, "The Iranian Revolution and Great Power Politics," paper presented at a symposium at the Center for International and Strategic Affairs at the University of California at Los Angeles, April 22–23, 1988.

12. Bernard Lewis, "Islamic Revolution," *The New York Review of Books,* January 21, 1988.

13. Said Amir Arjomand, *The Turban for the Crown: The Islamic Revolution in Iran*, page 4.

14. Simpson, op. cit., page 36.

15. "Imam's Family Background According to Ayatollah Pasandideh," from *Pasdar-e Islam*, in *Akhbaar News and Translation Service*, January 25, 1989, pages 6–8.

16. Henry Munson, Jr., *Islam and Revolution in the Middle East*, pages 41–45; John W. Limbert, *Iran: At War with History*, pages 78–82; Fischer, op. cit., pages 30–31 and 181–84.

17. Munson, op. cit.

18. Fischer, op. cit.

19. Limbert, op. cit.

20. "Imam's Family Background," op. cit.

21. *Current Biography*, November 1979, page 23; Amir Taheri, *The Spirit of Allah: Khomeini and the Islamic Revolution*, page 19.

22. *Current Biography*, op. cit.; David Hirst, *The Guardian*, March 17, 1979.

23. Mohsen M. Milani, *The Making of Iran's Islamic Revolution: From Monarchy to Islamic Republic*, pages 88–89.

24. Limbert, op. cit., page 85.

25. For brief but thorough accounts of Reza Shah's reign, see Limbert, op. cit., chapter 5, and Arthur Goldschmidt, Jr., *A Concise History of the Middle East*, pages 216–21.

26. Ibid.

27. "Imam's Family Background," op. cit.

28. Goldschmidt, op. cit., page 218.

29. Algar, op. cit., page 14.

30. "Imam, a Model in Everything," *Etalaat*, June 4 and June 7, 1988, in *Akhbaar News and Translation Service*, June 9, 1988.

31. Limbert, op. cit., page 88.

32. Algar, op. cit., pages 169–73.

33. Ibid., page 374.

34. Ibid., page 14.

35. Cole and Keddie, op. cit., pages 1–30.

36. John L. Esposito, *Islam and Politics*, pages 43–44 and 49–51.

37. Robin Wright, *Sacred Rage: The Wrath of Militant Islam*, pages 37–38.

38. Munson, op. cit., page 50.

39. Bill, op. cit., pages 26–35 and 53–72; Limbert, op. cit., pages 88–96.

40. Bill, op. cit., pages 71–72.

41. William H. Sullivan, *Mission to Iran*, pages 55–56.

42. Bill, op. cit., pages 147–56.

43. Taheri, op. cit., page 126.

44. Ibid., pages 134–46.

45. Algar, op. cit.

46. Bakhash, op. cit., page 32.

47. Algar, op. cit., pages 181–88.

48. Ibid.

49. Cheryl Benard and Zalmay Khalilzad, *The Government of God: Iran's Islamic Republic*, pages 12–13.

50. Ibid., page 12.

51. Algar, op cit., pages 35–36.

52. Bill, op. cit., pages 183–85.

53. Ibid.

54. Algar, op. cit., pages 200–208.

55. Munson, op. cit., page 20.
56. Esposito, op. cit., pages 10–15.
57. "Imam, a Model in Everything," op. cit.
58. Munson, op. cit., page 59; Taheri, op. cit., pages 182–83.
59. Bill, op. cit., page 233.
60. Sullivan, op. cit., page 90.

61. Taheri, op. cit., page 200.
62. Ibid., pages 222–23.
63. Bakhash, op. cit., pages 15–16.
64. Taheri, op. cit., page 233.
65. Bakhash, op. cit., pages 16–17; Taheri, op. cit., pages 234–35.
66. Sullivan, op. cit., page 57.
67. Interview in Tehran, June 1988.

Chapter Two

1. Dilip Hiro, *Iran Under the Ayatollahs*, page 106.
2. Algar, op. cit., page 282.
3. Tim Wells, *444 Days: The Hostages Remember*, pages 8–18. Wells's oral histories are the most comprehensive firsthand accounts of the hostage ordeal. The original interviews on which his book is based are housed at the Perkins Library at Duke University.
4. Interview with Colonel Holland, December 12, 1988.
5. Sullivan, op. cit., page 235.
6. Ibid., pages 254–56.
7. Wells, op. cit.
8. Holland interview, op. cit.
9. Wells, op. cit.
10. Sullivan, op. cit.; Wells, op. cit.
11. Sullivan, op. cit., pages 265–67.
12. Ibid., page 271.
13. Benard and Khalilzad, op. cit., page 105; Hiro, op. cit., page 104.
14. Bill, op. cit., page 264.
15. Ofra Bengio and Uriel Dann, "Iran," in *Middle East Contemporary Survey*, volume III, 1978–79, page 522.
16. Bakhash, op. cit., pages 52–55.
17. Crane Brinton, *The Anatomy of Revolution*, pages 128–84.
18. Milani, op. cit., pages 253–54.
19. Brinton, op. cit., page 141. Brinton's classic study of revolutions, first issued in 1938, applies as much to Iran's upheaval as it did to the English, American, French and Russian revolutions he studied. His section on the fate of revolutionary moderates, on pages 128–154, outlines why they are doomed to failure.
20. Simpson, op. cit., pages 82–83.
21. Milani, op. cit., pages 255–60; Bakhash, op. cit., pages 59–63.

22. Bakhash, op. cit., page 57.
23. Milani, op. cit.
24. Simpson, op. cit., page 93.
25. Bengio and Dann, op. cit., page 520.
26. Bakhash, op. cit.; Milani, op. cit.; Simpson, op. cit., pages 47–49.
27. *1980 Amnesty International Report*, page 52.
28. Milani, op. cit., pages 257–58; Bakhash, op. cit., pages 63–64.
29. Milani, op. cit., page 257.
30. Bengio and Dann, op. cit., page 518.
31. Ibid., page 521.
32. Holland interview, op. cit.
33. Bakhash, op. cit., page 75.
34. Algar, op. cit., page 170.
35. Both quotes were cited in Benard and Khalilzad, op. cit., page 110.
36. Milani, op. cit., page 262.
37. Benard and Khalilzad, op. cit., page 111.
38. Milani, op. cit., page 266.
39. Sullivan, op. cit., page 277.
40. Holland interview, op. cit.
41. Interview with Mike Metrinko, December 4, 1988.
42. Metrinko interview, op. cit.
43. John Kifner, "How a Sit-in Turned Into a Siege," Robert D. McFadden, Joseph B. Treaster, and Maurice Carroll, editors, *No Hiding Place*, pages 175–87. Kifner's discussions with members of the Students Following the Imam's Line after the embassy seizure provides an original and chilling account of what led to the ordeal.
44. Wells, op. cit., page 70.
45. Ibid., pages 86–88.
46. Ibid., pages 87–88.
47. Ibid., page 85.
48. Ibid., page 78.

49. Metrinko interview, op. cit.
50. Wells, op. cit., page 123.
51. Ibid., pages 123–24.

52. Kifner, op. cit., page 178.
53. Wells, op. cit., page 122.

Chapter Three

1. Radio Tehran, quoted in *Foreign Broadcast Information Service*, March 10, 1982.
2. David Menashri, "Iran," in *Middle East Contemporary Survey, 1979–80*, page 454.
3. Menashri, op. cit., page 486.
4. John Kifner, "Iraq Planes Strike 10 Airfields in Iran; Oil Area Imperiled," *The New York Times*, September 23, 1980; Hiro, op. cit., page 166.
5. Interview on CBS News's "Face the Nation," September 21, 1988, as quoted in wire service reports.
6. Edgar O'Ballance, *The Gulf War*, page 64.
7. "War in the Persian Gulf," October 6, 1980.
8. *The Guardian*, March 5, 1979, as quoted in Hiro, op. cit., page 153.
9. Hiro, op. cit., page 154.
10. Shahram Chubin and Charles Tripp, *Iran and Iraq at War*, page 36.
11. "War in the Persian Gulf," op. cit.
12. Chubin and Tripp, op. cit., page 40.
13. Henry Tanner, "Iraqis Intensifying Shelling of Abadan; Refinery in Flames," *The New York Times*, September 27, 1980.
14. Radio Tehran, quoted in *Foreign Broadcast Information Service*, October 21, 1980.
15. Menashri, op. cit., page 447.
16. Ibid., pages 448–49.
17. *The New York Times*, January 28, 1980, quoted in Menashri, op. cit., page 449.
18. Statistics provided by the press office of the Iranian parliament in interviews, June 1988.
19. *The Middle East* magazine, April 1980.
20. *Jomhuri Islami*, January 31, 1980.
21. *The Guardian*, June 28, 1980, as quoted in Menashri, op. cit., page 462.

22. "War in the Persian Gulf," op. cit., page 40.
23. Ibid.
24. Ami Ayalon, "The Iraqi-Iranian War," in *Middle East Contemporary Survey, 1979–80*, page 41; O'Ballance, op. cit., page 38.
25. O'Ballance, op. cit., page 38.
26. Bakhash, op. cit., page 136.
27. O'Ballance, op. cit., page 40.
28. Bakhash, op. cit., page 130.
29. O'Ballance, op. cit., pages 62–63.
30. *Kayhan*, January 15, 1981, as quoted in Bakhash, op. cit., page 149.
31. Interview with Mike Metrinko, January 5, 1989.
32. Holland and Metrinko interviews, op. cit.
33. Bakhash, op. cit., pages 127–35.
34. Hiro, op. cit., page 180.
35. Bakhash, op. cit., page 156.
36. Hiro, op. cit., pages 179–85; Bakhash, op. cit.
37. Hiro, op. cit., page 183.
38. Interviews with diplomats in Tehran, April 1982.
39. Hiro, op. cit., page 191.
40. "A Government Beheaded," *Time*, September 14, 1981.
41. *The Financial Times*, September 10, 1981, as quoted in Menashri, op. cit., page 545.
42. Bakhash, op. cit., page 220.
43. O'Ballance, op. cit., pages 66–67.
44. Ibid., pages 68–69.
45. Tom Baldwin, "Iranian Boys, as Young as 13, Fighting Against Iraq," Associated Press, April 10, 1982.
46. David Hirst, "How the Mullahs Fought to Win," *The Guardian*, April 16, 1982.
47. Interview during a trip to the Dezful-Ahvaz front, March-April 1982.
48. Interview with Iranian ground commanders during a tour of the front,

March-April 1982; O'Ballance, op. cit., pages 78–85.

49. Interview with Iranian ground commanders during a tour of the front, March-April 1982.

50. Interviews with prisoners of war at a camp near Dezful, March-April 1982.

51. Ibid.

52. Robin Wright, "Winning Streak Puts Iran in Quandary," *The Sunday Times* (London), April 4, 1982.

53. O'Ballance, op. cit., page 82.

54. Ibid., page 85.

55. Robin Wright, "Mullahs' Law: Think Our Way or Face Death," *The Sunday Times* (London), April 11, 1982.

56. R. W. Apple, "Khomeini's Islamic Regime Appears to Strengthen Its Grip; Opposition Fades," *The International Herald Tribune*, November 22, 1982.

57. David Menashri, "Iran," in *Middle East Contemporary Survey, 1982–83*, pages 522–25.

Chapter Four

Most of the research in this chapter is based on residence in Beirut between 1981 and 1984, eyewitness reporting of the Iranian involvement in Lebanon and interviews with Iranian leaders in Tehran in 1987 and 1988.

1. Ayatollah Ruhollah Khomeini, "Excerpts from Speeches and Messages of Imam Khomeini on the Unity of the Muslims," distributed by the Ministry of Islamic Guidance, Tehran.

2. Interview with Rafiqdoost in Tehran, June 14, 1988.

3. Wright, *Sacred Rage*, op. cit., pages 114–19.

4. *Newsweek*, May 31, 1982.

5. Interview, May 2, 1984.

6. David Menashri, "Iran," in *Middle East Contemporary Survey, 1981–82*, page 562.

7. *Foreign Broadcast Information Service*, March 3, 1982, page I–2.

8. Interview in Bahrain, May 19, 1984.

9. Interview in Beirut, September 1984.

10. *As Shiraa* magazine, November 29, 1983.

11. Interview with Rafiqdoost, op. cit.

12. "War and Power: The Rise of Syria," ABC television's "Close-up," June 14, 1984.

13. Interview with Mohtashami, June 7, 1988.

14. Wright, *Sacred Rage*, op. cit., pages 112–13.

15. Ibid., page 43; Menashri, "Iran," 1981–2, op. cit., page 562.

16. Menashri, "Iran," 1982–3, op. cit., pages 522–31.

17. David Menashri, "Iran," in *Middle East Contemporary Survey, 1983–84*, page 447.

18. Uriel Dann, "The Iraqi-Iranian War," in *Middle East Contemporary Survey, 1982–3*, page 259.

19. Uriel Dann, "The Iraqi-Iranian War," in *Middle East Contemporary Survey, 1983–4*, pages 183–86.

20. Robin Wright, "The Gulf Catches Fire," *The Sunday Times* (London), May 20, 1984.

Chapter Five

1. Reuters report reprinted in the *Beirut Daily Star*, August 15, 1984.

2. Tower Commission, *Report of the President's Special Review Board*, page B-109.

3. David Ottaway in *The Washington Post*, July 5, 1985, and *Newsweek*, July 15, 1985.

4. Interviews with National Security Council officials from the Reagan administration, fall 1988.

5. Byrne, *The Chronology: The Documented Day-by-Day Account of the Secret Military Assistance to Iran and the Contras*, published by the National Security Archive, page 122.

6. Anthony H. Cordesman, *The Iran-Iraq War and Western Security, 1984–1987: Strategic Implications and Policy Options,* page 79.

7. Chubin and Tripp, op. cit., pages 47–48.

8. Cordesman, op. cit., pages 75–79.

9. Interviews on the Iran-Iraq front, March-April 1982, and interviews in Tehran, August 1987.

10. Robin Wright, "Iran Was Seeking a Way to Reach Out to the West," *The Baltimore Sun,* December 28, 1986.

11. *The Chronology,* op. cit., pages 188–90.

12. Ibid., page 199.

13. David Menashri, "Iran," in *Middle East Contemporary Survey,* 1986, pages 329–31.

14. Ibid., pages 430–31.

15. Ibid., pages 433–35.

16. Hiro, op. cit., pages 264–66.

17. *The Chronology,* op. cit., pages 201–3.

18. Ibid., pages 213–20.

19. Ibid., page 225.

20. Ibid., page 271.

21. Ibid., page 293.

22. Cordesman, op. cit., pages 92–96.

23. Menashri, "Iran," 1986, op. cit., page 325.

24. *The Chronology,* op. cit., page 328.

25. Tower Commission, op. cit., pages B-85 and B-94; *The Chronology,* op. cit., pages 360, 370, 380.

26. Tower Commission, op. cit., page B-101.

27. Ibid., page B-114.

28. Ibid., page B-102.

29. Interviews with members of the McFarlane delegation, winter 1988, and interviews in Tehran, June and July 1989.

30. Tower Commission, op. cit., pages B-106 to B-109.

31. Ibid., page B-119.

32. Robin Wright, "On the Trail of a Deadly Terrorist," *Los Angeles Times,* November 26, 1988.

33. Tower Commission, op. cit., page B-117.

34. Ibid., page B-136.

35. Menashri, "Iran," 1986, op. cit., page 325.

36. Tower Commission, op. cit., page B-137.

37. Ibid., page B-147.

38. Ibid., page B-150.

39. Ibid., page B-152.

40. *The Chronology,* op. cit., pages 483–84.

41. Tower Commission, op. cit., pages B-157 to B-160.

42. Ibid., page III-18.

43. Ibid.

44. Ibid., pages B-166 to B-167.

45. *The Chronology,* op. cit., page 530.

46. Tower Commission, op. cit., page B-167.

47. Interviews with intelligence sources in Washington, March 9, 1989.

48. Interviews in Tehran, June 1988.

49. "Hashemi-Rafsanjani on Alleged McFarlane Visits," *Foreign Broadcast Information Service,* November 5, 1986, pages I-1 to I-5.

50. Ibid.

51. Menashri, "Iran," 1986, op. cit., page 331.

Chapter Six

1. "Excerpts from Khomeini's Speeches," *The New York Times,* August 4, 1987.

2. "Sermon on Social Matters," from Tehran Radio, *Foreign Broadcast Information Service,* December 28, 1987, pages 58–61.

3. Cordesman, op. cit., pages 122–124.

4. Ibid.

5. Interviews in Tehran, August 1987 and June 1988.

6. "Iranian Says U.S. 'Begged' for Ties," Associated Press report, *The New York Times,* December 6, 1986.

7. Robin Wright, "Life's Little Inconsistencies—They Abound in Iran's Islamic Revolution," *The Christian Science Monitor,* August 31, 1987.

8. *The Christian Science Monitor,*

December 12, 1986, as quoted in Cordesman, op. cit.

9. Cordesman, op. cit., pages 125–127.

10. Interviews with Reagan administration officials, Iran-Contra investigators and Pentagon officials, July 1988 and March and April 1989.

11. Interviews in Tehran, August 1987 and June 1988.

12. Ibid.

13. Loren Jenkins, "Tehran Sees a Rare Sign of War Dissent," *The Washington Post*, May 17, 1987.

14. Cordesman, op. cit., pages 132–134.

15. Robert Fisk, "Khomeini's Power Broker," *The Times* (London), August 6, 1987.

16. Cordesman, op. cit., page 131.

17. Gerald F. Seib, "Four Days in Iran Jail Leaves Reporter Seib Baffled as to Reasons," *The Wall Street Journal*, February 10, 1987.

18. Interview with Gerald Seib, March 13, 1989.

19. Seib, "Four Days," op. cit.

20. Interviews with European diplomats and Iranian officials in Tehran, June 1988; interviews with Lebanese Druze officials, September 1988.

21. Brian Michael Jenkins and Robin Wright, "The Kidnappings in Lebanon," *TVI Report*, volume 7, number 4, 1987.

22. Interviews with European envoys in Tehran, June 1988.

23. "Abolishing the Ruling Islamic Party: Why and for Whose Sake?," *The Middle East Reporter*, July 11, 1987, pages 13–15.

24. Andrew Gowers, "The Vice-Regency of the Prophet," *The Financial Times*, February 9, 1988.

25. Ed Blanche, "Khomeini, on Persian New Year, Appeals for Unity," Associated Press, March 21, 1987; "Iranian Leader Appeals for Unity," Reuters, March 21, 1987.

26. "Abolishing the Ruling Islamic Party," op. cit.

27. Patrick E. Tyler, "U.S. Flags Raised on Two Tankers," *The Washington Post*, July 22, 1987.

28. Gerald F. Seib and Barbara Rosewicz, "The Best Arab Friends Washington Has Are the Most Bitter Over Iran Arms Sale," *The Wall Street Journal*, December 11, 1986.

29. Tim Carrington and Gerald F. Seib, "Dire Straits: U.S. Ponders Response to Any Iranian Reprisals for Shielding Tankers," *The Wall Street Journal*, July 21, 1987.

30. Elaine Sciolino, "A Failed Bid for Safe Passage in the Gulf," *The New York Times*, January 10, 1988.

31. "Excerpts from Khomeini's Speeches," op. cit.

32. Mushahid Hussain, "Eyewitness in Mecca," *The Washington Post*, August 20, 1987; "402 Die in Mecca as Iranians Riot," *Facts on File*, August 7, 1987, pages 565–66.

33. Interviews in Tehran, August 1987.

34. "402 Die in Mecca," op. cit.

35. Tour of the two embassies, early August 1987.

36. Robin Wright, "Jockeying for Position in Post-Khomeini Iran," *The Christian Science Monitor*, August 25, 1987; interviews with Western and Asian diplomats in Tehran, August 1987.

37. Robin Wright, "Iran Takes Wait-and-See Stance on U.S. Gulf Moves," *The Christian Science Monitor*, August 17, 1987.

38. Visit to Revolutionary Guard headquarters in Tehran, June 1988.

39. John Kifner, "New Raids by Iraq," *The New York Times*, August 11, 1987.

40. Interview with President Khamenei at the United Nations, September 22, 1987; Paul Lewis, "Iranian, in U.N., Rebuffs Reagan on Ceasefire," *The New York Times*, September 23, 1987.

41. "Hashemi-Rafsanjani Delivers Friday Sermon," from Tehran Radio, in *Foreign Broadcast Information Service*, October 5, 1987, pages 53–58.

42. Interview in Tehran, June 1988; Wright, "A Reporter at Large," op. cit., pages 38–39.

43. "Excerpts from Khomeini's Speeches," op. cit.; Wright, "A Reporter at Large," op. cit.

44. Shaul Bakhash, "Iran: Recent Developments in Domestic and Foreign Policy," paper presented at the National Defense University, March 31, 1988.

45. *Foreign Broadcast Information Service,* January 7, 1988, pages 49–51; Vahe Petrossian, "Khomeini Opens the Way for Economic Reform," *Middle East Economic Digest,* January 16, 1988, page 10; Wright, "A Reporter at Large," op. cit.

46. Godfrey Jansen, "Khomeini's Heretical Delusions of Grandeur," *Middle East International,* January 23, 1988.

47. "Khomeini Answers Letter on Government Rulings," from Tehran Radio, in *Foreign Broadcast Information Service,* February 8, 1988, pages 55–62; Vahe Petrossian, "Khomeini Empowers Special Assembly to Act on Economy," *Middle East Economic Digest,* February 13, 1988, page 10.

48. Interview in Tehran, June 1988.

49. Interviews with eyewitnesses and tour of the missile damage in Tehran, June 1988.

50. Andrew Bilski, "Under a Cloud of Death," *Maclean's,* April 4, 1988.

51. Interviews with Reagan administration officials, July and August 1988, and with Pentagon officials, September 1988 and April 1989.

52. Interviews in Tehran, June and July 1988.

53. Wright, "A Reporter at Large," op. cit.

54. Interviews in Tehran, June 1988.

55. Interviews in Tehran, June 1988; Youssef M. Ibrahim, "Tehran Said to Reassess the Future of Its Dream," *The New York Times,* June 6, 1988; Youssef M. Ibrahim, "Economics of Revolution Bedevil Iran," *The New York Times,* July 11, 1988.

56. "Second Sermon on Elections, War," *Foreign Broadcast Information Service,* January 19, 1988, pages 75–77.

57. Interview in Tehran, June 1988.

Chapter Seven

1. "Leader Designate: We Must Redress Mistakes of Past Ten Years," from *Abrar,* in *Akhbaar News and Translation Service,* February 12, 1989, page 2.

2. *Akhbaar News and Translation Service,* June 25, 1988, page 11.

3. "Profile: Ali Akbar Hashemi Rafsanjani," *The Echo of Iran,* October 18, 1988, pages 19–20.

4. Interview with Mohammad Hashemi, Rafsanjani's brother, in Tehran, June 1988.

5. Ibid.

6. Patrick E. Tyler, "Iraq Recaptures Strategic Marshes," *The Washington Post,* June 26, 1988.

7. Youssef M. Ibrahim, "Iraqi Troops Recapture Big Oil Field," *The New York Times,* June 26, 1988.

8. Interviews with foreign military attachés in Tehran, June and July 1988.

9. Interviews with Revolutionary Guard members and foreign military envoys in Tehran, June 1988.

10. Interviews in Tehran, July 1988; Nadim Jaber, "Contemplating Peace," *Middle East International,* June 24, 1988.

11. From Tehran Television, "Hashemi-Rafsanjani Interviewed on New War Policy," in *Foreign Broadcast Information Service,* July 6, 1988, pages 59–61.

12. "Seven Minutes to Death," *Newsweek,* July 18, 1988.

13. Karen DeYoung, "Iran Buries Victims, Accuses U.S. of Conspiring with Iraq," *The Washington Post,* July 8, 1988.

14. Interview in Tehran, July 1988.

15. Interviews in Tehran after the airbus disaster, July 1988.

16. Long-distance interviews with foreign envoys in Tehran, September and October 1988, and interviews in Washington, August and September 1988.

17. Long-distance interviews with foreign envoys in Iran, August and September 1988.

18. "Revolution Aims," from *Jom-*

huri Islami, in *Akhbaar News and Translation Service,* August 21, 1988, pages 3–4.

19. "In Brief," from *Jomhuri Islami,* in *Akhbaar News and Translation Service,* August 30, 1988, page 3.

20. Patrick E. Tyler, "Offbeat Holjatoleslam Is the Talk of Tehran," *The Washington Post,* October 27, 1988; *Jomhuri Islami,* in *Akhbaar News and Translation Service,* October 5, 1988, pages 2–3.

21. *Jomhuri Islami,* in *Akhbaar News and Translation Service,* July 17, 1988, pages 3–4.

22. "Revolution Aims," op. cit.

23. "Hashemi-Rafsanjani Interviewed," op. cit.

24. "Revolution Aims," op. cit.

25. *Akhbaar News and Translation Service,* October 17, 1988.

26. *Foreign Broadcast Information Service,* September 16, 1988, page 60.

27. Youssef M. Ibrahim, "Iran Is Said to Be Moving Toward Policy of Moderation," *The New York Times,* September 23, 1988.

28. "Iran Opens Its Doors for Business," *The Financial Times,* September 12, 1988.

29. Safa Haeri, "Opening the Doors," *Middle East International,* September 9, 1988, pages 11–12.

30. Patrick E. Tyler, "Correspondence Indicates High-Level Rift in Iran," *The Washington Post,* November 11, 1988; "Confidential Letter," *The Echo of Iran,* October 18, 1988, page 21.

31. "Khomeini Writes Musavi," *Foreign Broadcast Information Service,* September 7, 1988, pages 40–41.

32. "Majlis Debates," from *Kayhan,* in *Foreign Broadcast Information Service,* September 23, 1988, pages 43–47.

33. "Editorial Assesses Relations with the United States," from *Jomhuri Islami,* in *Foreign Broadcast Information Service,* December 1, 1988, pages 61–63; "End of White House's Dreams About Iran," from *Jomhuri Islami,* in *Akhbaar News and Translation Service,* November 6, 1988, page 3.

34. "Deputy Foreign Minister Returns to Tehran After Talks with French, Italian and West German Officials," from *Kayhan,* in *Akhbaar News and Translation Service,* September 10, 1988, pages 8–9.

35. "Rapprochement with U.S.," from *Kayhan,* in *Akhbaar News and Translation Service,* September 3, 1988, page 8.

36. "Khomeini Letter on Guidelines for Reconstruction," from Tehran Radio, in *Foreign Broadcast Information Service,* October 4, 1988, pages 46–48; Scheherazade Daneshkhu and Safa Haeri, "Restoring Relations," *Middle East International,* October 7, 1988, pages 11–12.

37. Audrey Woods, "Amnesty International Reports Hundreds of Executions in Iran," Associated Press, December 12, 1988; "U.N. Report Expresses Concern About Human Rights in Iran," Reuters, November 11, 1988.

38. *Amnesty International Report on Political Executions in Iran,* December 12, 1988.

39. Youssef M. Ibrahim, "Montazeri's Evolution: An Heir Is Gone," *The New York Times,* April 2, 1989.

40. "Ayatollah Montazeri's Criticism of the Government," *The Echo of Iran,* October 18, 1988, page 9.

41. Patrick E. Tyler, "Ten Days of Dawn, Ten Years of Struggle," *The Washington Post Weekly,* February 6–12, 1989.

42. Patrick E. Tyler, "Khomeini: Father or Avenger?," *The Washington Post,* February 2, 1989.

43. "Khomeini Letter on Guidelines for Reconstruction," op. cit.

44. "Senior Officials Discuss Tenth Anniversary," from the Islamic Republic News Agency, in *Foreign Broadcast Information Service,* February 9, 1979, pages 52–55.

45. "Khomeini Predicts Hardships for Iran," Reuters, January 10, 1989.

46. Tyler, "Khomeini: Father or Avenger?," op. cit.

47. Ibid.

48. Robin Wright, "Khomeini's War on Book Seen as Bid to Unify Iran," *Los Angeles Times,* February 22, 1989.

49. "Khomeini Issues Message to

Religious Authorities," from Tehran Radio, in *Foreign Broadcast Information Service,* February 23, 1989, pages 44–48.

50. "Khomeini Puts Iran on Renewed Hardline Policy Over Rushdie," Reuters, February 23, 1989.

51. "Khomeini Issues Message to Religious Authorities," op. cit.

52. Elaine Sciolino, "Montazeri, Khomeini's Designated Successor in Iran, Quits Under Pressure," *The New York Times,* March 29, 1989.

Epilogue

Most of the vignettes in this chapter are drawn from various trips to Iran, particularly in 1987 and 1988.

1. Hugh Pope, "Khomeini Buried Amid Hysteria and His Policies Live On," Reuters, June 7, 1989.

2. Lord J. M. Balfour's 1921 evaluation of Persia cited in Benard and Khalilzad, op. cit., page 1.

3. "Hashemi Rafsanjani Notes Khomeini's Last Moments," from Tehran Television, in *Foreign Broadcast Information Service,* June 5, 1989, page 40.

4. Interview in Tehran, June 1988.

5. John Fullerton, "Khomeini Buried After Mourning Millions Delay Funeral," Reuters, June 7, 1989.

6. "Part I of Will and Testament," from Tehran Radio, in *Foreign Broadcast Information Service,* June 5, 1989, pages 41–47.

7. Interview with Mojahedin leaders, June 4, 1989.

8. Robin Wright, "Iran Faces Challenges at Home, Abroad," *Los Angeles Times,* June 5, 1989.

9. Patrick E. Tyler, "Clerics Ordered to Obey New Iranian Leader," *The Washington Post,* June 10, 1989.

10. "The Mystic Who Lit the Fires of Hatred," *Time,* January 7, 1980, pages 9–21.

11. Cottam, *Nationalism in Iran.*

12. Tyler, "Ten Days of Dawn," op. cit.

13. Scheherazade Daneshkhu, "Iran's Ten Years of Revolution: Achievements and Failures," *Middle East International,* February 3, 1989; Youssef M. Ibrahim, "Iran: Reality Tempers the Revolutionary Fervor," *International Herald Tribune,* January 27, 1989.

14. "Changes in Retail Prices of Some Basic Goods," from *The Islamic Republic News Agency Economic Bulletin,"* in *Akhbaar News and Translation Service,* April 15, 1989, page E-3.

15. "Iranians Stone 11 to Death for Prostitution," Reuters, April 24, 1989.

16. Interviews with Bush administration and intelligence sources, January–May 1989.

17. Youssef M. Ibrahim, "Iranian Urges Wider Terror Against West," *The New York Times,* May 6, 1989.

18. Halliday, op. cit.

Selected Bibliography

∼✦∼

Books

Afkhami, Gholam R. *The Iranian Revolution: Thanatos on a National Scale*. Washington, D.C.: Middle East Institute, 1985.

Afshar, Haleh, ed. *Iran: A Revolution in Turmoil*. Albany: State University of New York Press, 1985.

Ajami, Fouad. *The Arab Predicament: Arab Political Thought and Practice Since 1967*. New York: Cambridge University Press, 1982.

Akhavi, Shahrough. *Religion and Politics in Contemporary Iran: Clergy-State Relations in the Pahlavi Period*. Albany: State University of New York Press, 1980.

Al-e-Ahmad, Jalal. *Gharbzadegi*. Translated by John Green and Ahmad Alizadeh. Lexington, Ky.: Mazda, 1982.

———. *Iranian Society*. Anthology compiled and edited by Michael C. Hillman. Lexington, Ky.: Mazda, 1982.

Alexander, Yonah, and Allan Nanes, eds. *The United States and Iran*. Frederick, Md.: Alethia Books, 1980.

Algar, Hamid, tr. *Islam and Revolution: Writings and Declarations of Imam Khomeini*. Berkeley, Calif.: Mizan Press, 1981.

———. *Religion and State in Iran: 1795–1906*. Berkeley, Calif.: University of California Press, 1969.

———. *The Roots of the Islamic Revolution*. London: Open Press, 1983.

Amnesty International, ed. *Iran: Violations of Human Rights Documents Sent by Amnesty International to the Islamic Republic of Iran*. London: Amnesty International Publishers, 1987.

Arendt, Hannah. *On Revolution*. New York: Penguin, 1965.

Arjomand, Said Amir. *The Shadow of God and the Hidden Imam: Religion, Political Order and Societal Change in Shi'ite Iran from the Beginning to 1890*. Chicago and London: University of Chicago Press, 1984.

———. *The Turban for the Crown: The Islamic Revolution in Iran*. London: Oxford University Press, 1988.

Armstrong, Scott, et al., eds. *The Chronology: The Documented Day-by-Day Account of the Secret Military Assistance to Iran and the Contras*. New York: Warner Books, 1987.

Bakhash, Shaul. *The Reign of the Ayatollahs: Iran and the Islamic Revolution*. New York: Basic Books, 1984.

Bani-Sadr, Abolhassan. *Islamic Government*. Translated by M. R. Ghanoonparva. Lexington, Ky.: Mazda, 1981.

Bashiriyeh, Hossein. *The State and Revolution in Iran*. New York: St. Martin's Press, 1984.

Benard, Cheryl, and Zalmay Khalilzad. *The Government of God: Iran's Islamic Republic*. New York: Columbia University Press, 1984.

Bill, James A. *The Eagle and the Lion: The Tragedy of American-Iran Relations*. New Haven: Yale University Press, 1988.

———. *The Politics of Iran: Groups, Classes and Modernization*. Columbus, Ohio: Charles E. Merrill, 1972.

Bonine, Michael E., and Nikki R. Keddie, eds. *Modern Iran: The Dialectics of Continuity and Change*. Albany: State University of New York Press, 1981.

Brinton, Crane. *The Anatomy of Revolution*. New York: Vintage Books, 1965.

Byrne, Malcolm, ed. *The Chronology: The Documented Day-by-Day Account of the Secret Military Assistance to Iran and the Contras*. New York: Warner Books, 1987.

Carlsen, Robin W. *The Imam and His Islamic Revolution*. Victoria, B.C.: Snow Man Press, 1982.

Christopher, Warren, et al. *American Hostages in Iran: The Conduct of Crisis*. New Haven and London: Yale University Press, 1985.

Chubin, Shahram, and Charles Tripp. *Iran and Iraq at War*. Boulder: Westview Press, 1988.

Cordesman, Anthony H. *The Iran-Iraq War and Western Security 1984–1987: Strategic Implications and Policy Options*. London: Jane's Publishing Company, Ltd., 1987.

Cottam, Richard. *Nationalism in Iran*. Pittsburgh: University of Pittsburgh Press, 1979.

Cottrell, Alvin J., and Michael L. Moodie. *The United States and the Persian Gulf: Past Mistakes, Present Needs*. New York: National Strategy Information Center, 1984.

Dietl, Wilhelm. *Holy War*. Translated by Martha Humphreys. New York: Macmillan, 1984.

Dorman, William A., and Mansour Farhang. *The U.S. Press and Iran.* Berkeley: University of California Press, 1987.

El Azhary, M. S., ed. *The Iran-Iraq War.* London: Croom Helm, 1984.

Enayat, Hamid. *Modern Islamic Political Thought.* Austin, Tex.: University of Texas Press, 1982.

Esposito, John L. *Islam and Politics.* Syracuse: Syracuse University Press, 1984.

Europa Publications. *The Middle East and North Africa: 1986–87.* London: Europa Publications, 1987.

Fadlallah, Sheikh Mohammed Hussein. *Islam and the Logic of Force.* Beirut: Al Dar Al Islamiya, 1981.

Findly E., Y. Haddad and B. Haines, eds. *The Islamic Impact.* Syracuse: Syracuse University Press, 1984.

Fischer, Michael M. J. *Iran: From Religious Dispute to Revolution.* Cambridge, Mass.: Harvard University Press, 1984.

Ghayasuddin, M. *The Impact of Nationalism on the Modern World.* London: The Open Press, Al-Hoda Publishers, 1986.

Gibb, H.A.R. *Islam: An Historical Survey.* Oxford, New York, Toronto, Melbourne: Oxford University Press, 1949.

Graham, Robert. *Iran: The Illusion of Power.* New York: St. Martin's Press, 1979.

Green, Jerrold D. *Revolution in Iran: The Politics of Countermobilization.* New York: Praeger Publishers, 1982.

Grumman, Stephen. *The Iran-Iraq War.* Washington, D.C.: Council on Foreign Relations, 1982.

Guillaume, Alfred. *Islam.* New York and Middlesex: Penguin Books, 1954.

Halliday, Fred. *Iran: Dictatorship and Development.* London: Penguin Books, 1979.

Heikal, Mohammed. *Iran: The Untold Story.* New York: Pantheon, 1982.

Hendra, Tony, ed. *Sayings of the Ayatollah Khomeini.* New York: Bantam Books, 1979.

Hickman, William F. *Ravaged and Reborn: The Iranian Army.* Washington, D.C.: Brookings Institution, 1982.

Hiro, Dilip. *Iran Under the Ayatollahs.* London: Routledge & Kegan Paul, 1985.

Holt, P. M., Ann K. S. Lambton and Bernard Lewis, eds. *The Cambridge History of Islam: The Central Islamic Lands Since 1918*, Vol. 1B. Cambridge and New York: Cambridge University Press, 1970.

Hooglund, Eric J. *Land and Revolution in Iran, 1960–1980.* Austin, Tex.: University of Texas Press, 1982.

———. *Reform and Revolution in Rural Iran.* Austin, Tex.: University of Texas Press, 1982.

Huyser, General Robert E. *Mission to Tehran.* New York: Harper & Row, 1986.

Irfani, Suroosh. *Revolutionary Islam in Iran: Popular Liberation or Religious Dictatorship?* London: Zed Books Ltd., 1983.

Islamic Student Followers of the Imam's Policy. *Revelations from the Nest of Espionage.* Approximately 35 volumes to date. N.p., n.d. In English and Persian.

Jansen, Godfrey H. *Militant Islam.* London: Pan Books, 1979.

Kapuscinski, Ryszard. *Shah of Shahs.* San Diego: A Helen and Kurt Wolff Book/Harcourt Brace Jovanovich, 1985.

Keddie, Nikki R. *Roots of Revolution: An Interpretative History of Modern Iran.* New Haven: Yale University Press, 1981.

————, ed. *Religion and Politics in Iran: Shi'ism from Quietism to Revolution.* New Haven and London: Yale University Press, 1983.

————, ed. *Scholars, Saints and Sufis: Muslim Religious Institutions Since 1500.* Berkeley & Los Angeles: University of California Press, 1983.

Keddie, Nikki R., and Eric Hooglund, eds. *The Iranian Revolution and the Islamic Republic.* Conference Proceedings of the Woodrow Wilson International Center for Scholars, May 21–22, 1982. Washington, D.C.: Middle East Institute and Woodrow Wilson Center, 1982.

Khadduri, Majid. *The Gulf War: The Origins and Implications of the Iraq-Iran Conflict.* New York and Oxford: Oxford University Press, 1988.

Khateeb, Muhibbudeen al. *Broad Aspects of the Shi'ite Religion: An Exposition and Refutation.* Burnaby, Canada: Majlis of Al Haq Publication Society, 1983.

Khomeini, Ayatollah Ruhollah. *Islam and Revolution: Writings and Declarations of Imam Khomeini.* Translated and annotated by Hamid Algar. Berkeley, Calif.: Mizam Press, 1981.

Kramer, Martin. *Political Islam.* Beverly Hills: Sage Publications, 1980.

————. *Shi'ism, Resistance, and Revolution.* Boulder: Westview Press, 1987.

Kuniholm, Bruce R. *Persian Gulf & U.S. Policy: A Guide to Issues and References.* Regina Guides to Contemporary Issues. Claremont, Calif.: Regina Books, 1984.

Ledeen, Michael, and William Lewis. *Debacle: The American Failure in Iran.* New York: Vintage Books, 1982.

Lewis, Bernard. *Islam in History.* New York: The Library Press, 1973.

Limbert, John W. *Iran: At War with History.* Boulder: Westview Press, 1987.

McFadden, Robert D, Joseph B. Treaster and Maurice Carroll. *No Hiding Place.* New York: Times Books, 1981.

Middle East Contemporary Survey, Volumes 1978–79, 1979–80, 1980–81, 1981–2, 1982–3, 1983–4, 1984–5, and 1986. Various editors at the Dayan Center for Middle Eastern and African Studies, the Shiloah Institute, Tel Aviv University. Boulder: Westview Press.

Milani, Mohsen M. *The Making of Iran's Islamic Revolution: From Monarchy to Islamic Republic.* Boulder: Westview Press, 1988.

Mortimer, Edward. *Faith and Power: The Politics of Islam*. New York: Vintage Books, 1982.

Mottahedeh, Roy P. *The Mantle of the Prophet*. New York: Pantheon, 1986.

Munson, Henry, Jr. *Islam and Revolution in the Middle East: Religion and Politics in Iran*. New Haven: Yale University Press, 1987.

Naipaul, V. S. *Among the Believers: An Islamic Journey*. New York: Vintage Books, 1981.

Neff, Donald. *Warriors for Jerusalem: The Six Days That Changed the Middle East*. New York: Simon and Schuster, 1984.

North, Oliver L. *Taking the Stand: The Testimony of Lieutenant Colonel Oliver L. North*. New York: Pocket Books, 1987.

Norton, Augustus Richard. *Amal and the Shi'i: The Struggle for the Soul of Lebanon*. Austin, Tex.: University of Texas Press, 1987.

O'Ballance, Edgar. *The Gulf War*. London: Brassey's Defence Publishers, 1988.

Parsons, Anthony. *The Pride and the Fall*. London: Jonathan Cape, 1984.

Pipes, Daniel. *In the Path of God: Islam and Political Power*. New York: Basic Books, 1983.

Piscatori, James P., ed. *Islam in the Political Process*. New York: Cambridge University Press, 1983.

Rafizadeh, Mansur. *Witness: From the Shah to the Secret Arms Deal, An Insider's Account of U.S. Involvement in Iran*. New York: William Morrow & Co., 1987.

Rajaee, Farhang. *Islamic Values and World View: Khomayni on Man, the State and International Politics*. Lanham, Md.: University Press of America, 1983.

Ramazani, Rouhollah K. *Iran's Foreign Policy 1941–1973*. Charlottesville, Va.: University of Virginia Press, 1975.

———. *The Persian Gulf: Iran's Role*. Charlottesville, Va.: University of Virginia Press, 1972.

———. *Revolutionary Iran: Challenge and Response in the Middle East*. Baltimore: The Johns Hopkins University Press, 1986.

———. *The United States and Iran: The Patterns of Influence*. New York: Praeger, 1982.

Roosevelt, Kermit. *Countercoup: The Struggle for Control in Iran*. New York: McGraw-Hill, 1979.

Rosen, Barry M., ed. *Iran Since the Revolution*. New York: Brooklyn College Program on Society in Change, 1985.

Rubin, Barry. *Paved with Good Intentions: The American Experience in Iran*. New York: Penguin Books, 1981.

Ruthven, Malise. *Islam in the World*. New York and Middlesex: Penguin Books, 1984.

Said, Edward. *Covering Islam: How the Media and the Experts Determine How We See the Rest of the World*. New York: Pantheon, 1981.

Sanii, Kuross A. *Involvement by Invitation: American Strategies of Containment in Iran.* University Park: The Pennsylvania State University Press, 1987.

Schahgaldian, Nikola B. (with the assistance of Gena Barkhordarian). *The Iranian Military Under the Islamic Republic.* Santa Monica: Rand Corporation, 1987.

Scott, Col. Charles W. *Pieces of the Game.* Atlanta: Peachtree Publishers, 1984.

Segev, Samuel. *The Iranian Triangle: The Untold Story of Israel's Role in the Iran-Contra Affair.* New York: Free Press/Macmillan, 1988.

Shari'ati, Ali. *Marxism and Other Western Fallacies.* Translated by R. Campbell. Berkeley, Calif.: Mizan Press, 1980.

———. *On the Sociology of Islam.* Translated and edited by Hamid Algar. Berkeley, Calif.: Mizan Press, 1979.

Sick, Gary. *All Fall Down.* New York: Random House, 1985.

Simpson, John. *Inside Iran: Life Under Khomeini's Regime.* New York: St. Martin's Press, 1988.

Sivan, Emmanuel. *Radical Islam: Medieval Theology and Modern Politics.* New Haven: Yale University Press, 1985.

Smith, Peter. *The Babi and Baha'i Religions: From Messianic Shi'ism to a World Religion.* New York and Cambridge: Cambridge University Press, 1987.

Stempel, John D. *Inside the Iranian Revolution.* Bloomington: Indiana University Press, 1981.

Sullivan, William H. *Mission to Iran.* New York: W. W. Norton, 1981.

Tabataba'i, Allameh Sayyid Muhammad Husayn. *Shi'ite Islam.* Translated and edited by Seyyed Hossein Nasr. Albany: State University of New York Press, 1975.

Taheri, Amir. *Holy Terror: Inside the World of Islamic Terrorism.* Bethesda, Md.: Adler & Adler, Inc., 1987.

———. *The Spirit of Allah: Khomeini and the Islamic Revolution.* Bethesda, Md.: Adler & Adler, 1986.

Taleqani, Mahmood. *Islam and Ownership.* Translated from the Persian by Ahmad Jabbari and Farhang Rajaee. Lexington, Ky.: Mazda, 1983.

Tower Commission. *Report of the President's Special Review Board.* Washington, D.C.: U.S. Government Printing Office, 1987.

United Nations Security Council. *Report of the Mission Dispatched by the Secretary General to Investigate Allegations of the Use of Chemical Weapons in the Conflict Between the Islamic Republic of Iran and Iraq.* New York: March 12, 1986 (original English), May 8, 1987 (original English and Spanish) and May 18, 1987 (original English).

———. *Report of the Specialists Appointed by the Secretary General to Investigate Allegations by the Islamic Republic of Iran Concerning the Use of Chemical Weapons.* New York: March 26, 1984 (original English).

Wells, Tim. *444 Days: The Hostages Remember.* New York: Harcourt Brace Jovanovich, 1985.

Wright, Robin. *Sacred Rage: The Wrath of Militant Islam.* New York: Linden Press/Simon and Schuster, 1985.

Zabih, Sepehr. *Iran Since the Revolution.* Baltimore, Md.: The Johns Hopkins University Press, 1982.

———. *The Mossadegh Era: Roots of the Iranian Revolution.* Chicago: Lake View Press, 1982.

Zonis, Marvin. "Iran." In *The Middle East: Handbooks to the Modern World.* New York: Facts-on-File Publications, 1988.

———. *The Political Elite of Iran.* Princeton, N.J.: Princeton University Press, 1971.

Zonis, Marvin, and Daniel Brumberg. *Khomeini, The Islamic Republic of Iran, and the Arab World.* Cambridge, Mass.: Harvard University Center for Middle Eastern Studies, 1987.

Articles

Ajami, Fouad. "Iran: The Impossible Revolution." *Foreign Affairs,* Winter 1988–89, pp. 135–55.

Arjomand, Said, Eric Hooglund, William Royce and Steven Heydemann. "The Iranian Islamic Clergy: Governmental Politics and Theocracy." Washington, D.C.: The Middle East Institute, 1984.

Ayobb, Mohammed. "The Revolutionary Thrust of Islamic Political Tradition." *Third World Quarterly,* April 1981, pp. 269–76.

Bakhash, Shaul. "Who Lost Iran?" *New York Review of Books,* June 26, 1980, pp. 17–22.

Bill, James A. "Islam, Politics, and Shi'ism in the Gulf." *Middle East Insight,* January–February 1984.

———. "Power and Religion in Revolutionary Iran." *Middle East Journal* 36 (Winter 1982): 22–46.

———. "Resurgent Islam in the Persian Gulf." *Foreign Affairs,* Fall 1984, pp. 108–27.

Carswell, Robert. "Economic Sanctions and the Iran Experience." *Foreign Affairs,* Winter 1981/82, pp. 247–65.

Congressional Research Service. Library of Congress, Report Prepared for Committee on Foreign Relations, U.S. House of Representatives. "The Iran Hostage Crisis: A Chronology of Daily Developments." 97th Cong., 1st Sess.

Cottam, Richard W. "Khomeini, The Future, and U.S. Options." Muscatine, Iowa: Policy Paper 38, Stanley Foundation, 1987.

Giazzone, Laura. "Gulf Cooperation Council: The Security Policies." London: International Institute for Strategic Studies, March/April 1988.

Hunter, Shireen, ed. "Internal Developments in Iran." Washington, D.C.: CSIS Significant Issues Series, vol. 7, no. 3, Center for Strategic and International Studies, Georgetown University, 1985.

"Islamic Renewal: Iran's Continuing Revolution," *Harvard International Review* May/June 1984. Articles by Shaul Bakhash, Shapour Bakhtiar, Abolhassan Bani-Sadr, Sheryl Bernard, James A. Bill, John L. Esposito, Mansour Farhang, Zalmay Khalilzad, Ardeshir Mohassess, Said Rajai Khorassani.

Karsh, Efraim. "Military Power and Foreign Policy Goals: The Iran-Iraq War Revisited." *International Affairs,* vol. 64, no. 1, Winter 1987/88. The Royal Institute of International Affairs.

Keddie, Nikki R., and Eric Hooglund, eds. "The Iranian Revolution and the Islamic Republic." Washington, D.C.: Conference Proceedings, Middle East Institute, 1982.

Khomeini, Ayatollah Ruhollah. "Excerpts from Speeches and Messages of Imam Khomeini on the Unity of the Muslims." Tehran: Distributed by the Ministry of Islamic Guidance, n.d.

Koury, Enver M., and Charles G. MacDonald, eds. "Revolution in Iran: A Reappraisal." Hyattsville, Md.: Institute of Middle Eastern and North African Affairs, 1982.

Lewis, Flora. "Upsurge in Islam." Four-part series in *The New York Times,* December 28–31, 1979.

Mottahedeh, Roy. "Iran's Foreign Devils." *Foreign Policy* 38 (Spring 1980): 19–34.

Norton, Augustus R.. "Shi'ism and Social Protest in Lebanon." In *Shi'ism and Social Protest,* edited by Nikki Keddie and Juan Cole. New Haven: Yale University Press, 1985.

Pars News Agency, ed. "Highlights of Imam Khomeini's Speeches, Nov. 5, 1980–April 28, 1981." Compiled by the Muslim Student Association, 1981.

Precht, Henry. "Ayatollah Realpolitik." *Foreign Policy* 70 (Spring 1988): 109–128.

Ramazani, Rouhollah K. "Iran's Islamic Revolution and the Persian Gulf." *Current History,* January 1985, pp. 5–6, 40–41.

———. "Who Lost America? The Case of Iran." *Middle East Journal* 36 (Winter 1982).

Rouleau, Eric. "Khomeini's Iran." *Foreign Affairs,* Fall 1980, pp. 1–19.

Rubin, Barry. "Iran's Future Crises, Contingencies, and Continuities." Washington, D.C.: Johns Hopkins Foreign Policy Institute, 1987.

Sciolino, Elaine. "Iran's Durable Revolution," *Foreign Affairs,* Spring 1983, pp. 893–920.

Wright, Robin. "A Reporter at Large: Teheran Summer," *The New Yorker,* September 5, 1988.

Zonis, Marvin, and Daniel Brumberg. "An Ideological Justification of Terrorism and Violence: Ayatollah Khomeini Interprets Shi'ism." Paper delivered at the Conference on Shi'ism, Resistance and Revolution, Israel, December 12–21, 1984.

Index

277

PHOTO CREDITS

ABOUT THE AUTHOR

ROBIN WRIGHT is a three-time nominee for the Pulitzer Prize and is the winner of the 1989 National Magazine Award for her reportage from Iran for *The New Yorker*. A veteran international correspondent, she has reported from over sixty nations for *The Sunday Times* of London, CBS News, *The Washington Post, The Christian Science Monitor* and the *Los Angeles Times*. The winner of the Overseas Press Club's Bob Considine Award for "best reporting in any medium requiring exceptional courage and initiative," she is also the author of *Sacred Rage*.